CHAPTER 5 ONE TO CALL "FRIEND"

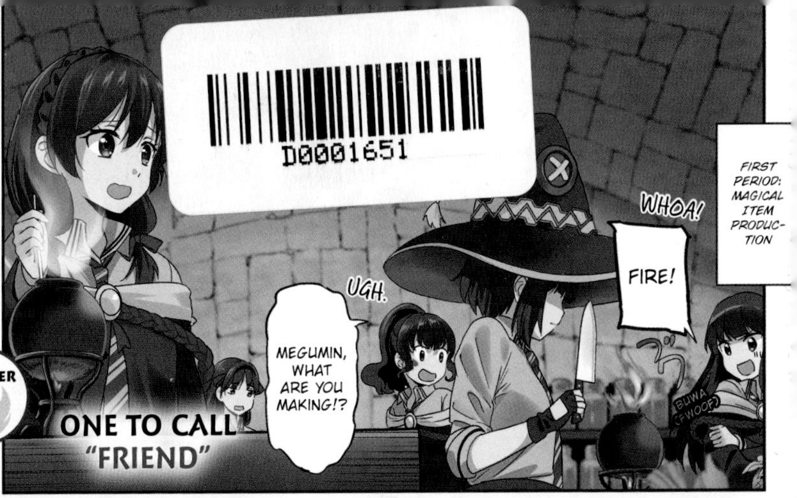
FIRST PERIOD: MAGICAL ITEM PRODUCTION
WHOA!
FIRE!
BUWA (FWOOF)
UGH.
MEGUMIN, WHAT ARE YOU MAKING!?
CHAPTER 5
ONE TO CALL "FRIEND"

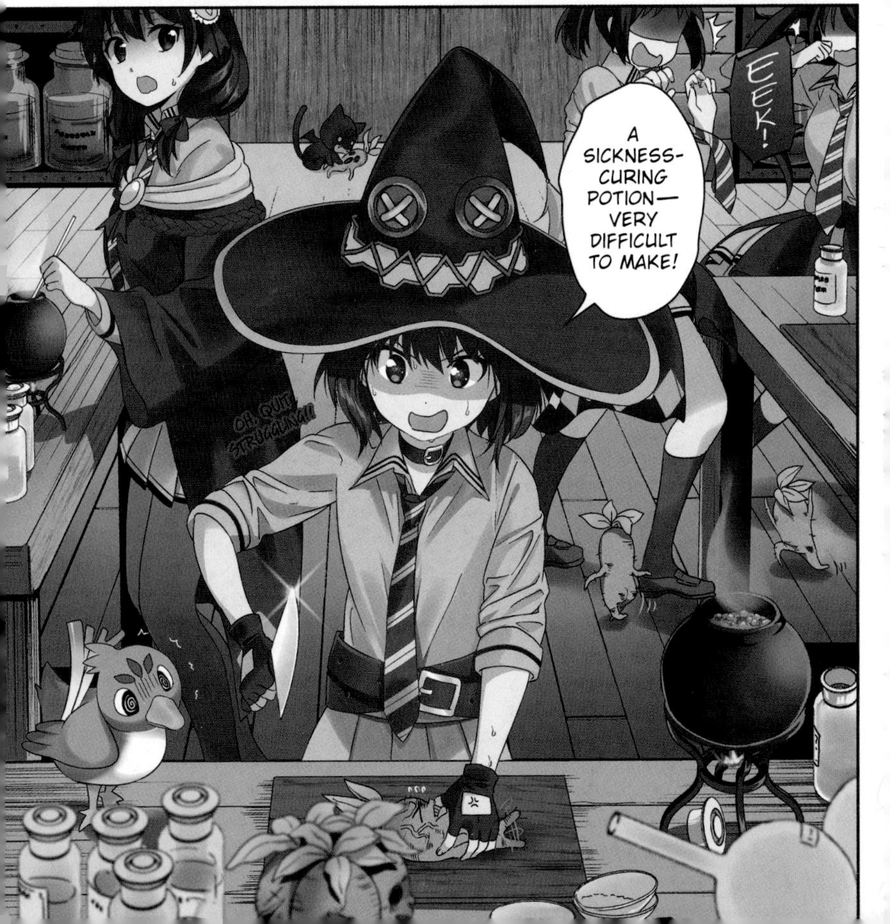
EEK!
A SICKNESS-CURING POTION—VERY DIFFICULT TO MAKE!
OH, QUIT STRUGGLING!!

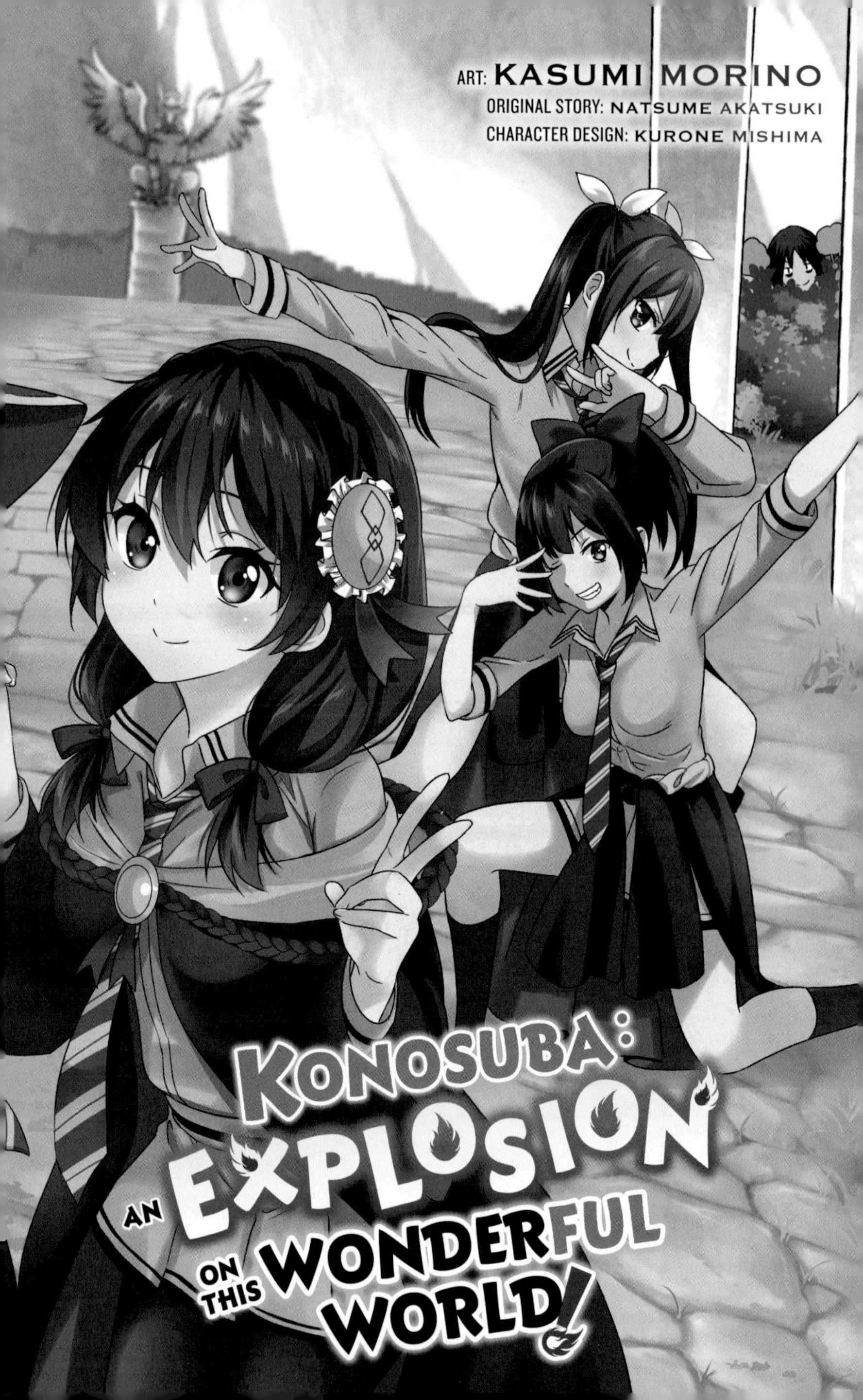
ART: KASUMI MORINO
ORIGINAL STORY: NATSUME AKATSUKI
CHARACTER DESIGN: KURONE MISHIMA
KONOSUBA:
AN EXPLOSION
ON THIS WONDERFUL
WORLD!

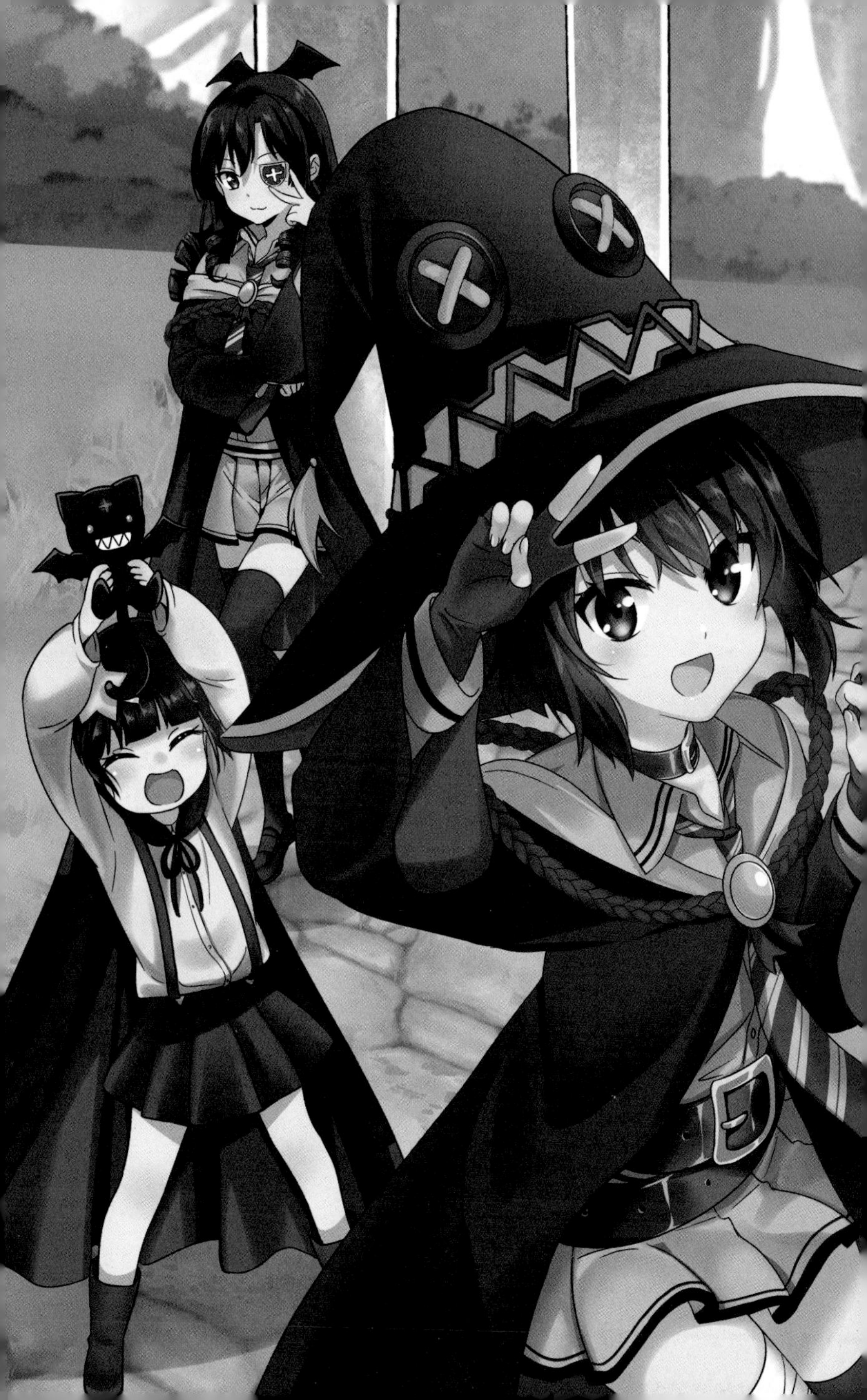

CONTENTS

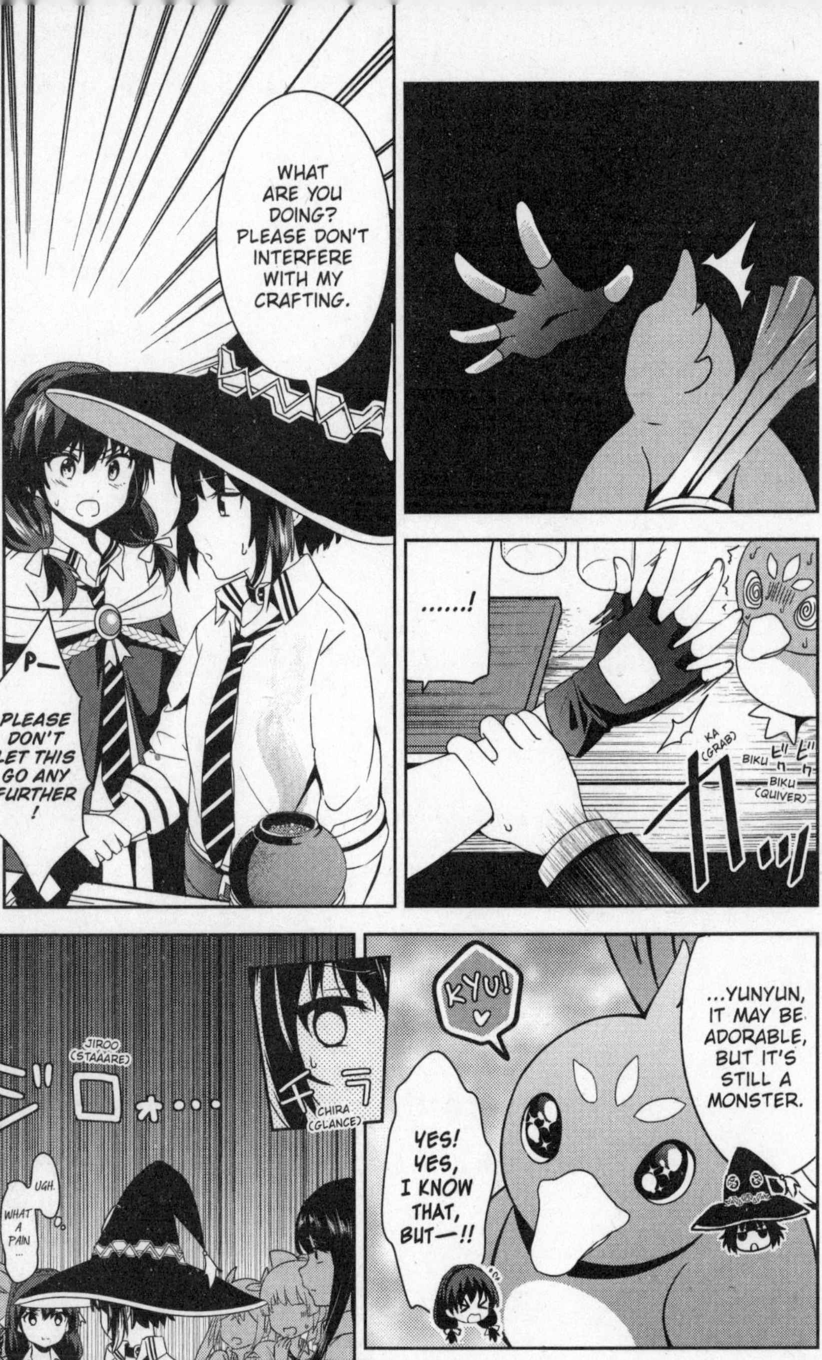
......!
KA (GRAB)
BIKU BIKU (QUIVER)
WHAT ARE YOU DOING? PLEASE DON'T INTERFERE WITH MY CRAFTING.
P—
PLEASE DON'T LET THIS GO ANY FURTHER!
...YUNYUN, IT MAY BE ADORABLE, BUT IT'S STILL A MONSTER.
KYU! ♥
YES! YES, I KNOW THAT, BUT—!!
CHIRA (GLANCE)
JIROO (STAAARE)
UGH.
WHAT A PAIN...

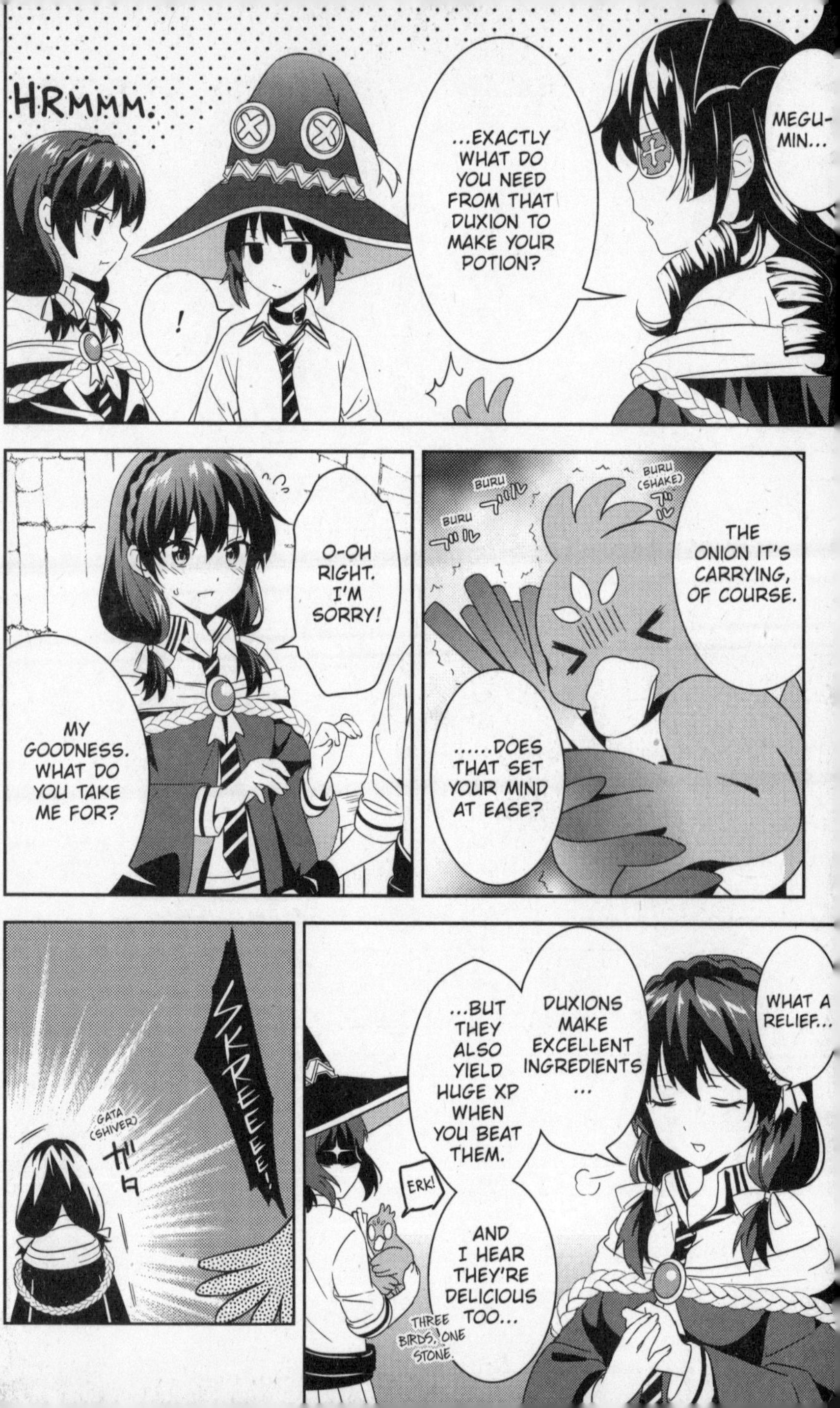
MEGU-MIN...
...EXACTLY WHAT DO YOU NEED FROM THAT DUXION TO MAKE YOUR POTION?
!
HRMMM.
BURU (SHAKE)
BURU
BURU
THE ONION IT'S CARRYING, OF COURSE.
......DOES THAT SET YOUR MIND AT EASE?
O-OH RIGHT. I'M SORRY!
MY GOODNESS. WHAT DO YOU TAKE ME FOR?
WHAT A RELIEF...
DUXIONS MAKE EXCELLENT INGREDIENTS...
...BUT THEY ALSO YIELD HUGE XP WHEN YOU BEAT THEM.
ERK!
AND I HEAR THEY'RE DELICIOUS TOO...
THREE BIRDS, ONE STONE.
SKREEEE!!
GATA (SHIVER)

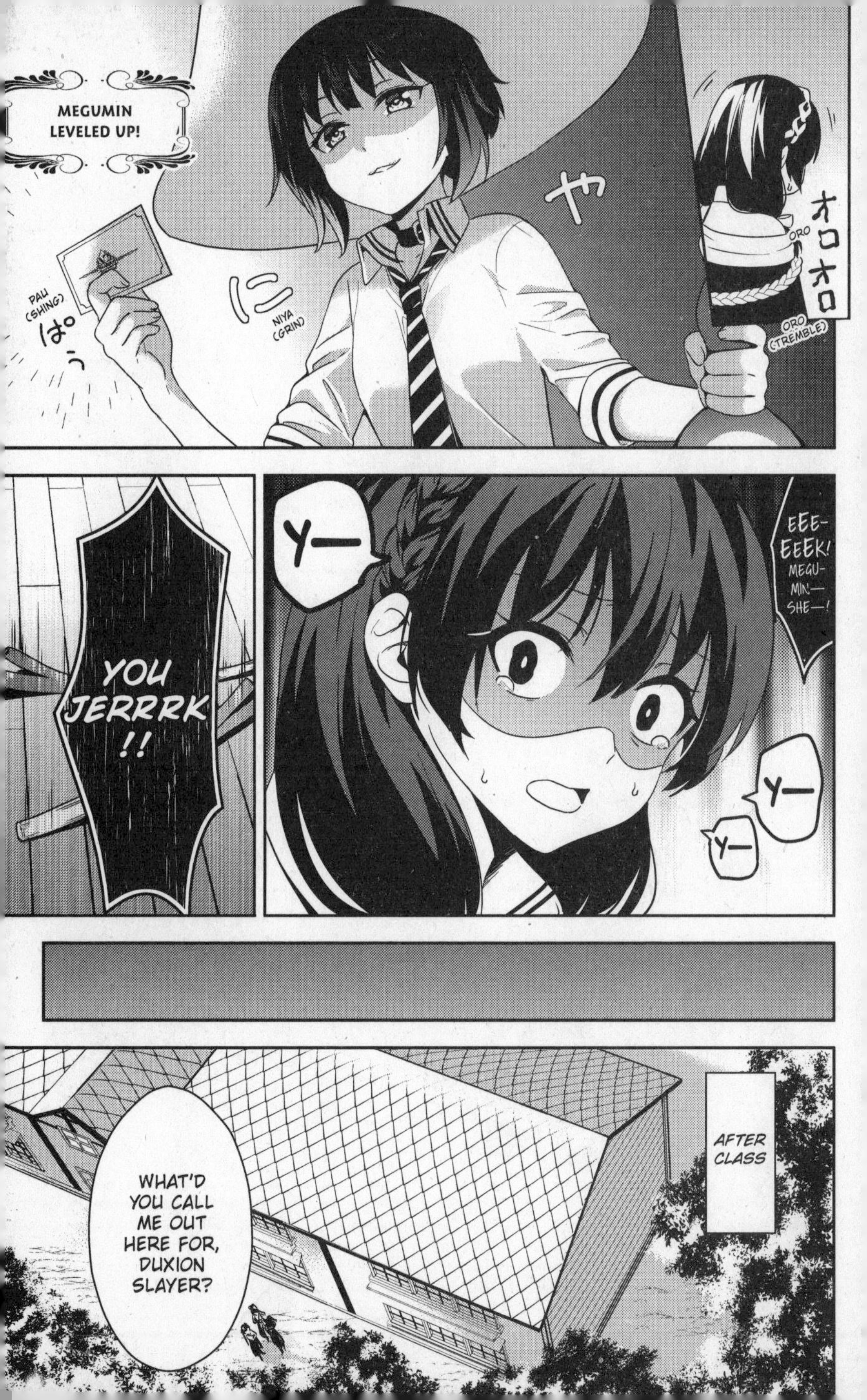
オロオロ
ORO ORO (TREMBLE)
ヤ
に
NIYA (GRIN)
ぱう
PAU (SHING)
MEGUMIN LEVELED UP!
EEE-EEEK! MEGUMIN—SHE—!
Y—
Y—
Y—
YOU JERRRK!!
AFTER CLASS
WHAT'D YOU CALL ME OUT HERE FOR, DUXION SLAYER?

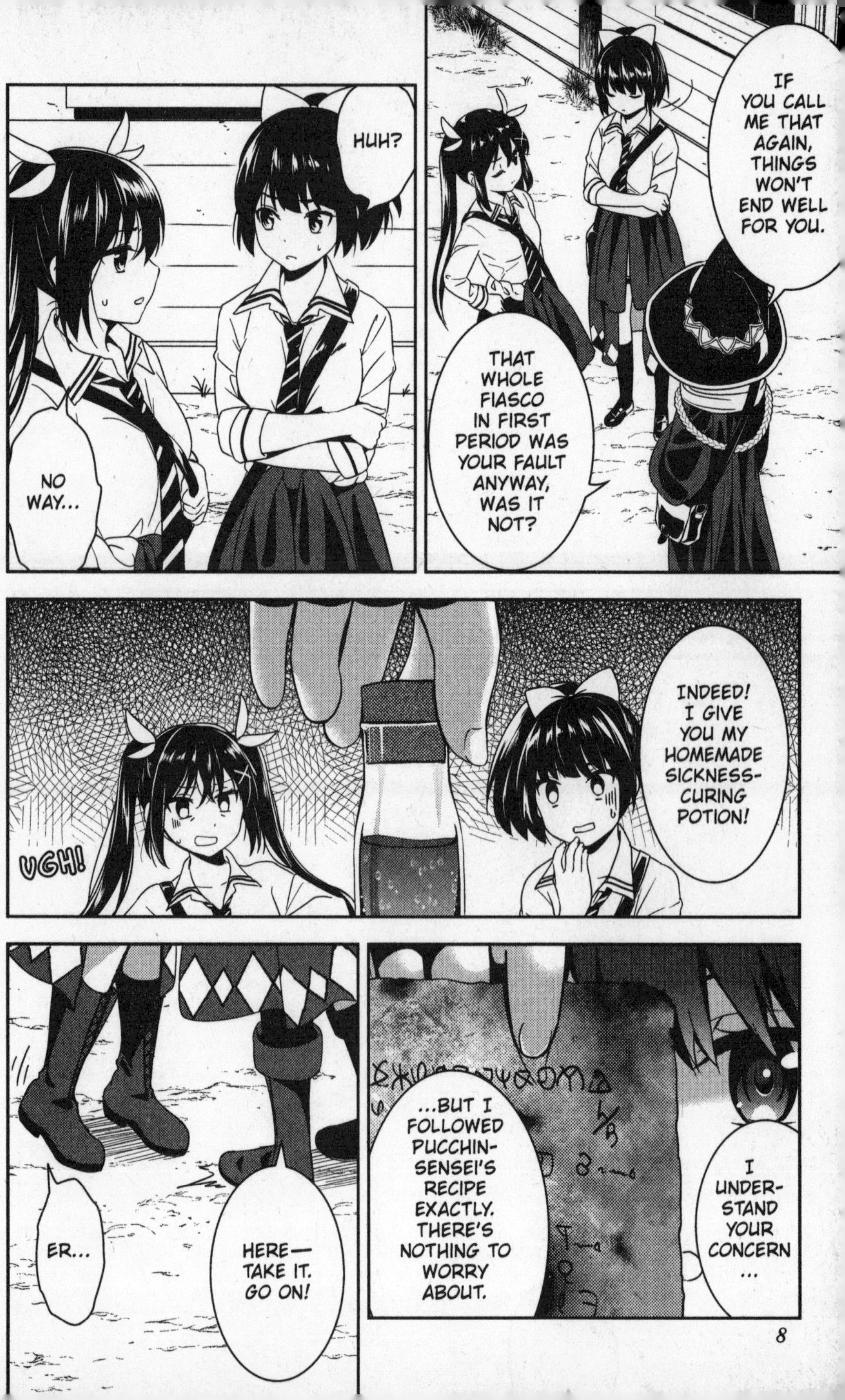
IF YOU CALL ME THAT AGAIN, THINGS WON'T END WELL FOR YOU.
THAT WHOLE FIASCO IN FIRST PERIOD WAS YOUR FAULT ANYWAY, WAS IT NOT?
HUH?
NO WAY...
INDEED! I GIVE YOU MY HOMEMADE SICKNESS-CURING POTION!
UGH!
I UNDERSTAND YOUR CONCERN...
...BUT I FOLLOWED PUCCHIN-SENSEI'S RECIPE EXACTLY. THERE'S NOTHING TO WORRY ABOUT.
HERE—TAKE IT. GO ON!
ER...

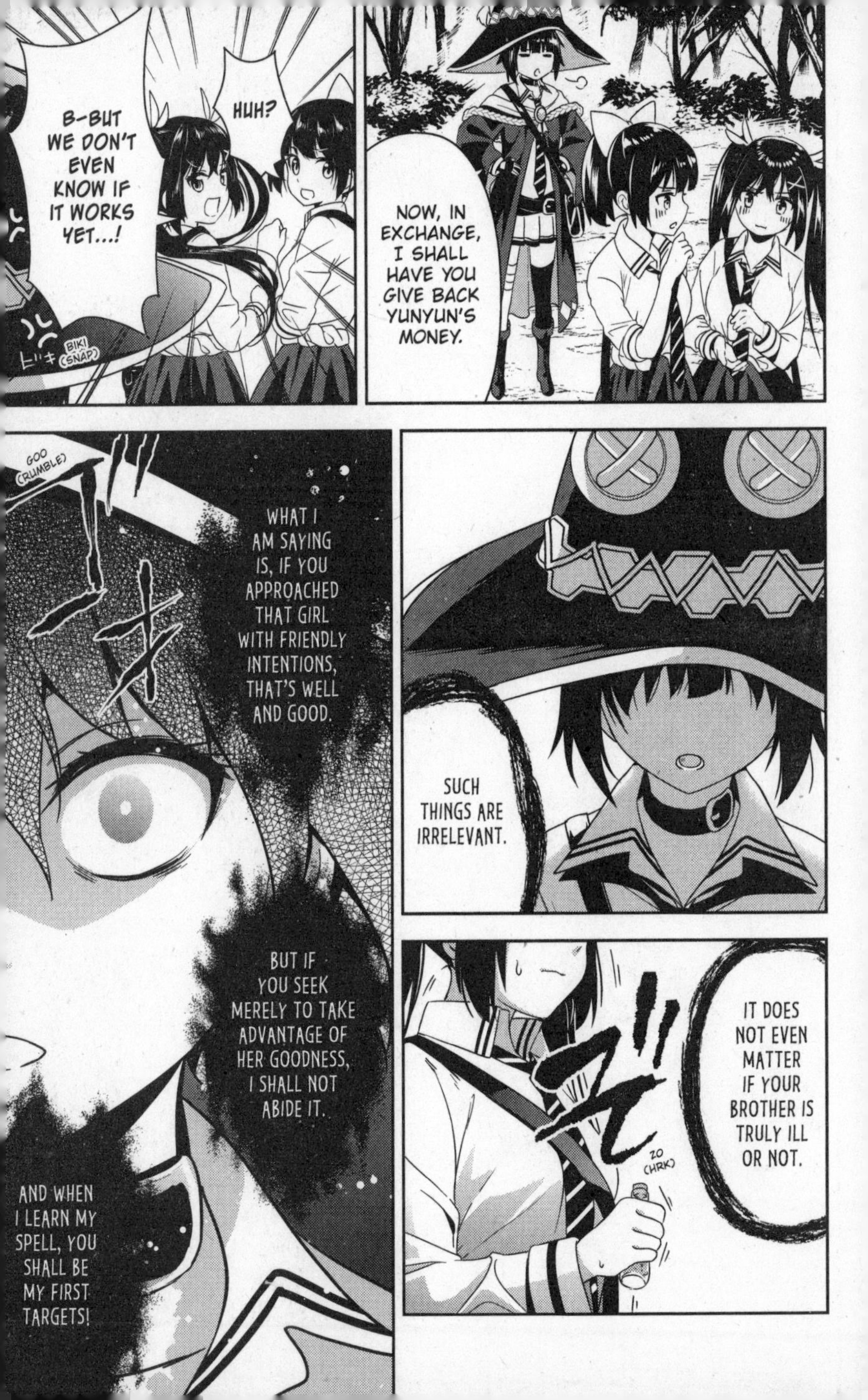
NOW, IN EXCHANGE, I SHALL HAVE YOU GIVE BACK YUNYUN'S MONEY.
HUH?
B-BUT WE DON'T EVEN KNOW IF IT WORKS YET...!
BIKI (SNAP)
SUCH THINGS ARE IRRELEVANT.
IT DOES NOT EVEN MATTER IF YOUR BROTHER IS TRULY ILL OR NOT.
ZO (HRK)
GOO (RUMBLE)
WHAT I AM SAYING IS, IF YOU APPROACHED THAT GIRL WITH FRIENDLY INTENTIONS, THAT'S WELL AND GOOD.
BUT IF YOU SEEK MERELY TO TAKE ADVANTAGE OF HER GOODNESS, I SHALL NOT ABIDE IT.
AND WHEN I LEARN MY SPELL, YOU SHALL BE MY FIRST TARGETS!

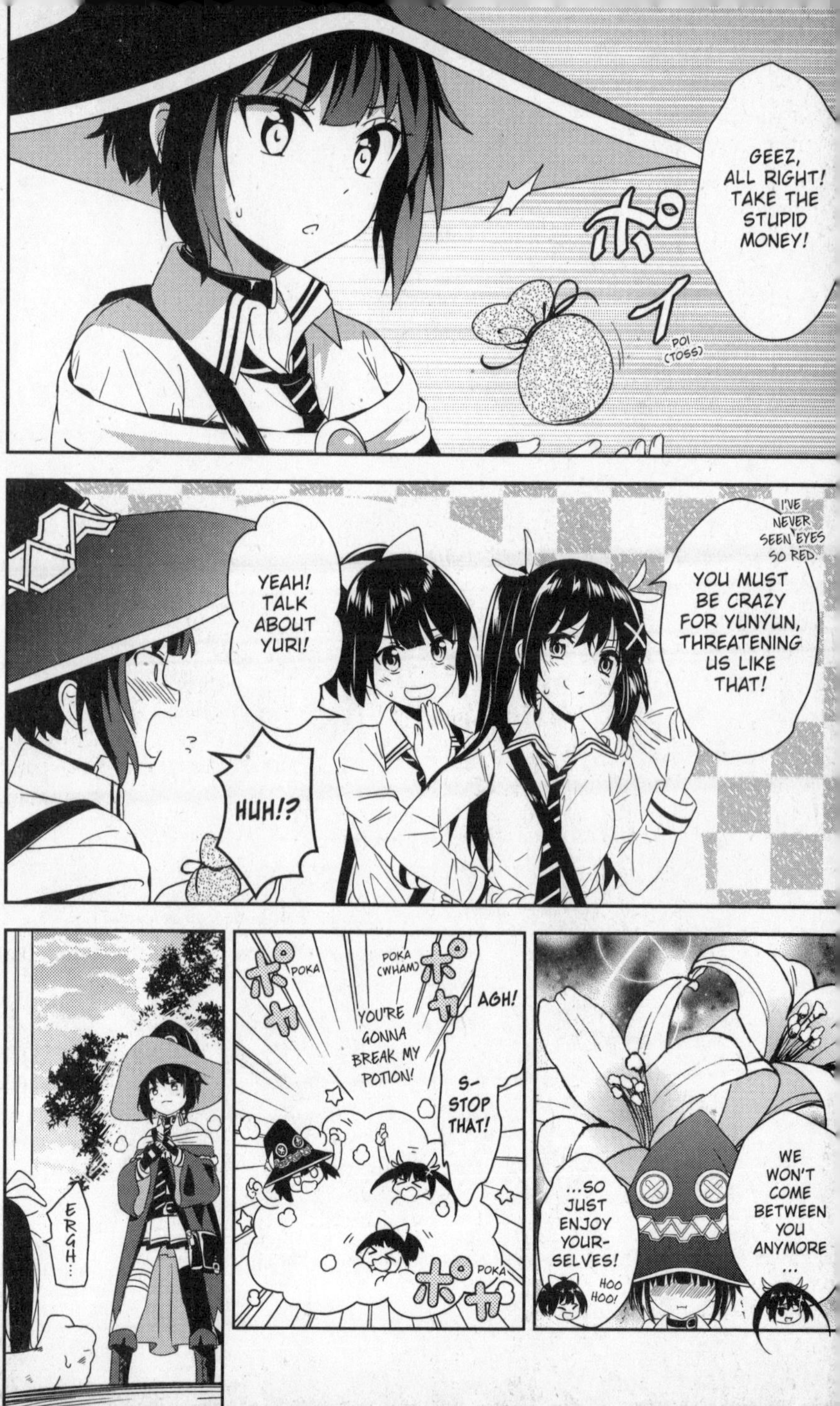
GEEZ, ALL RIGHT! TAKE THE STUPID MONEY!
ポイ
POI (TOSS)
I'VE NEVER SEEN EYES SO RED.
YOU MUST BE CRAZY FOR YUNYUN, THREATENING US LIKE THAT!
YEAH! TALK ABOUT YURI!
HUH!?
WE WON'T COME BETWEEN YOU ANYMORE ...
...SO JUST ENJOY YOUR-SELVES!
HOO HOO!
AGH!
ポカ
POKA (WHAM)
S-STOP THAT!
YOU'RE GONNA BREAK MY POTION!
ポカ
POKA
ポカ
POKA
ERGH...

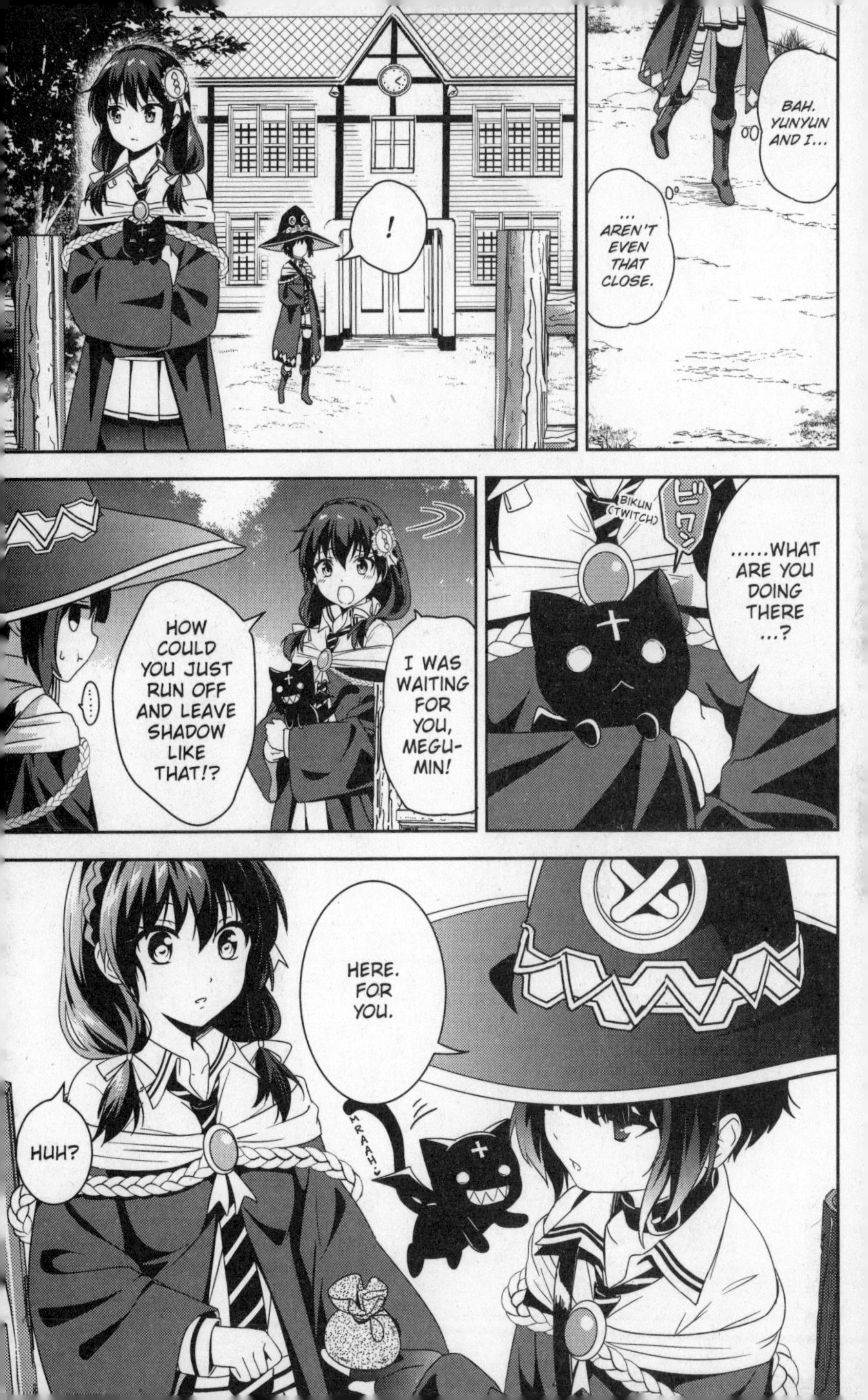
BAH. YUNYUN AND I...
...AREN'T EVEN THAT CLOSE.
!
BIKUN (TWITCH)
......WHAT ARE YOU DOING THERE ...?
I WAS WAITING FOR YOU, MEGU-MIN!
HOW COULD YOU JUST RUN OFF AND LEAVE SHADOW LIKE THAT!?
...
HERE. FOR YOU.
MRAAH♪
HUH?

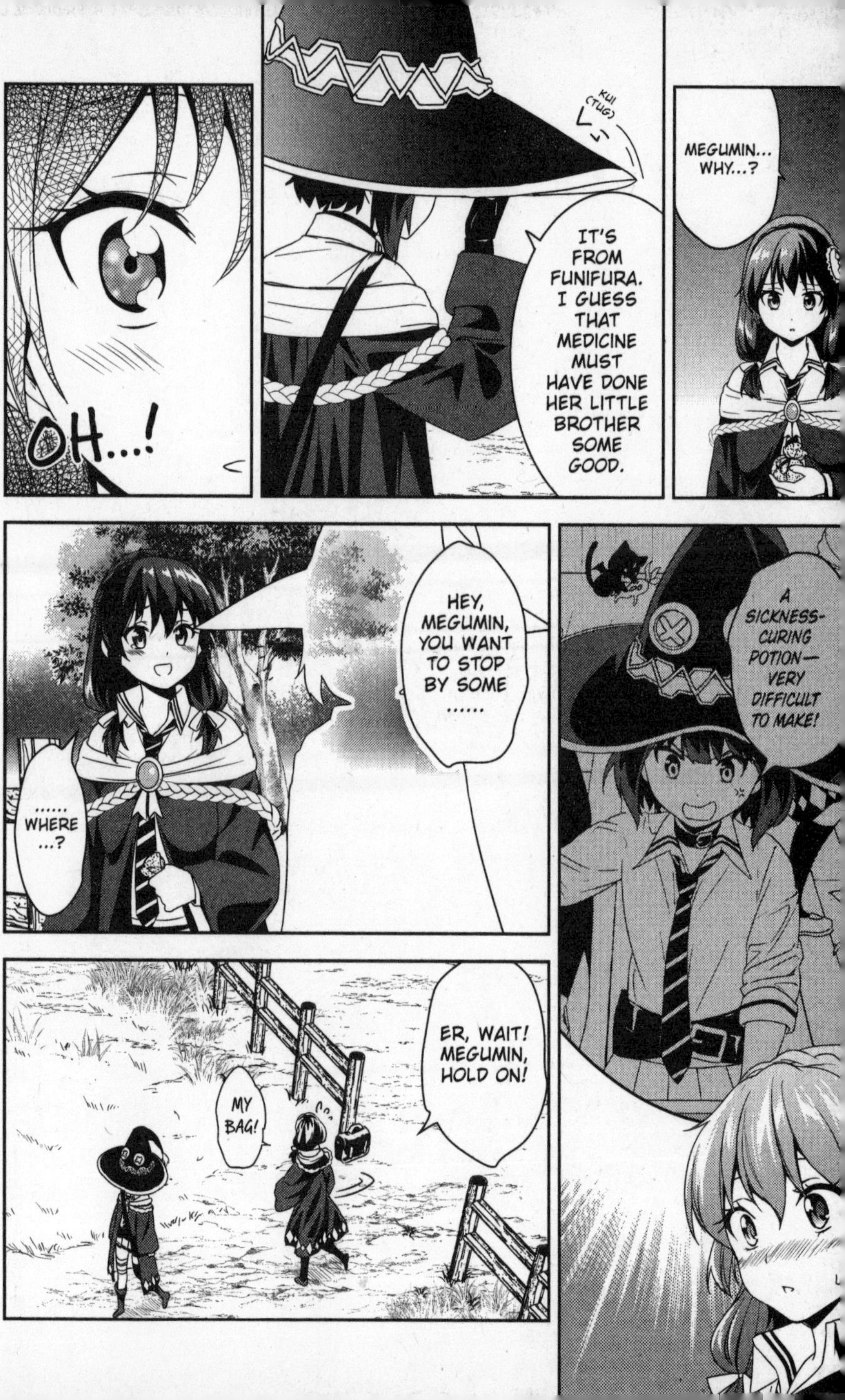
MEGUMIN... WHY...?
KUI (TUG)
IT'S FROM FUNIFURA. I GUESS THAT MEDICINE MUST HAVE DONE HER LITTLE BROTHER SOME GOOD.
OH...!
A SICKNESS-CURING POTION—VERY DIFFICULT TO MAKE!
HEY, MEGUMIN, YOU WANT TO STOP BY SOME ......
...... WHERE ...?
ER, WAIT! MEGUMIN, HOLD ON!
MY BAG!

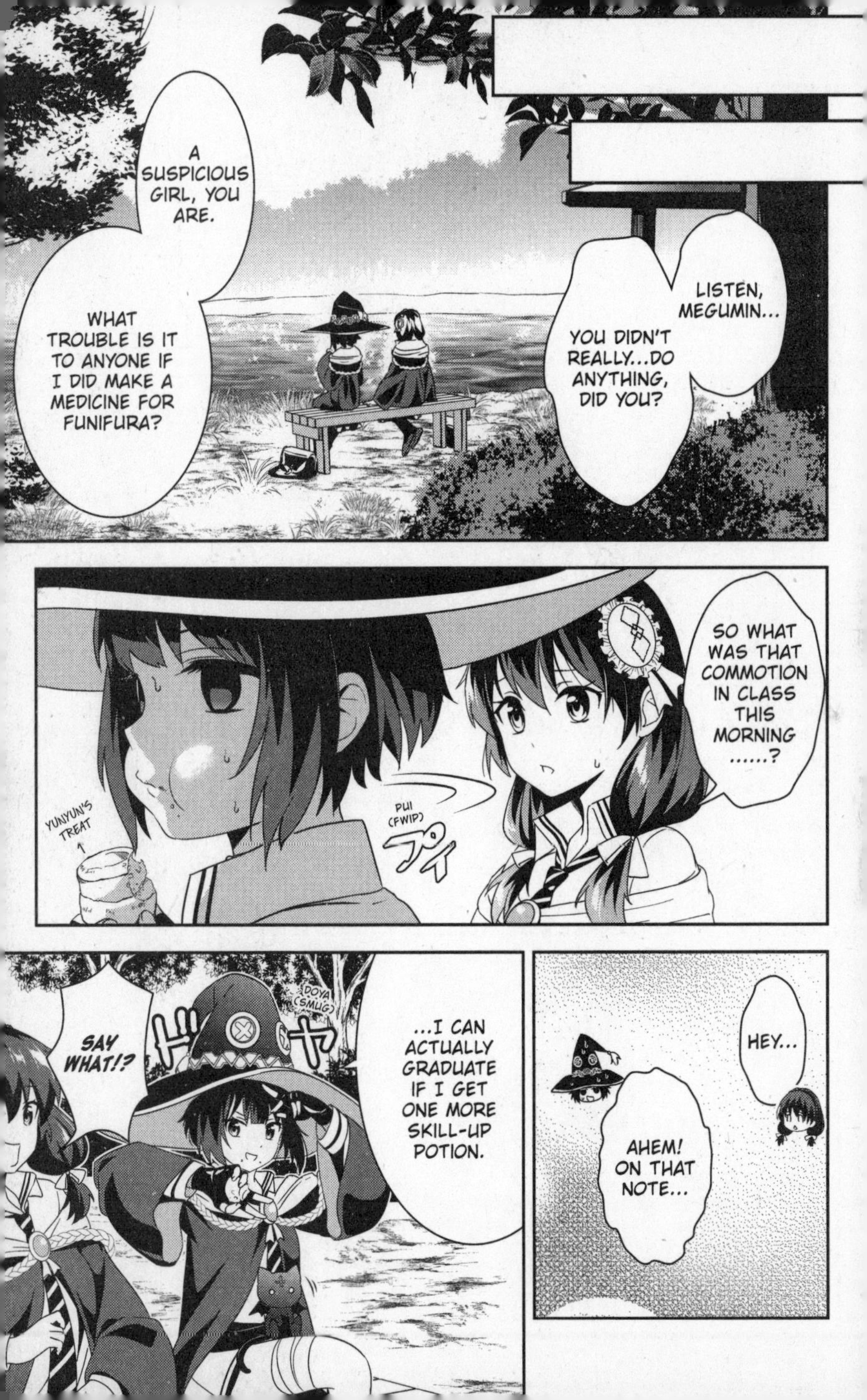
LISTEN, MEGUMIN...
YOU DIDN'T REALLY...DO ANYTHING, DID YOU?
A SUSPICIOUS GIRL, YOU ARE.
WHAT TROUBLE IS IT TO ANYONE IF I DID MAKE A MEDICINE FOR FUNIFURA?
SO WHAT WAS THAT COMMOTION IN CLASS THIS MORNING ......?
PUI (FWIP)
YUNYUN'S TREAT
HEY...
AHEM! ON THAT NOTE...
...I CAN ACTUALLY GRADUATE IF I GET ONE MORE SKILL-UP POTION.
DOYA (SMUG)
SAY WHAT!?

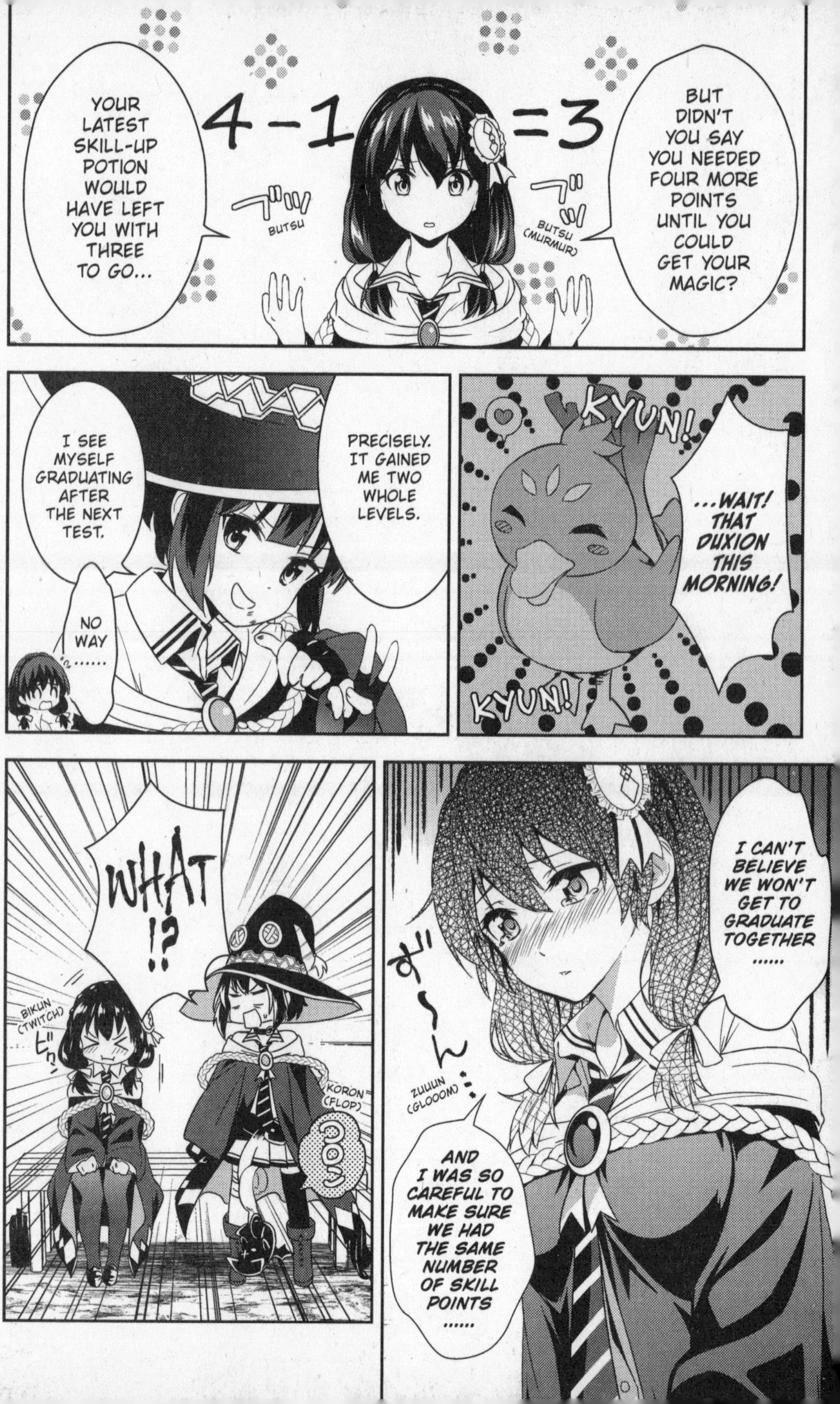
BUT DIDN'T YOU SAY YOU NEEDED FOUR MORE POINTS UNTIL YOU COULD GET YOUR MAGIC?
4 - 1 = 3
BUTSU (MURMUR)
BUTSU
YOUR LATEST SKILL-UP POTION WOULD HAVE LEFT YOU WITH THREE TO GO...
KYUN!
...WAIT! THAT DUXION THIS MORNING!
KYUN!
PRECISELY. IT GAINED ME TWO WHOLE LEVELS.
I SEE MYSELF GRADUATING AFTER THE NEXT TEST.
NO WAY ......
I CAN'T BELIEVE WE WON'T GET TO GRADUATE TOGETHER ......
ZUUUN (GLOOOM)
AND I WAS SO CAREFUL TO MAKE SURE WE HAD THE SAME NUMBER OF SKILL POINTS ......
WHAT !?
KORON (FLOP)
BIKUN (TWITCH)

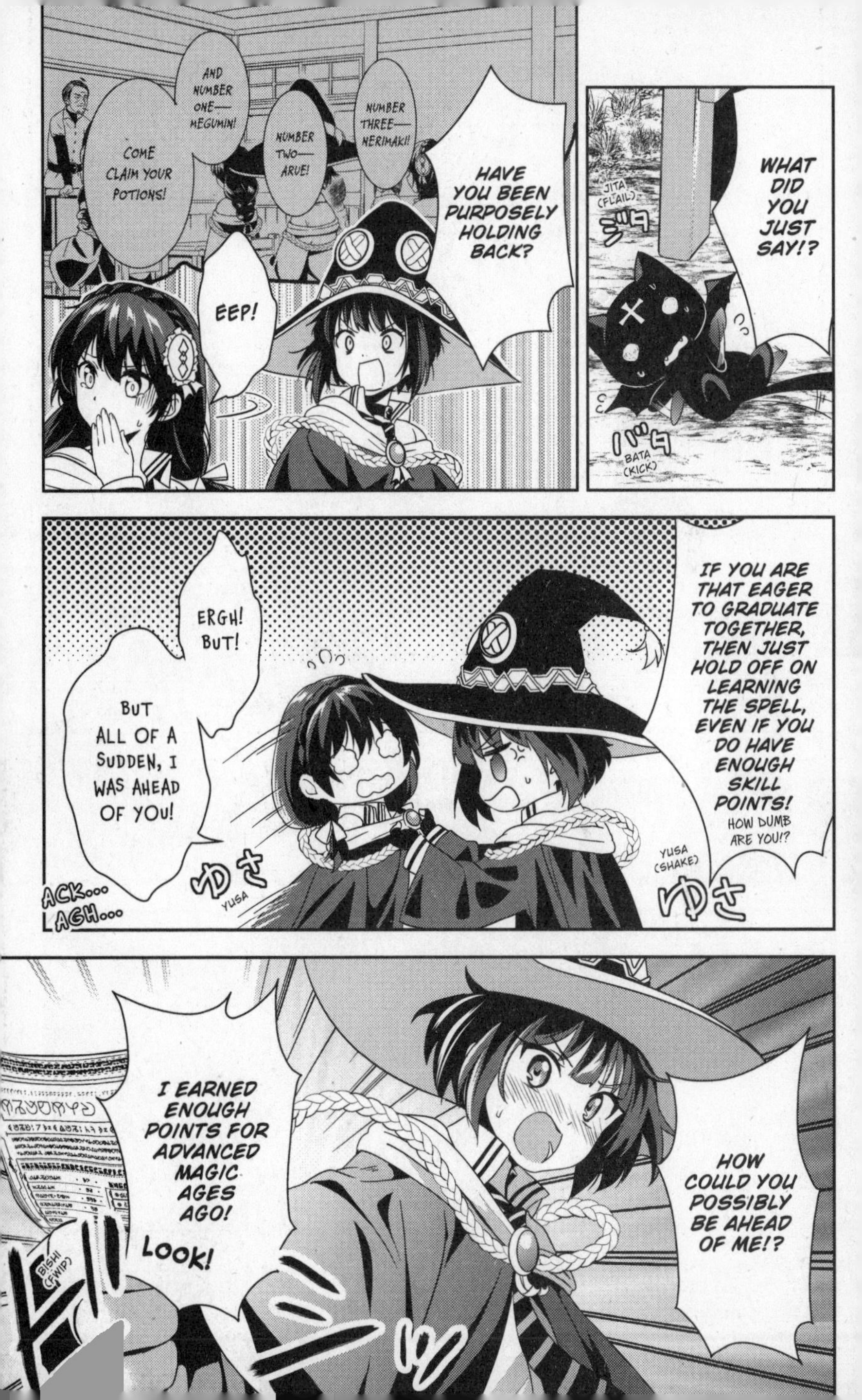
WHAT DID YOU JUST SAY!?
JITA (FLAIL)
BATA (KICK)
HAVE YOU BEEN PURPOSELY HOLDING BACK?
NUMBER THREE— NERIMAKI!
NUMBER TWO— ARUE!
AND NUMBER ONE— MEGUMIN!
COME CLAIM YOUR POTIONS!
EEP!
IF YOU ARE THAT EAGER TO GRADUATE TOGETHER, THEN JUST HOLD OFF ON LEARNING THE SPELL, EVEN IF YOU DO HAVE ENOUGH SKILL POINTS!
HOW DUMB ARE YOU!?
YUSA (SHAKE)
ERGH! BUT!
BUT ALL OF A SUDDEN, I WAS AHEAD OF YOU!
YUSA
ACK... AGH...
HOW COULD YOU POSSIBLY BE AHEAD OF ME!?
I EARNED ENOUGH POINTS FOR ADVANCED MAGIC AGES AGO!
LOOK!
BISHI (FWIP)

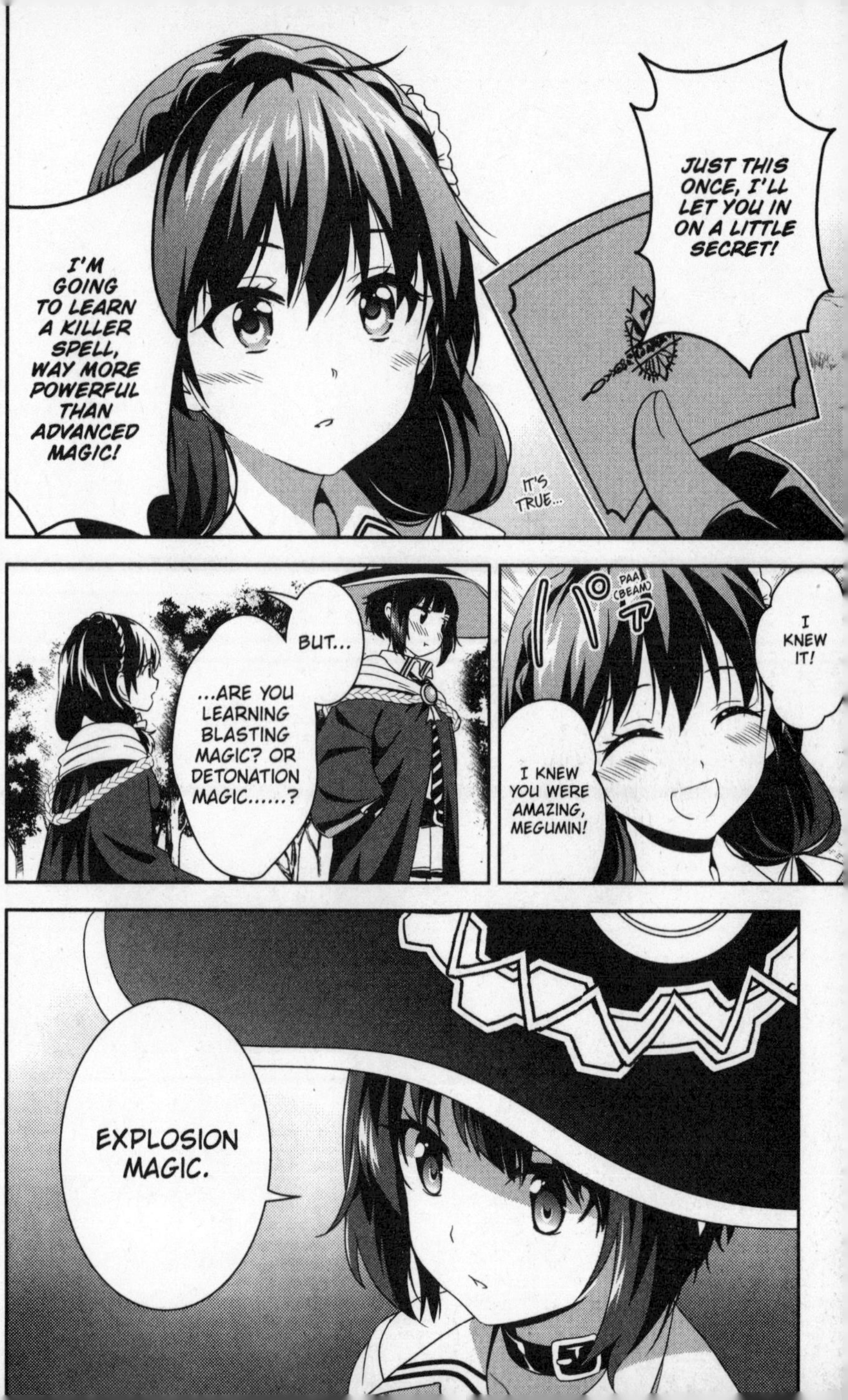
JUST THIS ONCE, I'LL LET YOU IN ON A LITTLE SECRET!
I'M GOING TO LEARN A KILLER SPELL, WAY MORE POWERFUL THAN ADVANCED MAGIC!
IT'S TRUE...
パァ
PAA (BEAM)
I KNEW IT!
I KNEW YOU WERE AMAZING, MEGUMIN!
BUT...
...ARE YOU LEARNING BLASTING MAGIC? OR DETONATION MAGIC......?
EXPLOSION MAGIC.

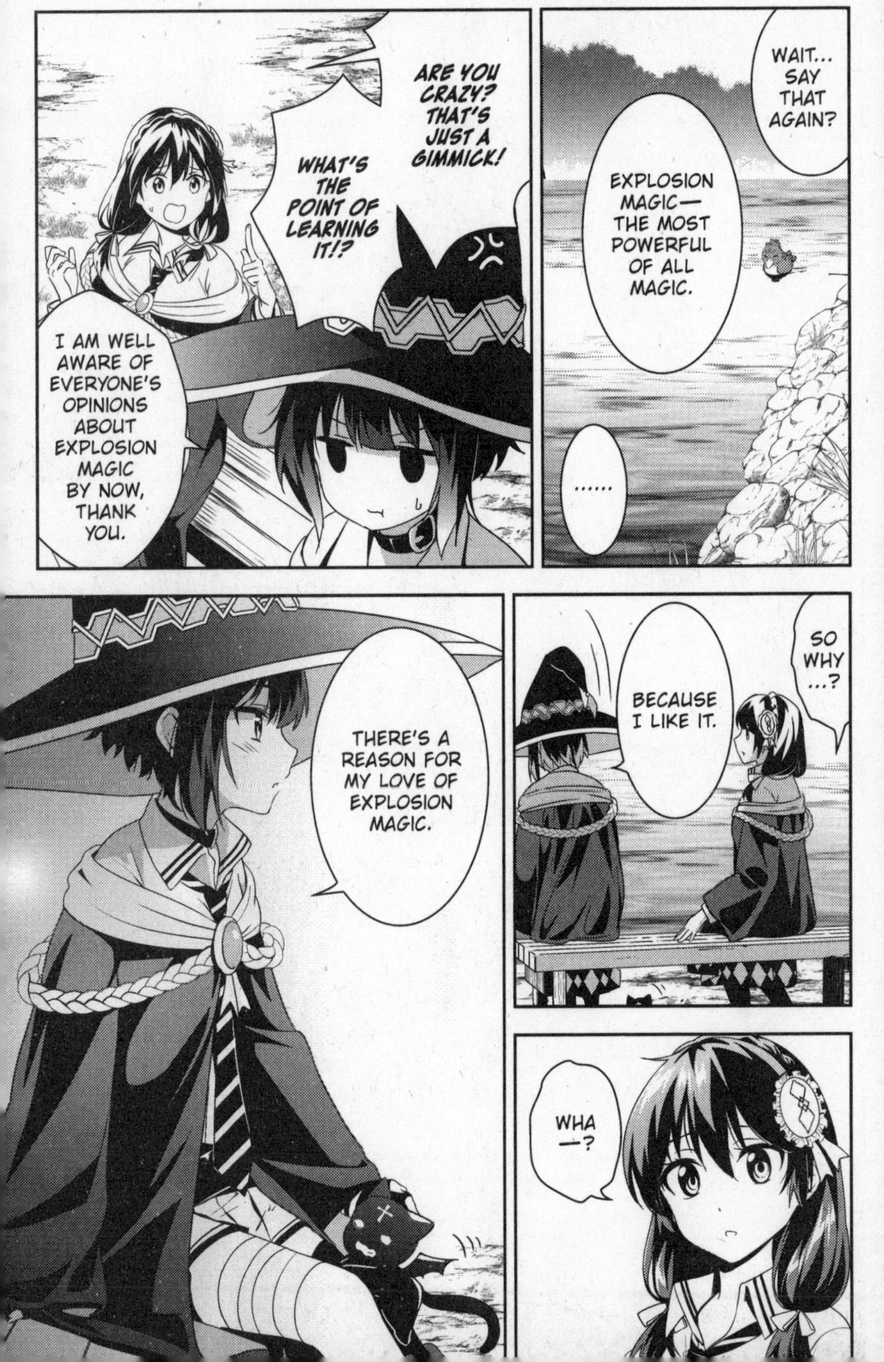
WAIT... SAY THAT AGAIN?
EXPLOSION MAGIC— THE MOST POWERFUL OF ALL MAGIC.
......
ARE YOU CRAZY? THAT'S JUST A GIMMICK!
WHAT'S THE POINT OF LEARNING IT!?
I AM WELL AWARE OF EVERYONE'S OPINIONS ABOUT EXPLOSION MAGIC BY NOW, THANK YOU.
SO WHY ...?
BECAUSE I LIKE IT.
WHA—?
THERE'S A REASON FOR MY LOVE OF EXPLOSION MAGIC.

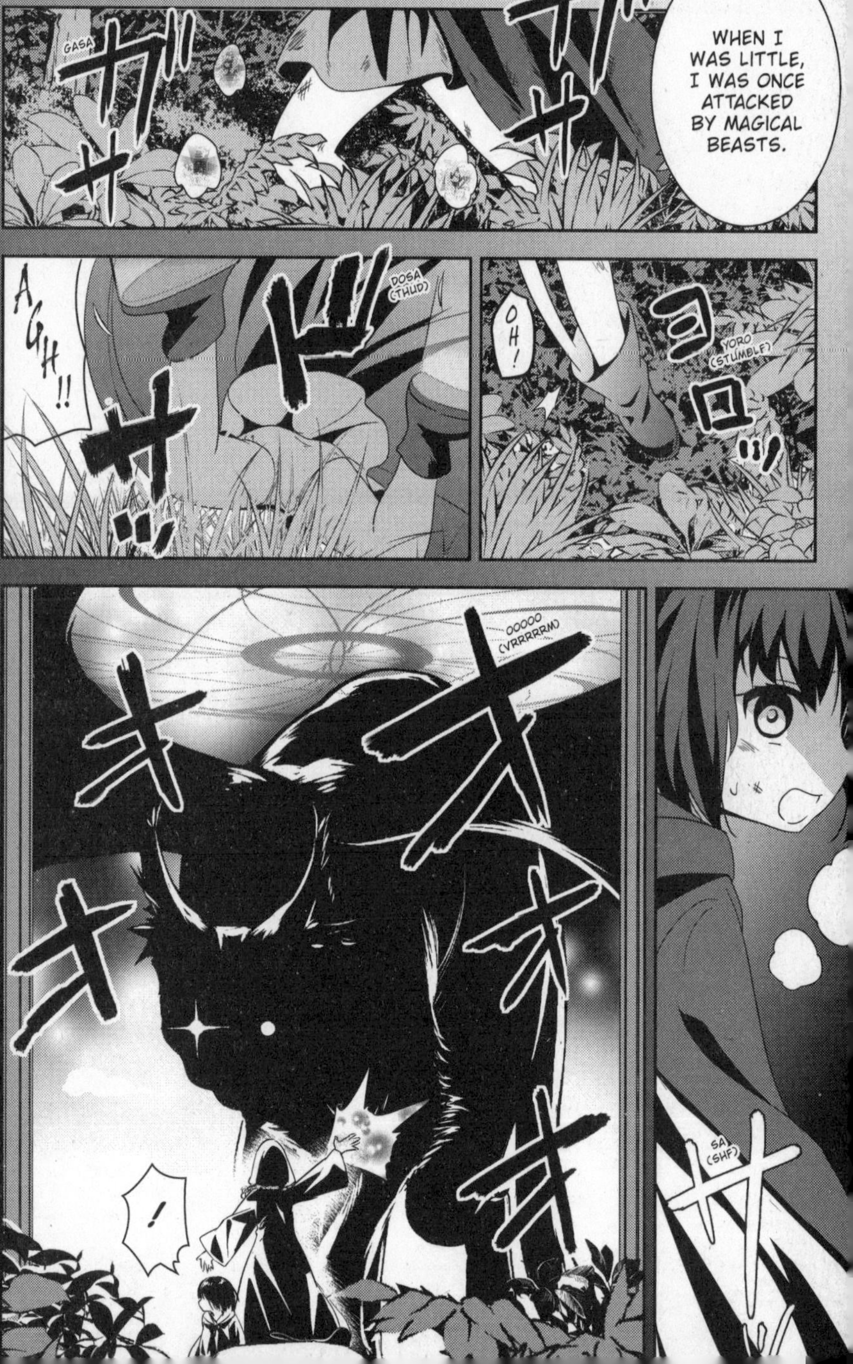
WHEN I WAS LITTLE, I WAS ONCE ATTACKED BY MAGICAL BEASTS.
GASA (RUSTLE)
GASA
YORO (STUMBLE)
OH!
DOSA (THUD)
AGH!!
SA (SHF)
OOOOO (VRRRRRM)
!

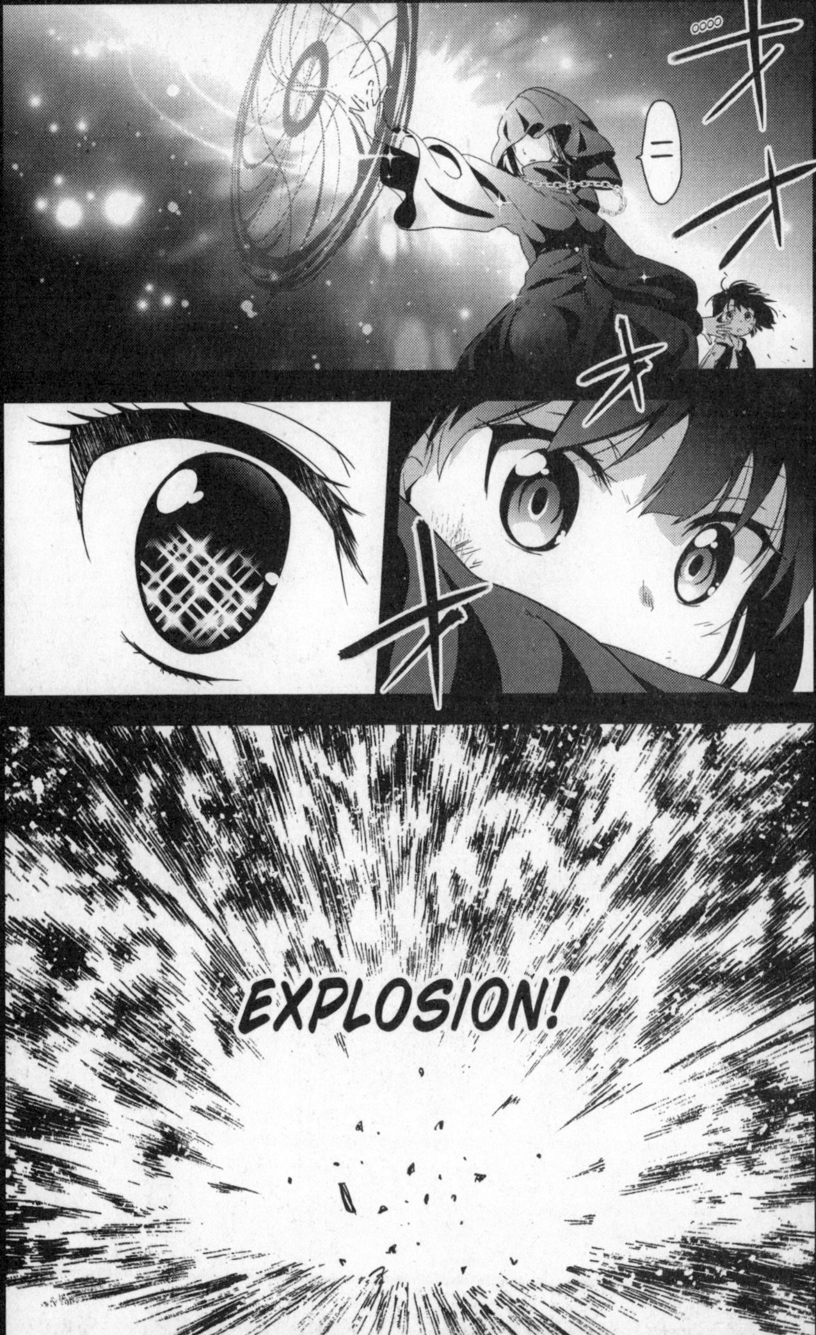
oooo
オオオオ
EXPLOSION!

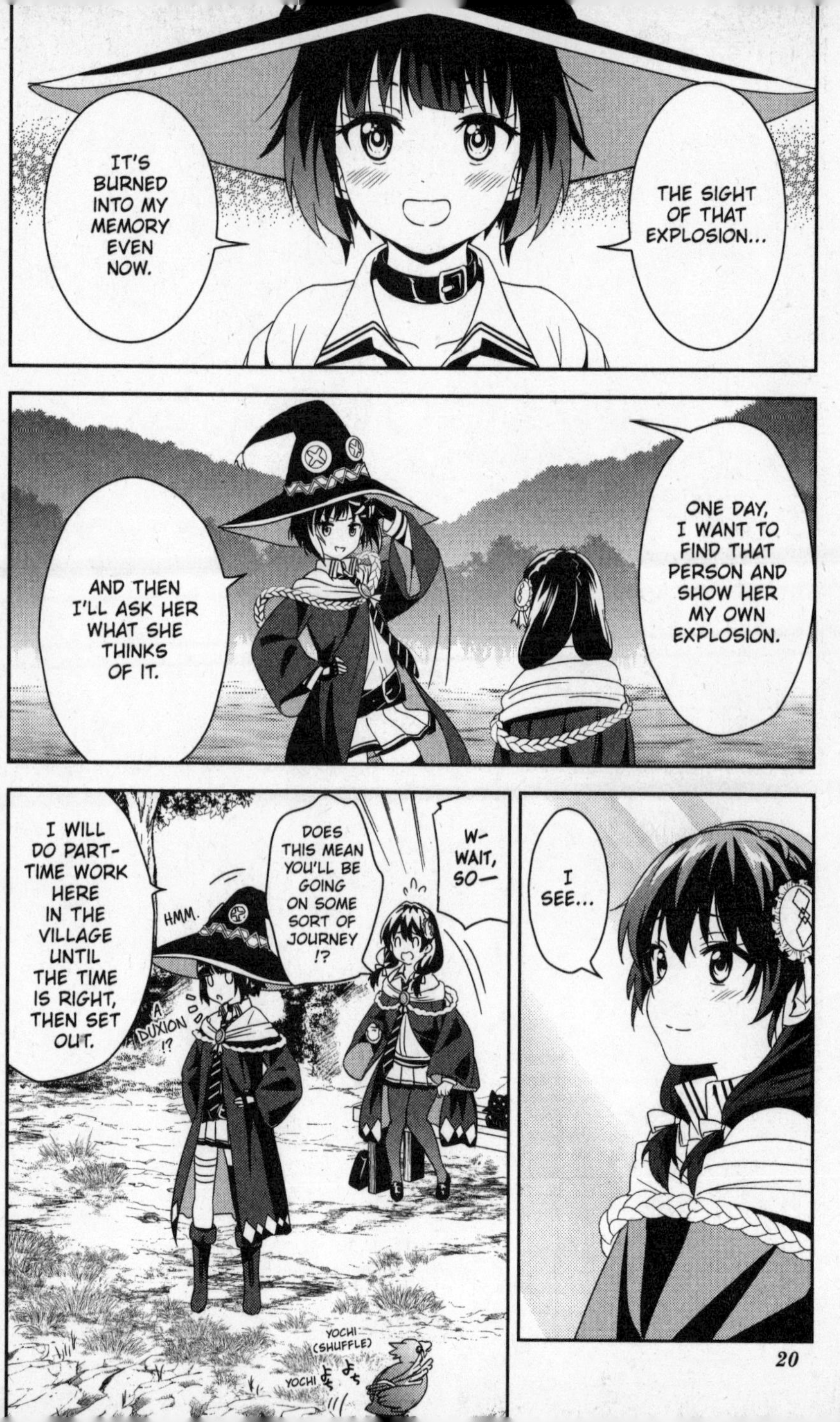
THE SIGHT OF THAT EXPLOSION...
IT'S BURNED INTO MY MEMORY EVEN NOW.
ONE DAY, I WANT TO FIND THAT PERSON AND SHOW HER MY OWN EXPLOSION.
AND THEN I'LL ASK HER WHAT SHE THINKS OF IT.
I SEE...
W-WAIT, SO—
DOES THIS MEAN YOU'LL BE GOING ON SOME SORT OF JOURNEY!?
HMM.
I WILL DO PART-TIME WORK HERE IN THE VILLAGE UNTIL THE TIME IS RIGHT, THEN SET OUT.
A DUXION!?
YOCHI (SHUFFLE)
YOCHI

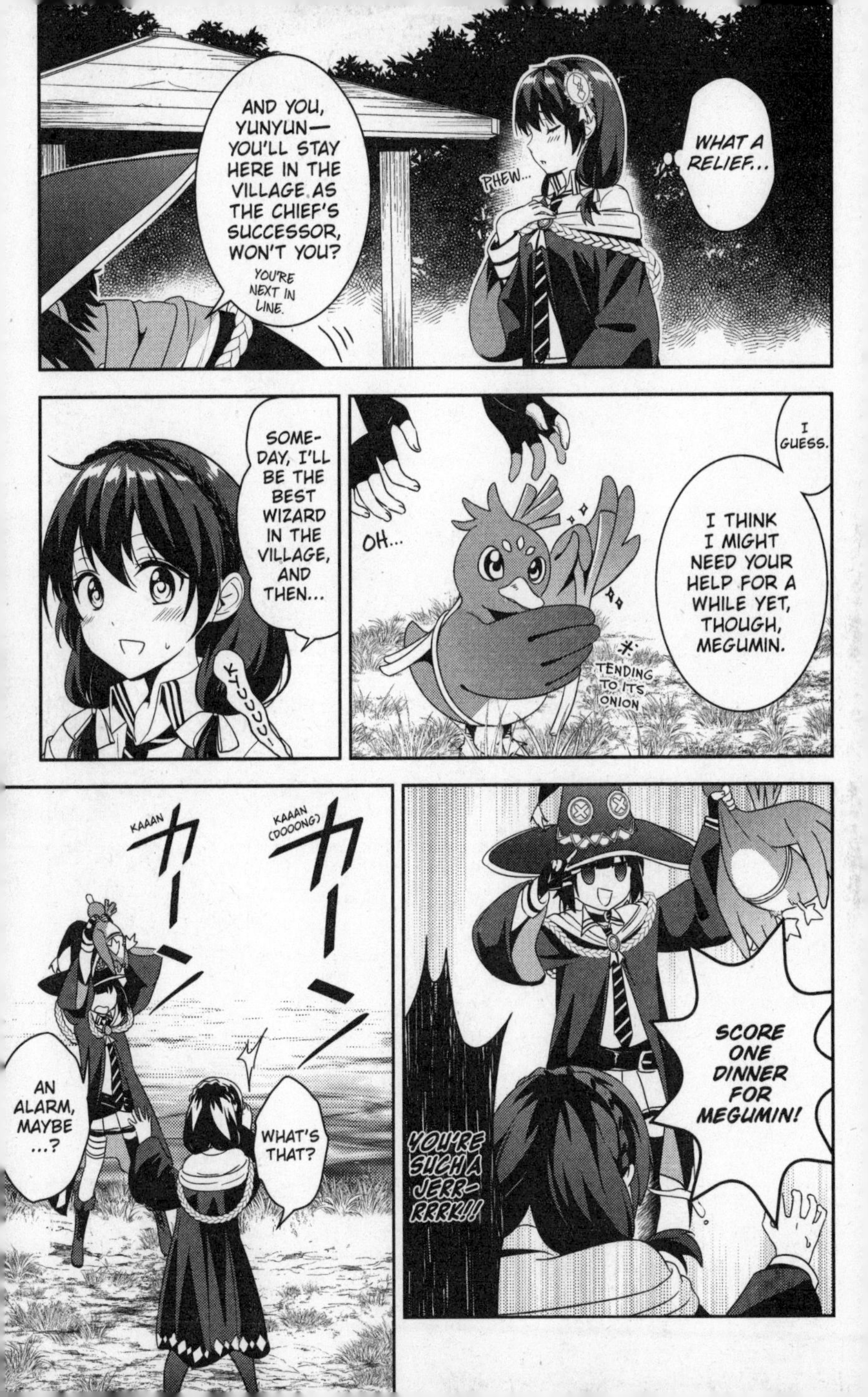
WHAT A RELIEF...
PHEW...
AND YOU, YUNYUN—YOU'LL STAY HERE IN THE VILLAGE AS THE CHIEF'S SUCCESSOR, WON'T YOU?
YOU'RE NEXT IN LINE.
I GUESS.
I THINK I MIGHT NEED YOUR HELP FOR A WHILE YET, THOUGH, MEGUMIN.
TENDING TO ITS ONION
OH...
SOMEDAY, I'LL BE THE BEST WIZARD IN THE VILLAGE, AND THEN...
KTUUUU!
SCORE ONE DINNER FOR MEGUMIN!
YOU'RE SUCH A JERR-RRRK!!
KAAAN (DOOONG)
KAAAN
WHAT'S THAT?
AN ALARM, MAYBE...?

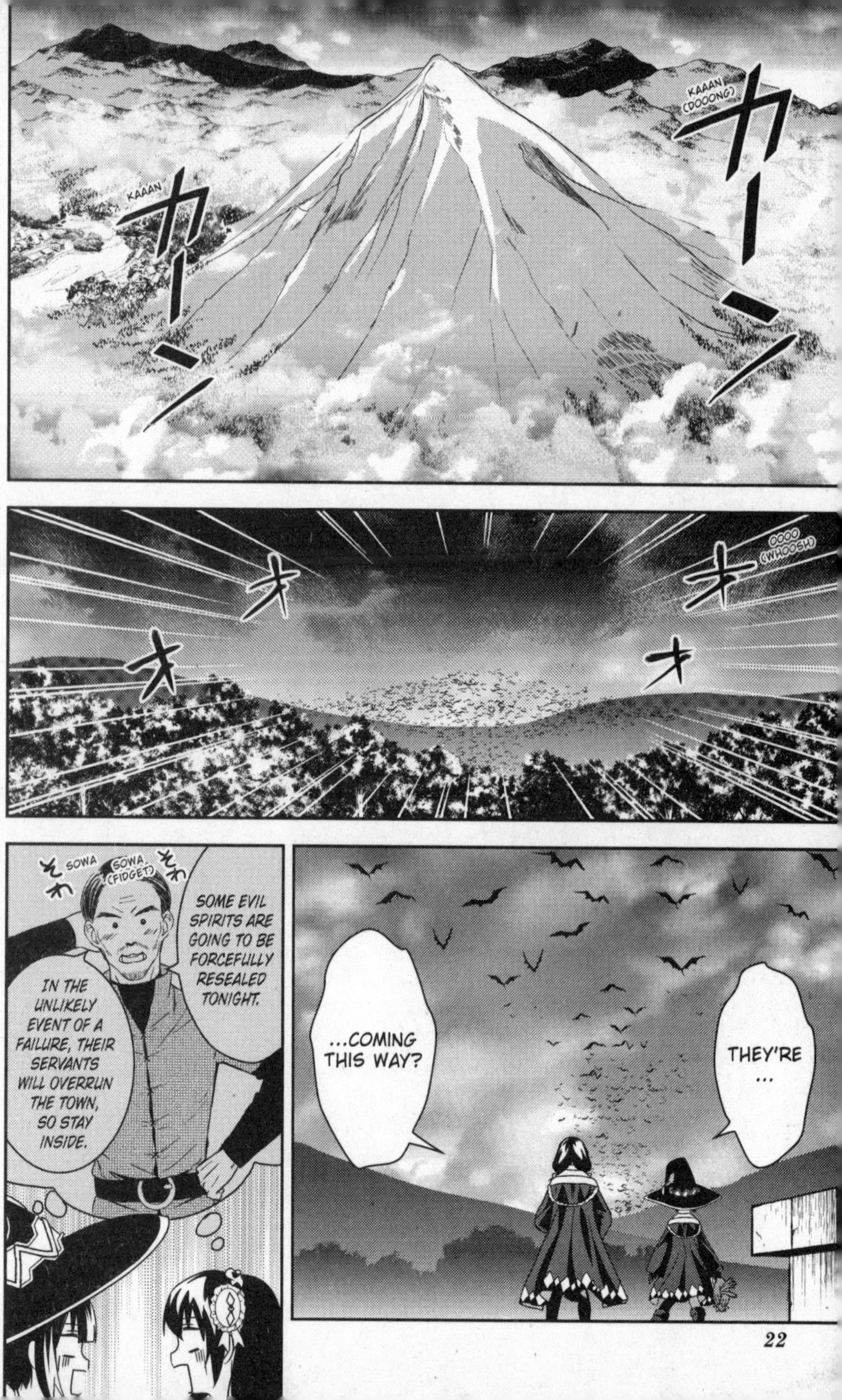
KAAAN (DOOONG)
KAAAN
OOOO (WHOOSH)
THEY'RE ...
...COMING THIS WAY?
SOWA SOWA (FIDGET)
SOME EVIL SPIRITS ARE GOING TO BE FORCEFULLY RESEALED TONIGHT.
IN THE UNLIKELY EVENT OF A FAILURE, THEIR SERVANTS WILL OVERRUN THE TOWN, SO STAY INSIDE.

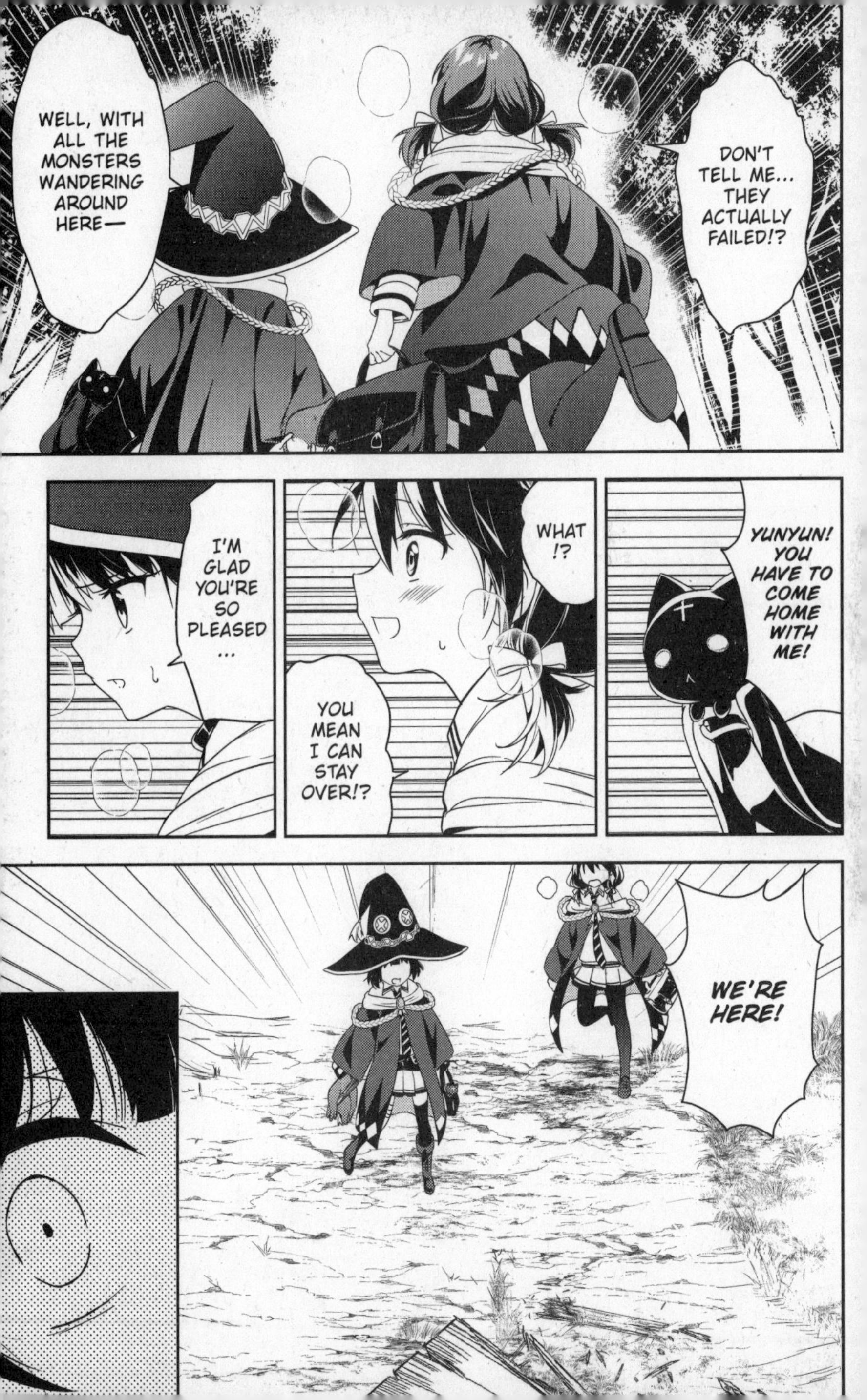
DON'T TELL ME... THEY ACTUALLY FAILED!?
WELL, WITH ALL THE MONSTERS WANDERING AROUND HERE—
YUNYUN! YOU HAVE TO COME HOME WITH ME!
WHAT!?
YOU MEAN I CAN STAY OVER!?
I'M GLAD YOU'RE SO PLEASED...
WE'RE HERE!

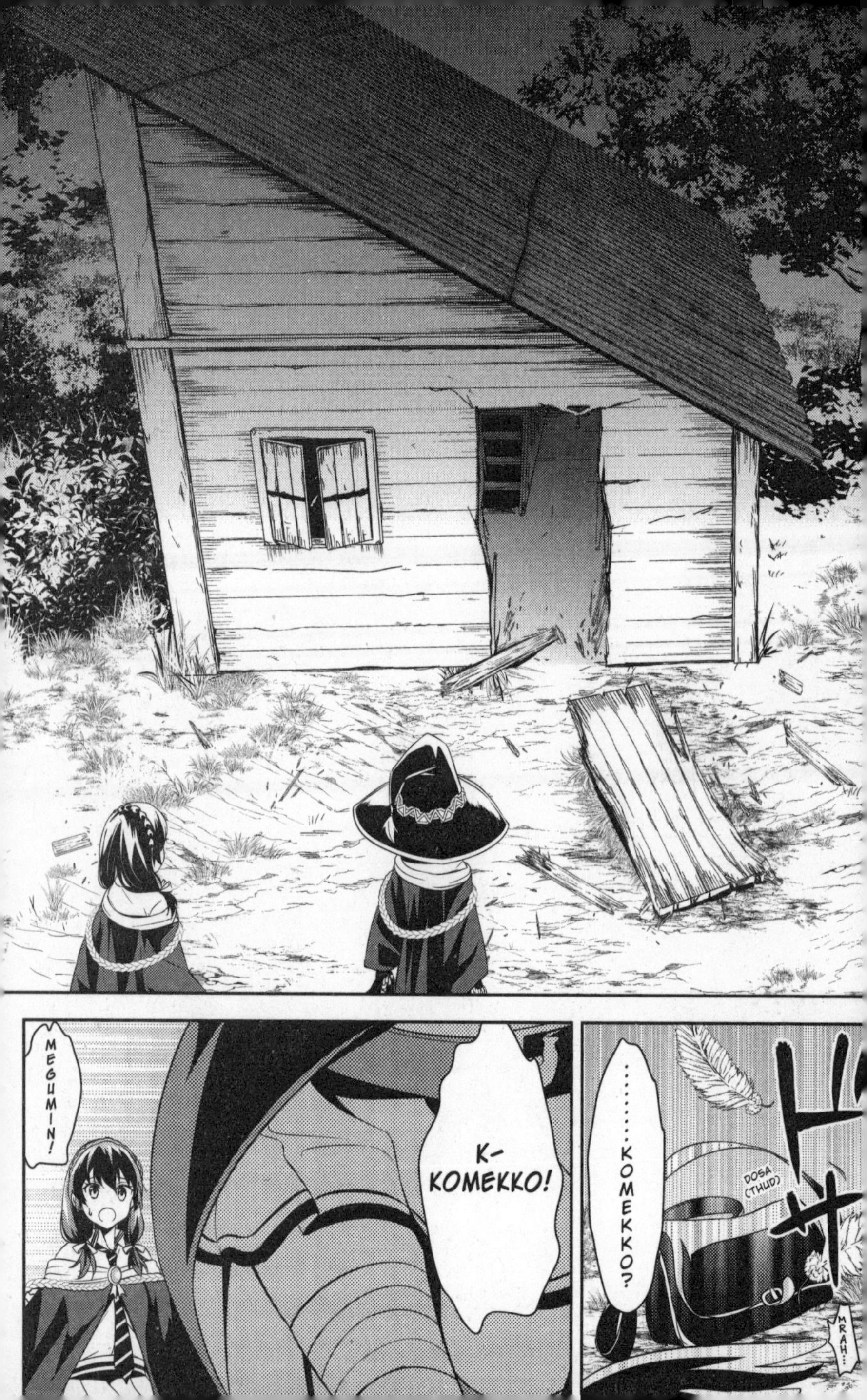
......KOMEKKO?
DOSA (THUD)
MRAH...
K-KOMEKKO!
MEGUMIN!

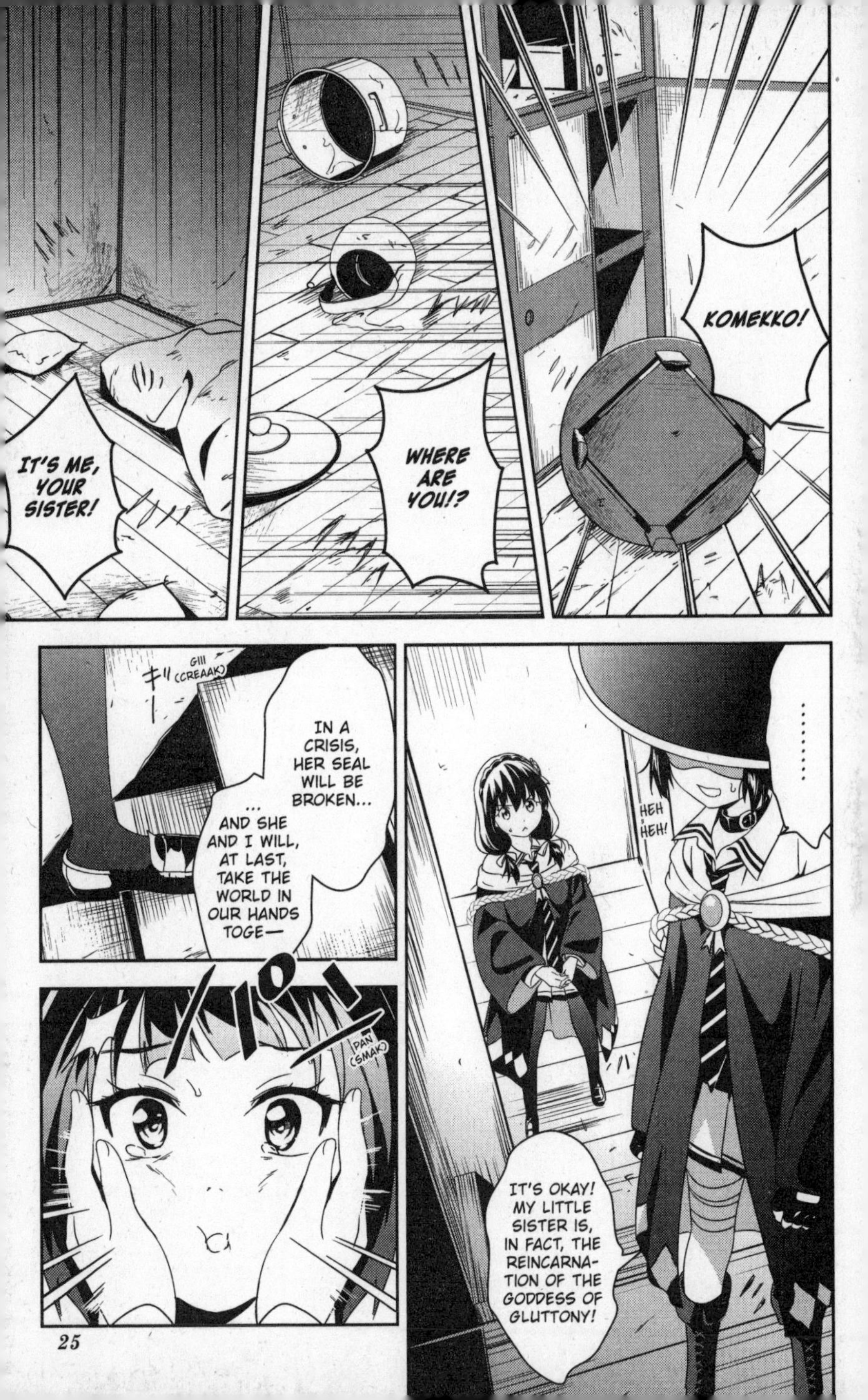
KOMEKKO!
WHERE ARE YOU!?
IT'S ME, YOUR SISTER!
....
HEH HEH!
IT'S OKAY! MY LITTLE SISTER IS, IN FACT, THE REINCARNATION OF THE GODDESS OF GLUTTONY!
GIII (CREAAK)
IN A CRISIS, HER SEAL WILL BE BROKEN...
...AND SHE AND I WILL, AT LAST, TAKE THE WORLD IN OUR HANDS TOGE—
PAN (SMAK)

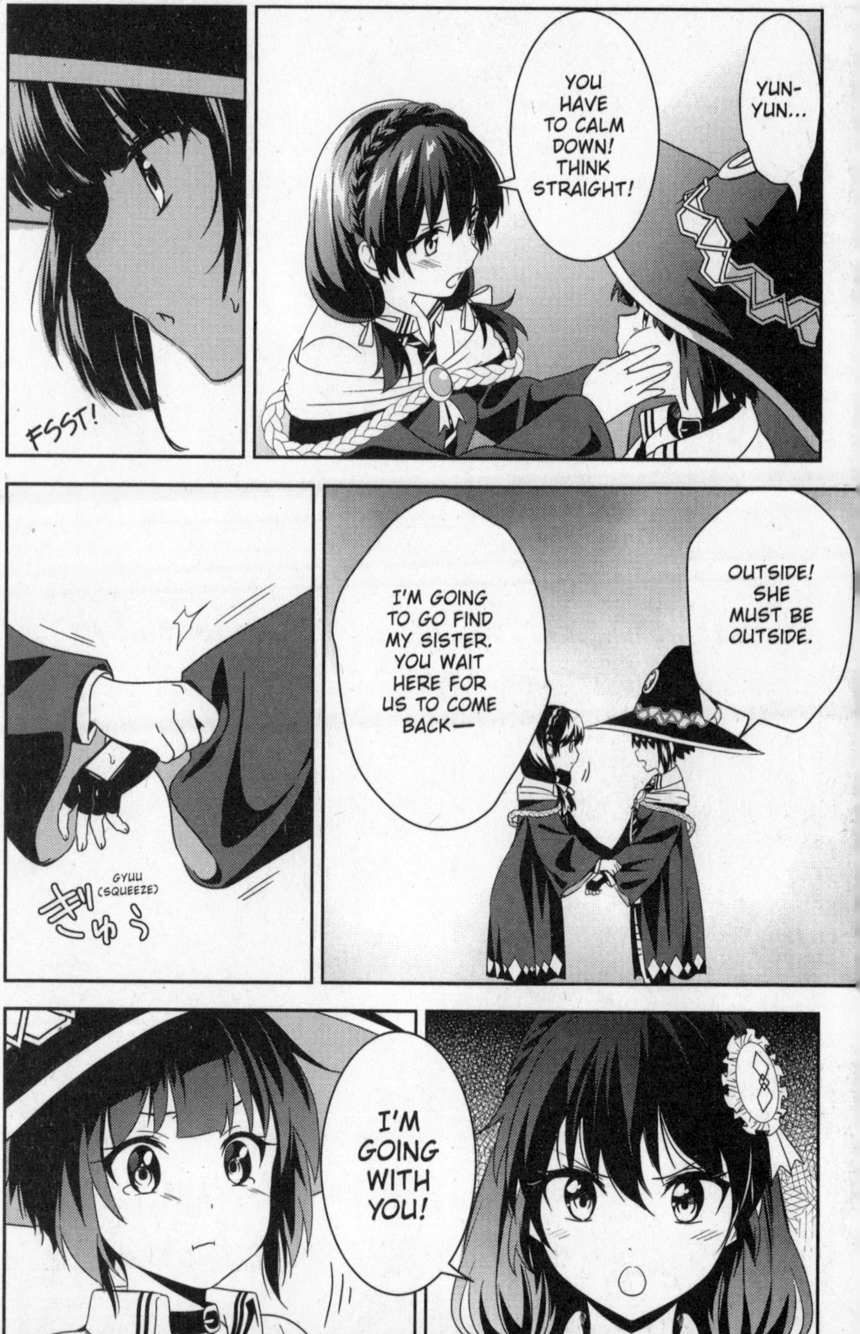
YUN-YUN...
YOU HAVE TO CALM DOWN! THINK STRAIGHT!
FSST!
OUTSIDE! SHE MUST BE OUTSIDE.
I'M GOING TO GO FIND MY SISTER. YOU WAIT HERE FOR US TO COME BACK—
GYUU (SQUEEZE)
ぎゅう
I'M GOING WITH YOU!

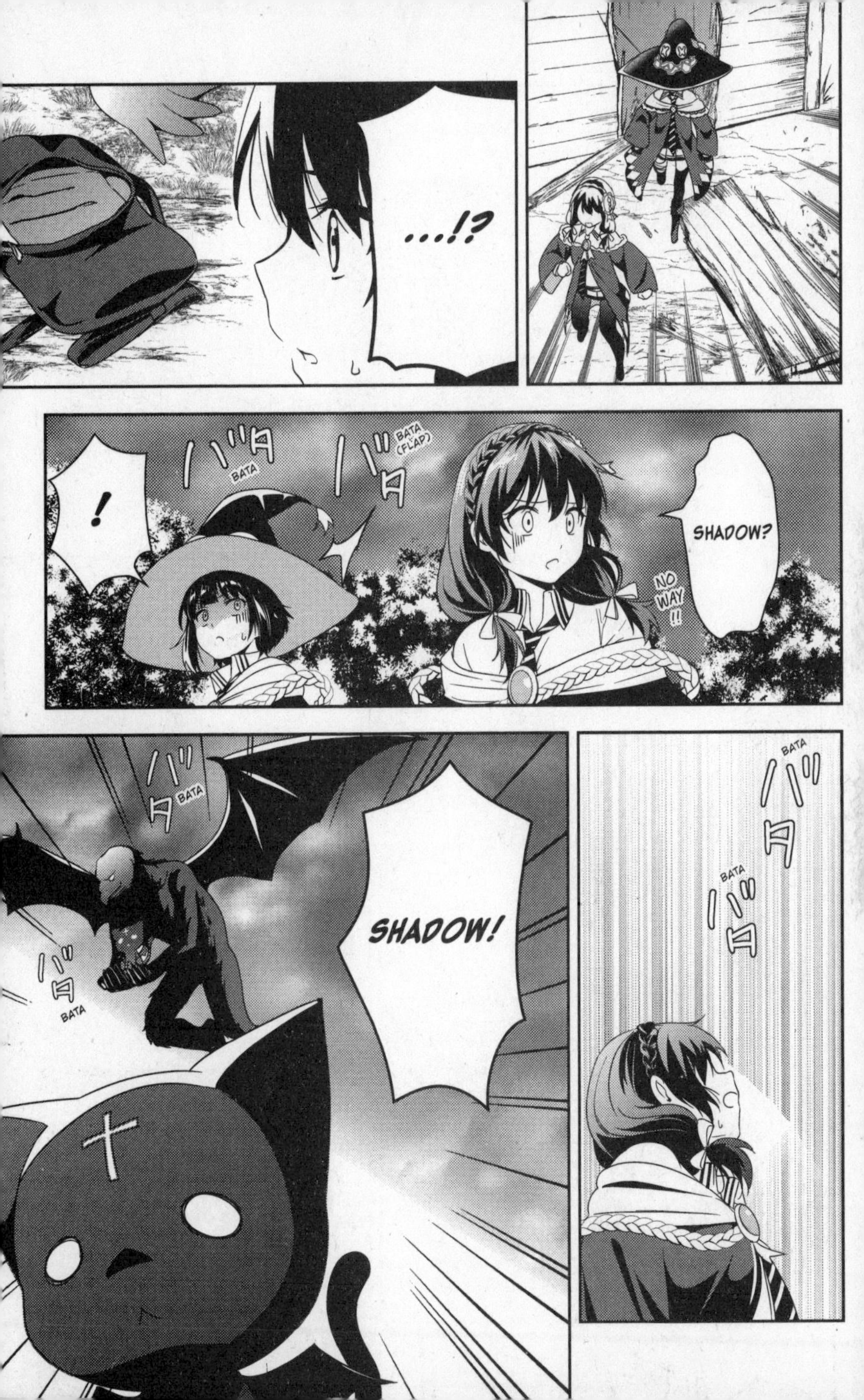
...!?
SHADOW?
NO WAY!!
BATA (FLAP)
BATA
!
BATA
BATA
SHADOW!
BATA
BATA

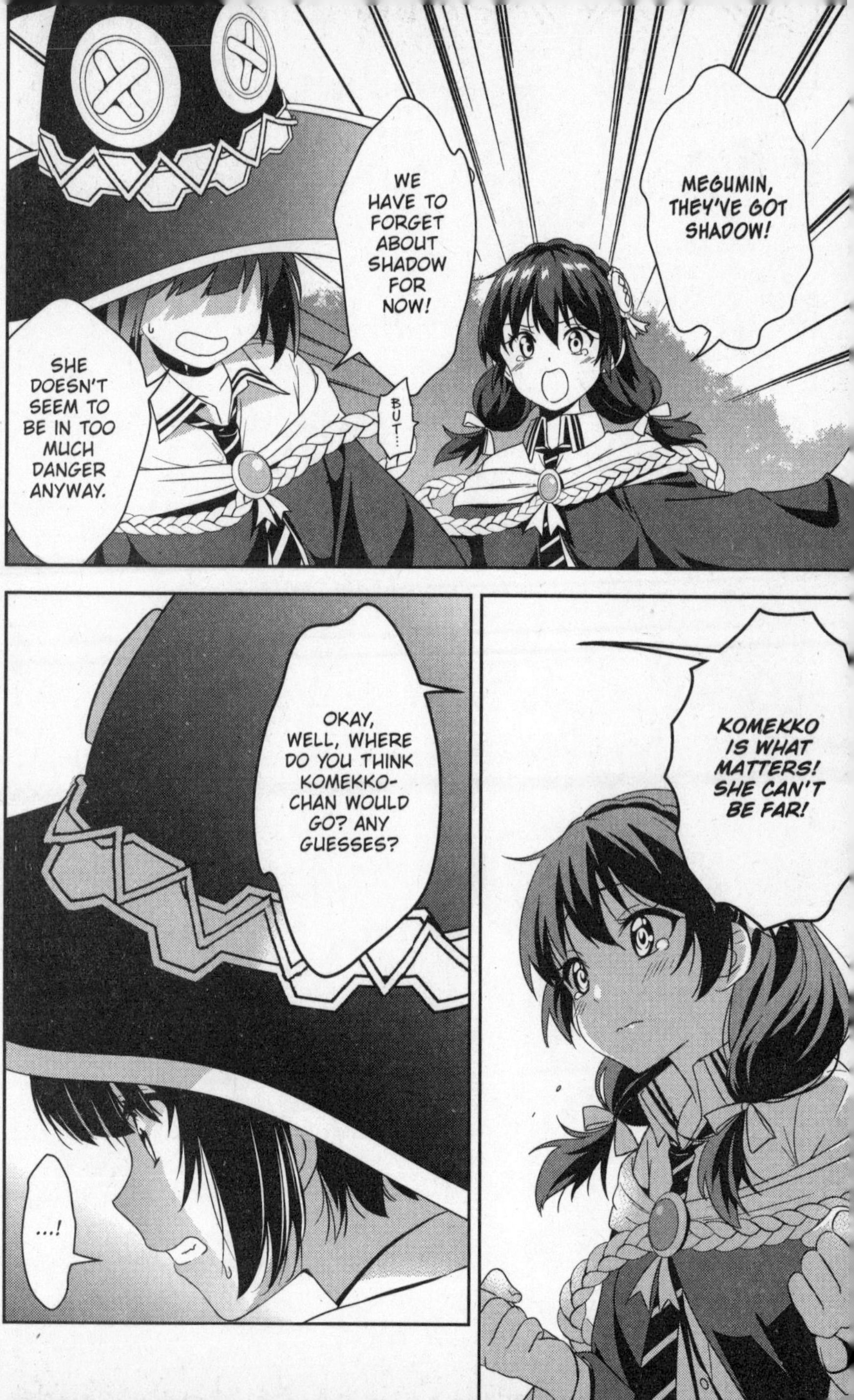
MEGUMIN, THEY'VE GOT SHADOW!
WE HAVE TO FORGET ABOUT SHADOW FOR NOW!
BUT...
SHE DOESN'T SEEM TO BE IN TOO MUCH DANGER ANYWAY.
KOMEKKO IS WHAT MATTERS! SHE CAN'T BE FAR!
OKAY, WELL, WHERE DO YOU THINK KOMEKKO-CHAN WOULD GO? ANY GUESSES?
...!

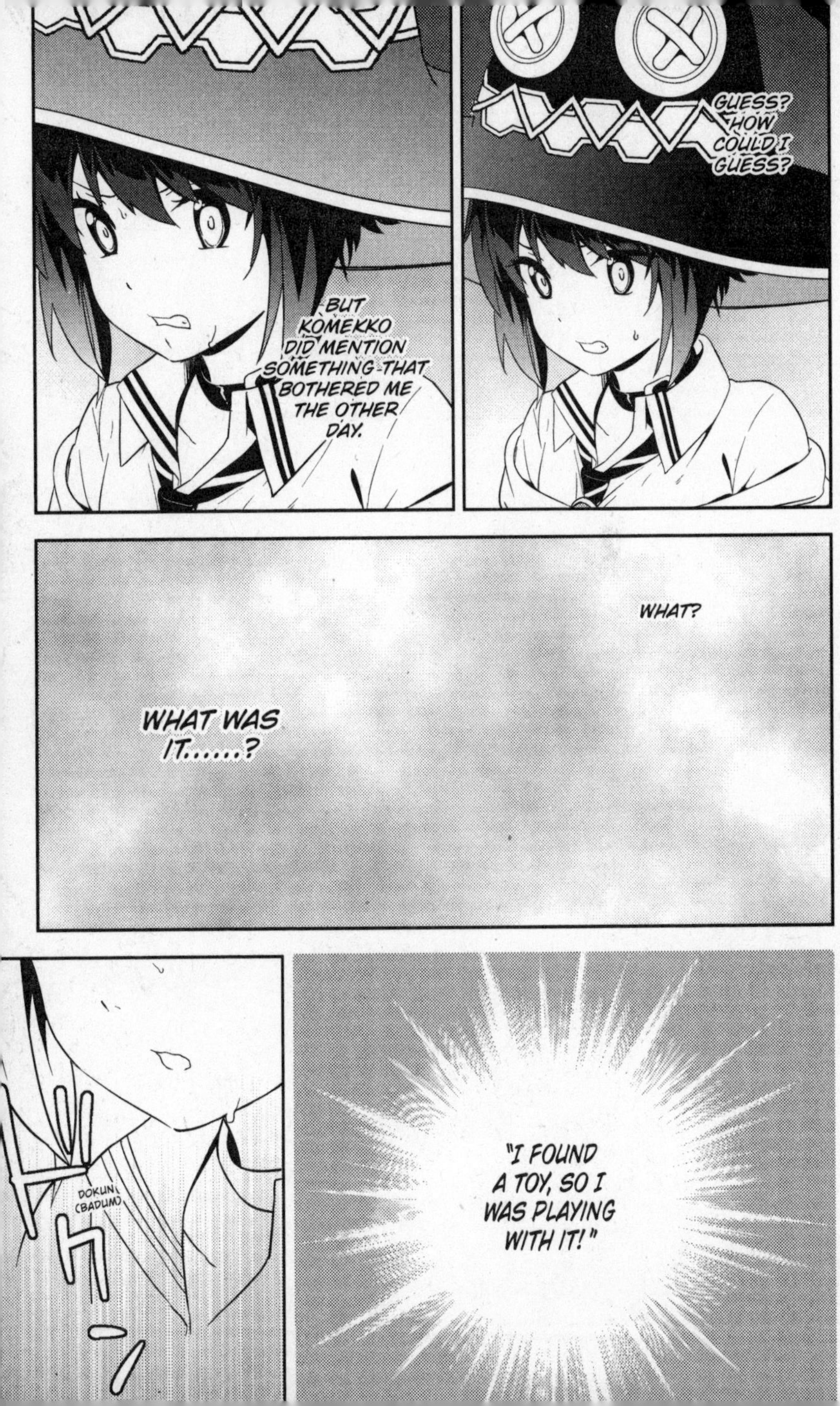
GUESS? HOW COULD I GUESS?
BUT KOMEKKO DID MENTION SOMETHING THAT BOTHERED ME THE OTHER DAY.
WHAT?
WHAT WAS IT......?
"I FOUND A TOY, SO I WAS PLAYING WITH IT!"
DOKUN (BADUM)

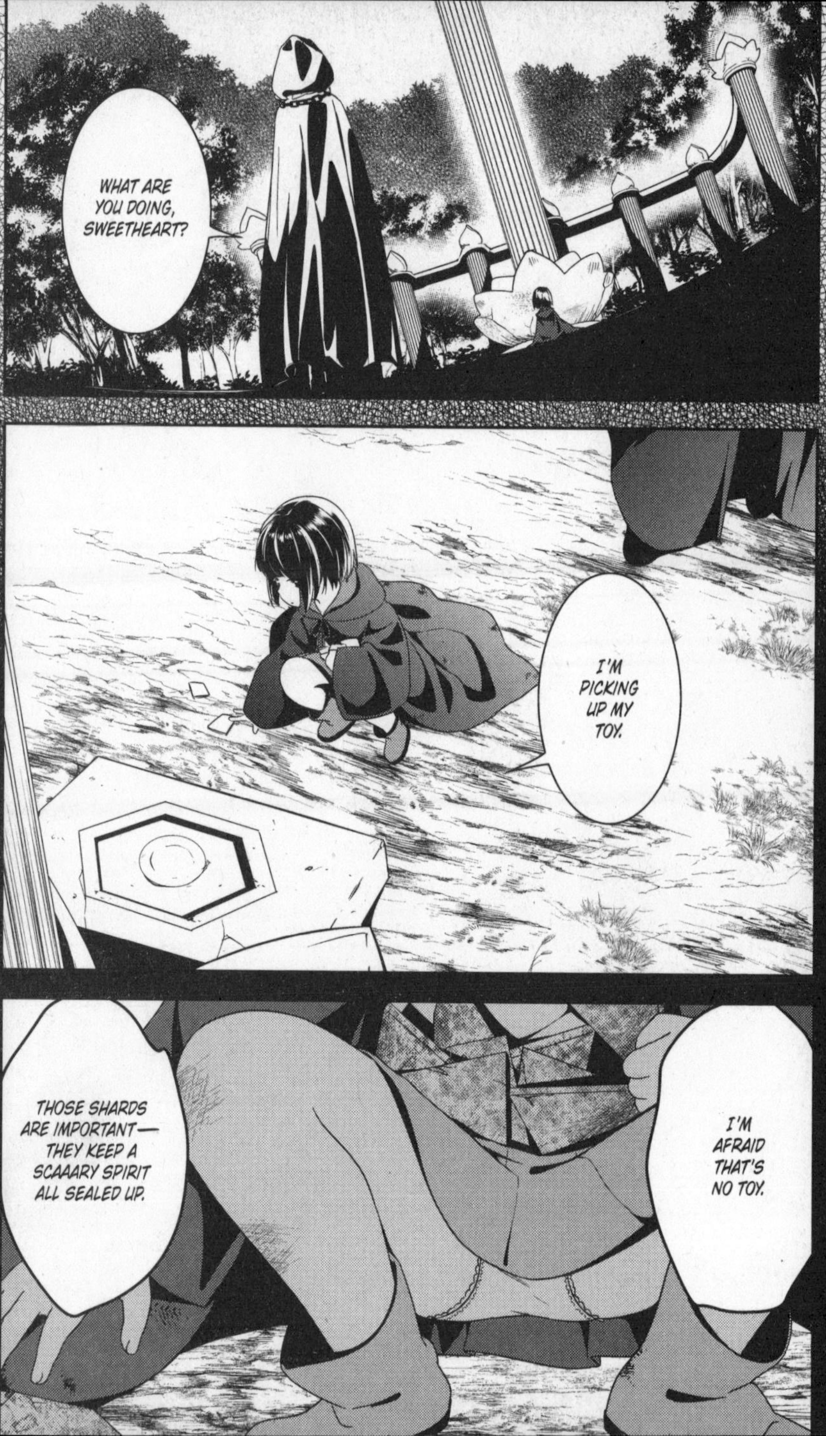
WHAT ARE YOU DOING, SWEETHEART?
I'M PICKING UP MY TOY.
I'M AFRAID THAT'S NO TOY.
THOSE SHARDS ARE IMPORTANT— THEY KEEP A SCAAARY SPIRIT ALL SEALED UP.

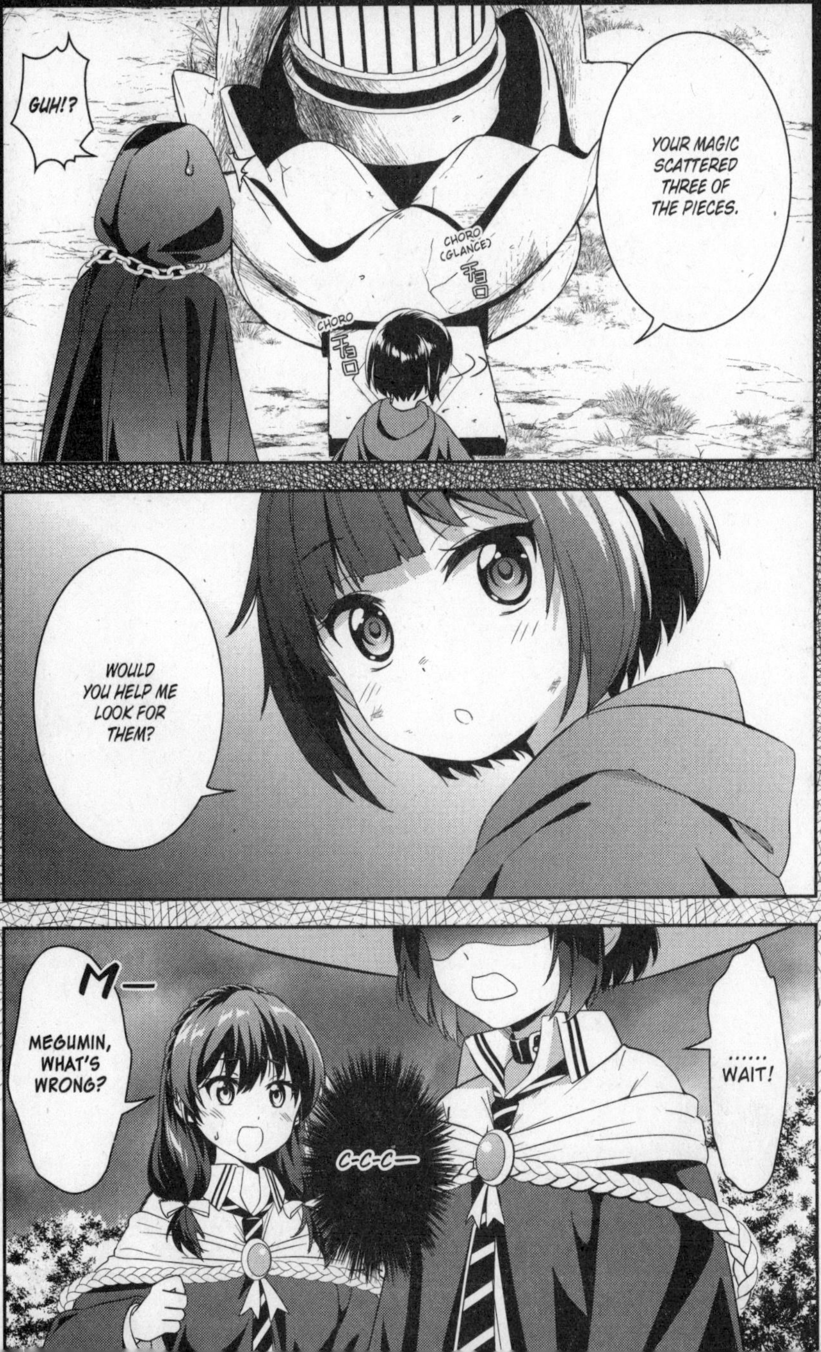
YOUR MAGIC SCATTERED THREE OF THE PIECES.
CHORO (GLANCE)
チョロ
CHORO
チョロ
GUH!?
WOULD YOU HELP ME LOOK FOR THEM?
......WAIT!
C-C-C—
M—
MEGUMIN, WHAT'S WRONG?

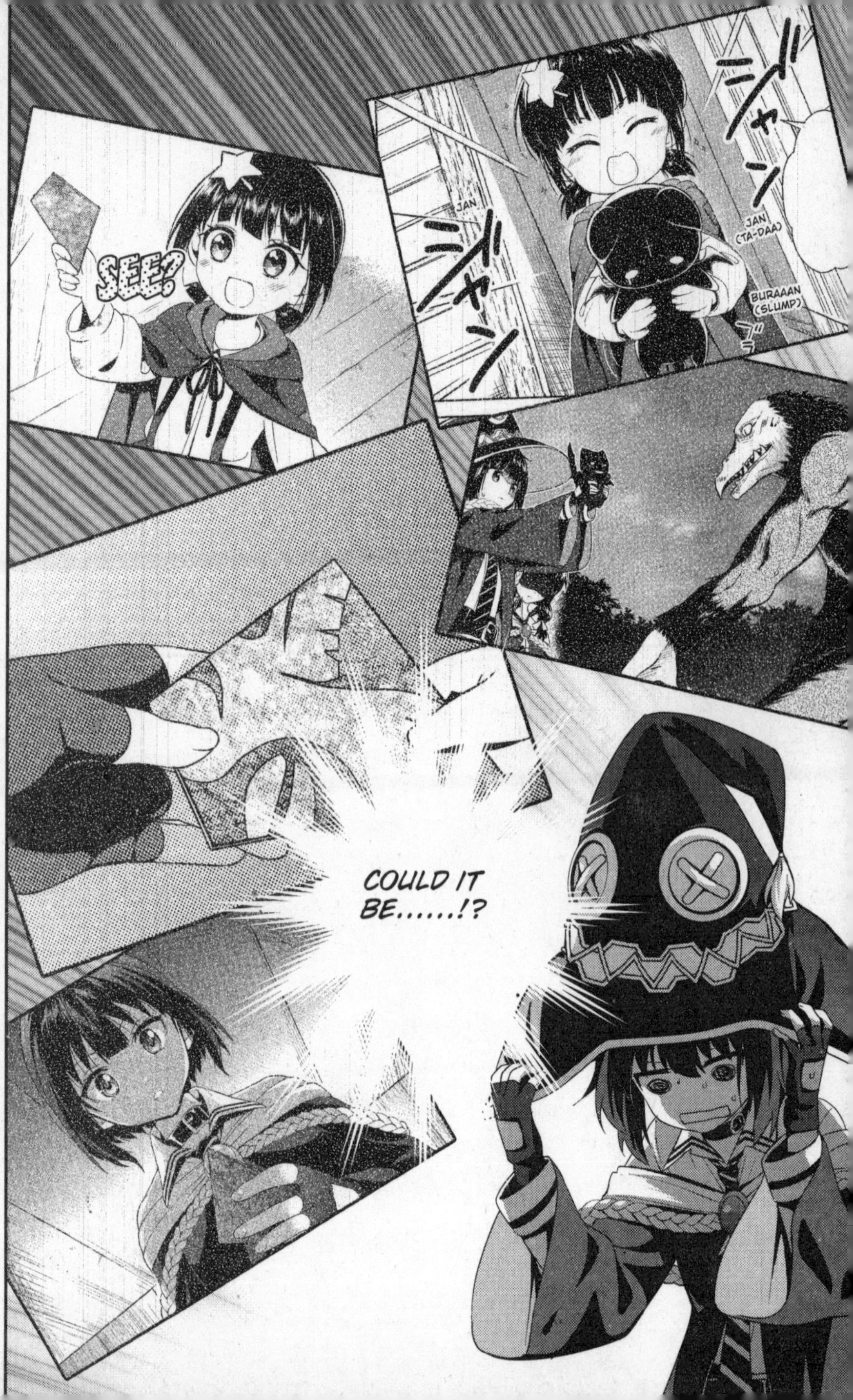
ジャン
JAN (TA-DAA)
BURAAAN (SLUMP)
JAN
ジャン
SEE?
COULD IT BE......!?

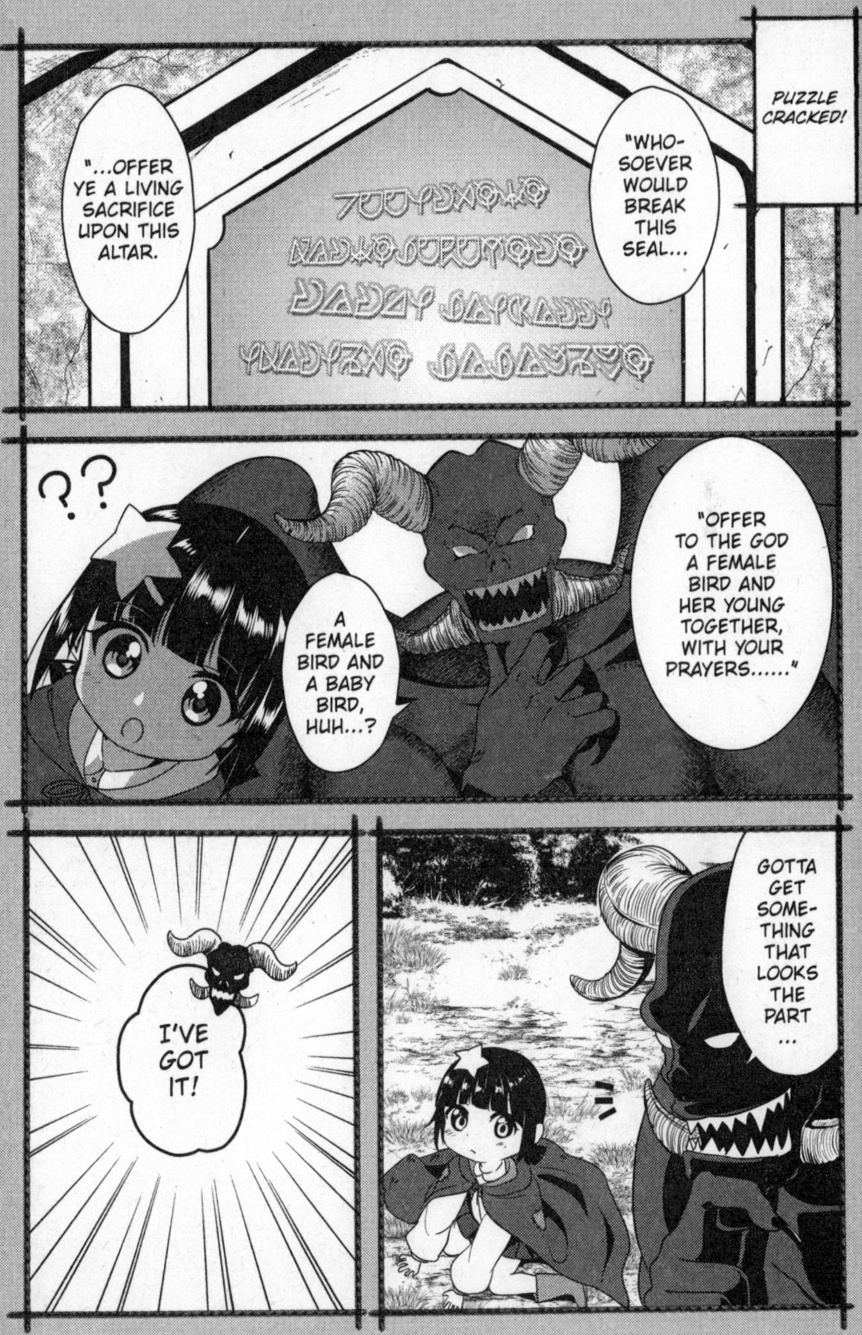
PUZZLE CRACKED!
"WHO-SOEVER WOULD BREAK THIS SEAL...
"...OFFER YE A LIVING SACRIFICE UPON THIS ALTAR.
"OFFER TO THE GOD A FEMALE BIRD AND HER YOUNG TOGETHER, WITH YOUR PRAYERS......"
A FEMALE BIRD AND A BABY BIRD, HUH...?
??
GOTTA GET SOME-THING THAT LOOKS THE PART ...
I'VE GOT IT!

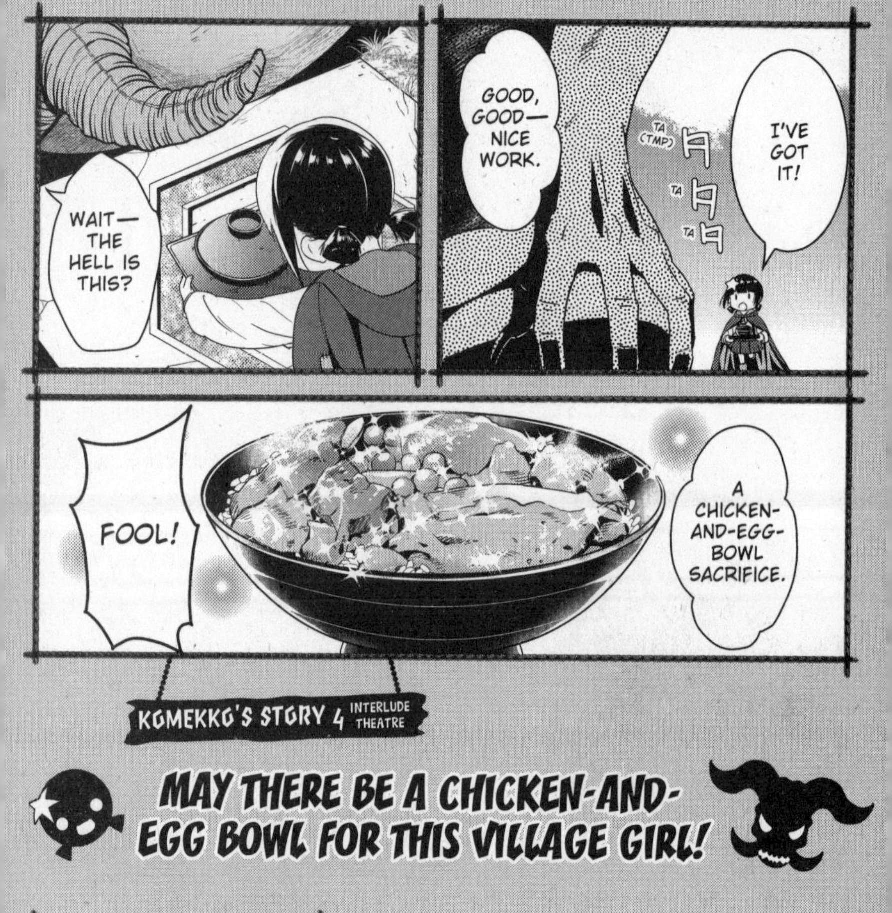
I'VE GOT IT!
TA (TMP) TA TA TA
GOOD, GOOD— NICE WORK.
WAIT— THE HELL IS THIS?
A CHICKEN-AND-EGG-BOWL SACRIFICE.
FOOL!

KOMEKKO'S STORY 4 INTERLUDE THEATRE

MAY THERE BE A CHICKEN-AND-EGG BOWL FOR THIS VILLAGE GIRL!

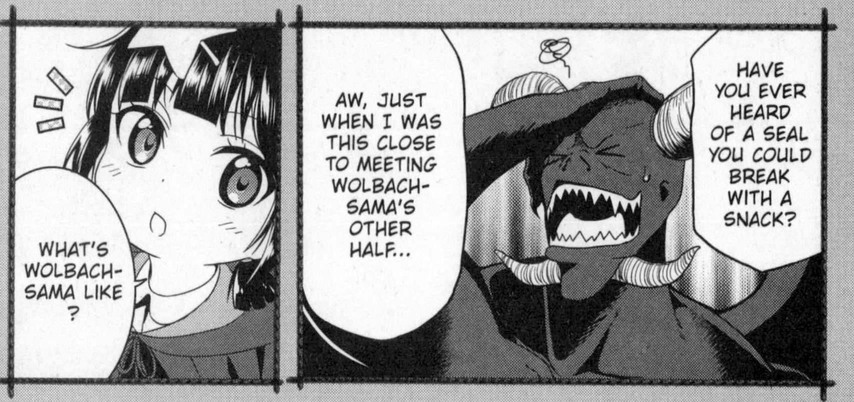
HAVE YOU EVER HEARD OF A SEAL YOU COULD BREAK WITH A SNACK?
AW, JUST WHEN I WAS THIS CLOSE TO MEETING WOLBACH-SAMA'S OTHER HALF...
WHAT'S WOLBACH-SAMA LIKE?

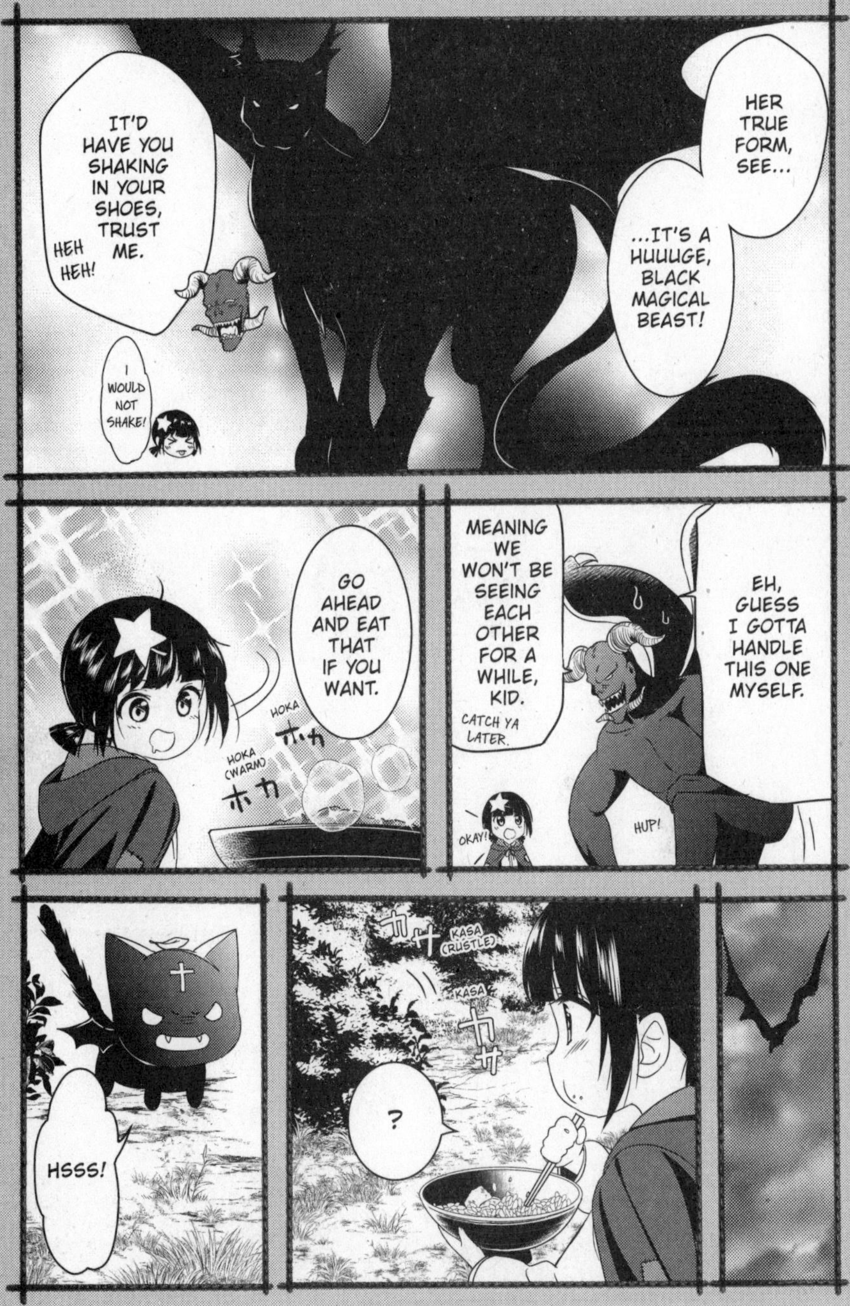
HER TRUE FORM, SEE...
...IT'S A HUUUGE, BLACK MAGICAL BEAST!
IT'D HAVE YOU SHAKING IN YOUR SHOES, TRUST ME.
HEH HEH!
I WOULD NOT SHAKE!
EH, GUESS I GOTTA HANDLE THIS ONE MYSELF.
MEANING WE WON'T BE SEEING EACH OTHER FOR A WHILE, KID.
CATCH YA LATER.
HUP!
OKAY!
GO AHEAD AND EAT THAT IF YOU WANT.
HOKA
HOKA (WARM)
KASA (RUSTLE)
KASA
?
HSSS!

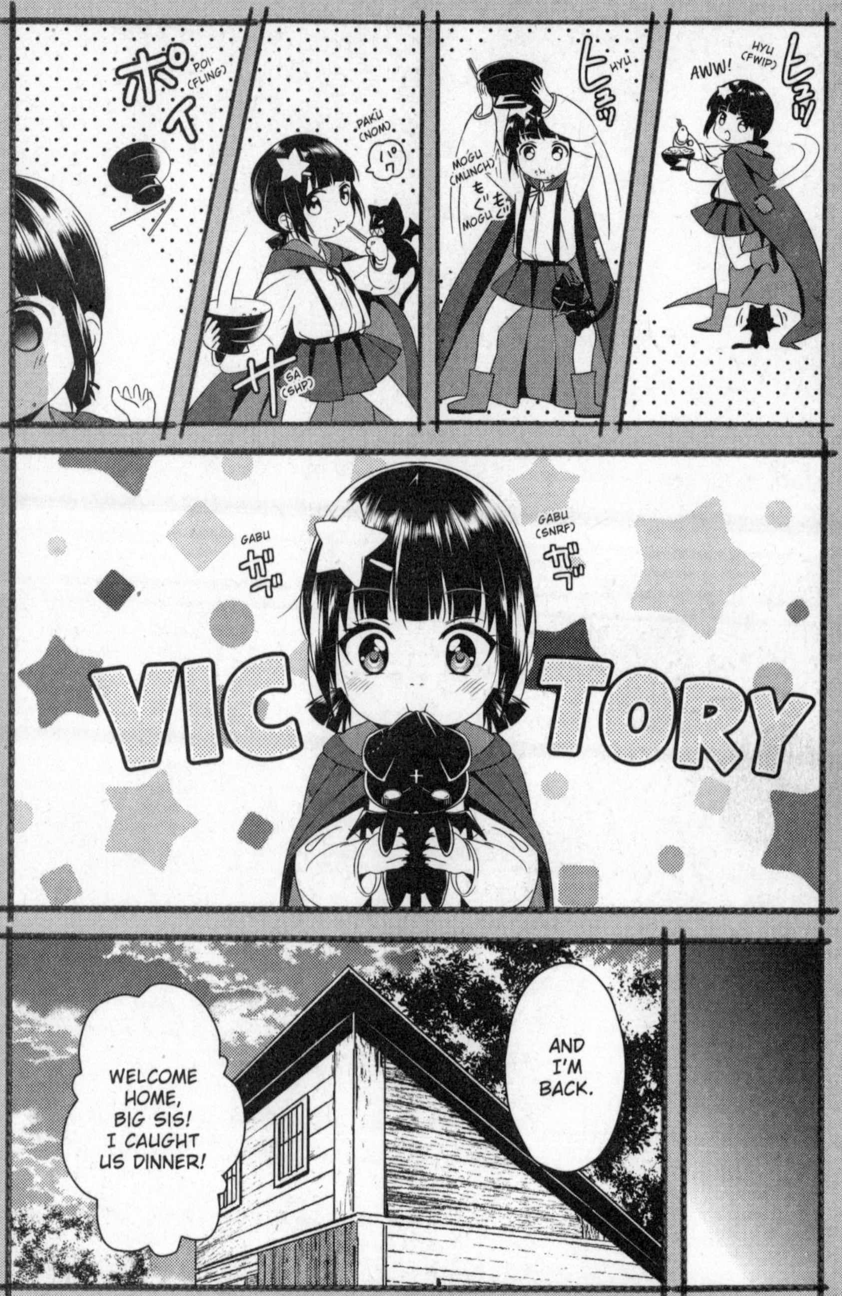
ヒュッ
HYU (FWIP)
AWW!
ヒュッ
HYU
もぐもぐ
MOGU (MUNCH)
MOGU
PAKU (NOM)
パク
SA (SHP)
ポイ
POI (FLING)
GABU (SNRF)
ガブ
GABU
ガブ
VIC TORY
AND I'M BACK.
WELCOME HOME, BIG SIS! I CAUGHT US DINNER!

KONOSUBA: AN EXPLOSION ON THIS WONDERFUL WORLD!

KONOSUBA: AN EXPLOSION ON THIS WONDERFUL WORLD!

PRELUDE TO EXPLOSION MADNESS

CHAPTER 6

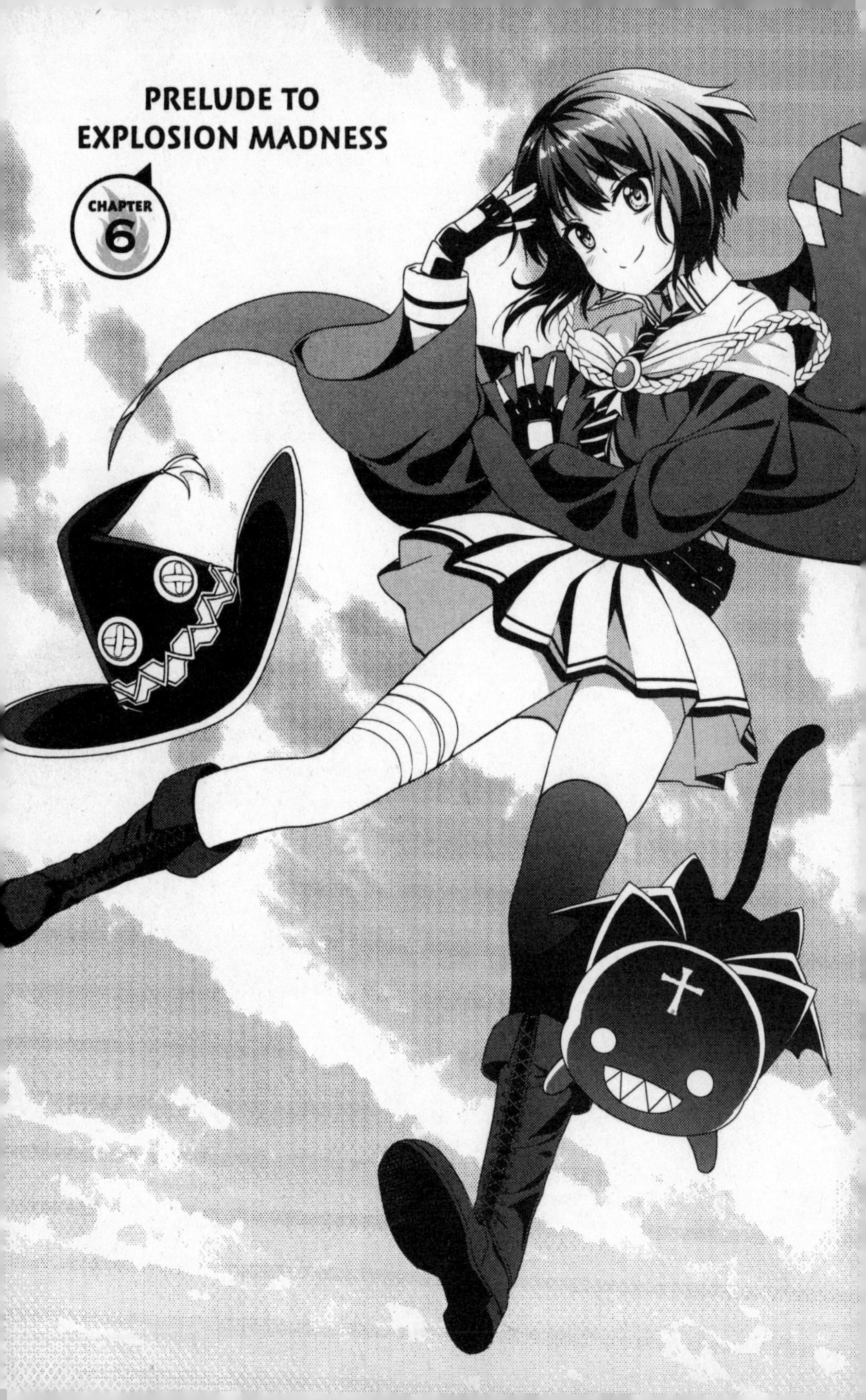

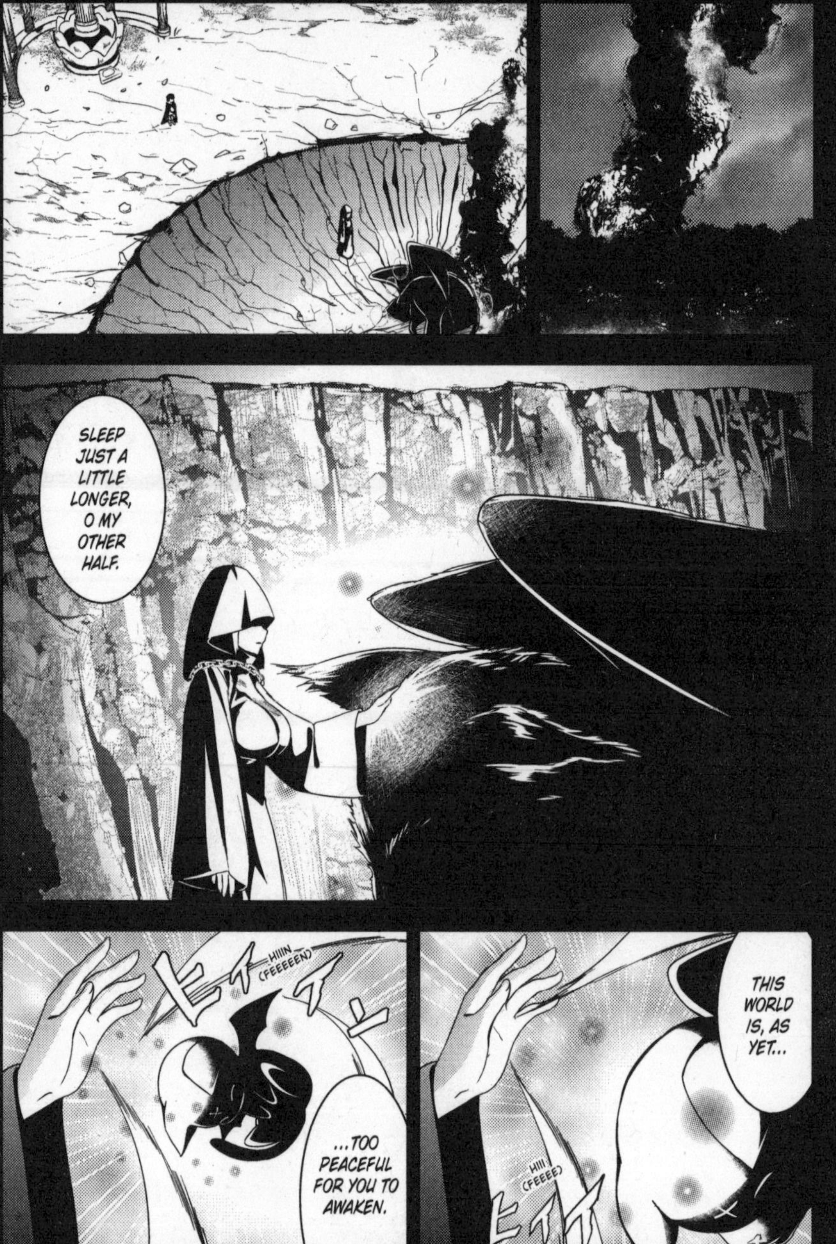
SLEEP JUST A LITTLE LONGER, O MY OTHER HALF.
THIS WORLD IS, AS YET...
HIII (FEEEE)
HIIIN (FEEEEEN)
...TOO PEACEFUL FOR YOU TO AWAKEN.

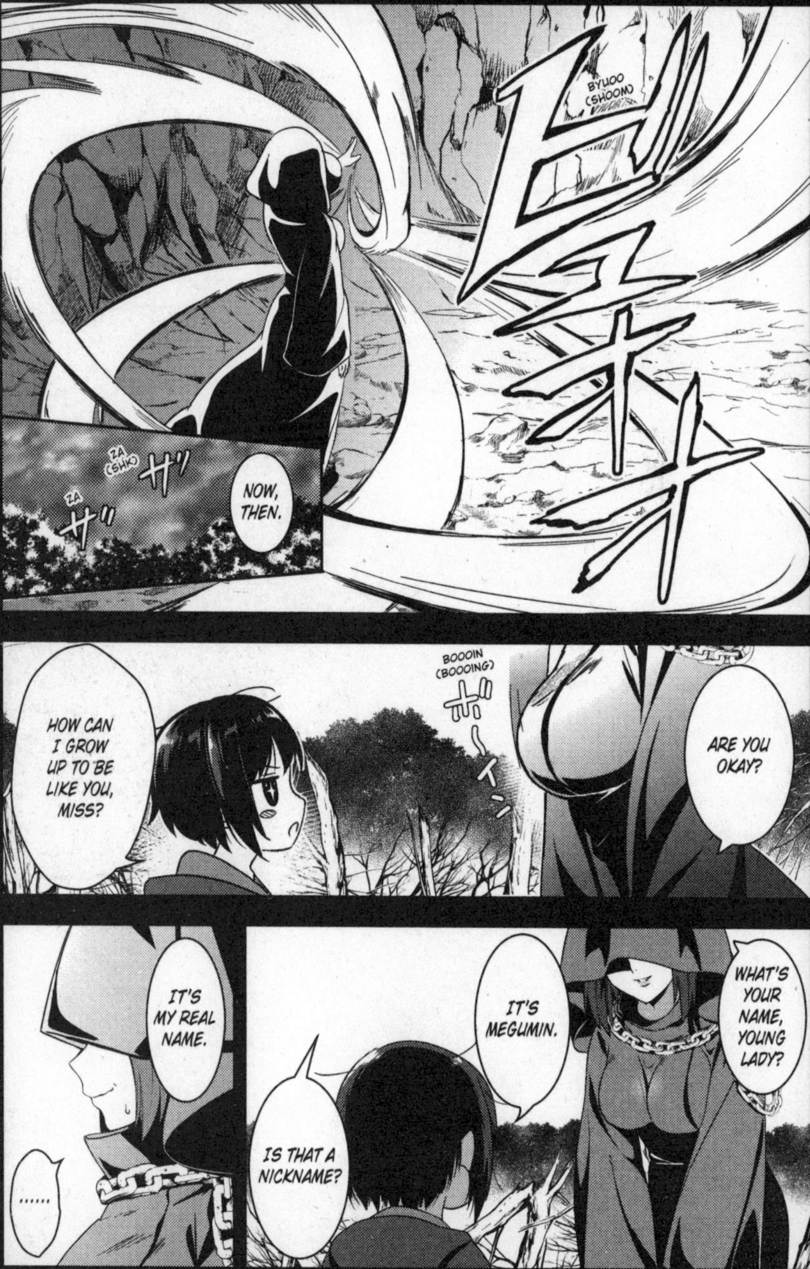

BYUOO (SHOOM)
ZA (SHK)
ZA
NOW, THEN.
ARE YOU OKAY?
BOOOIN (BOOOING)
HOW CAN I GROW UP TO BE LIKE YOU, MISS?
WHAT'S YOUR NAME, YOUNG LADY?
IT'S MEGUMIN.
IS THAT A NICKNAME?
IT'S MY REAL NAME.
……

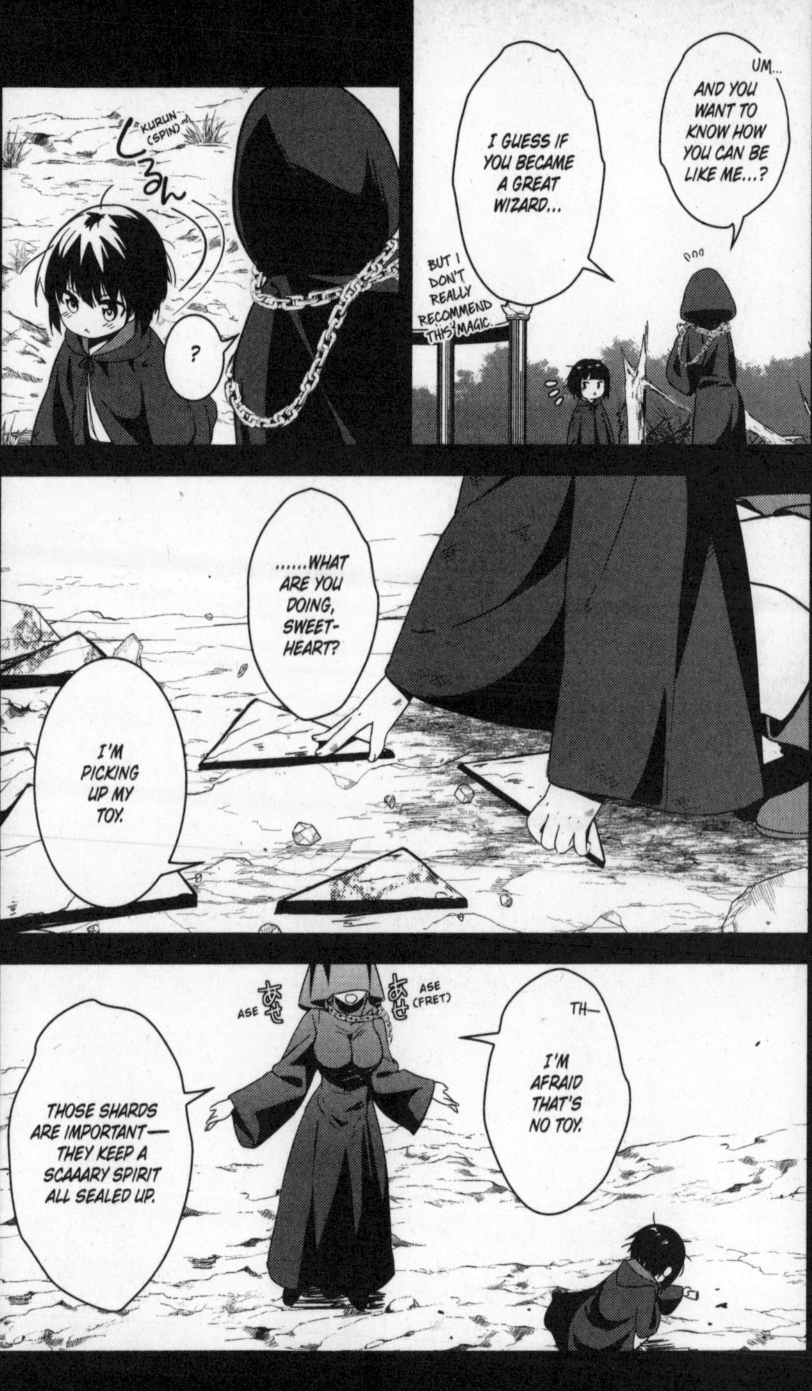
UM... AND YOU WANT TO KNOW HOW YOU CAN BE LIKE ME...?
I GUESS IF YOU BECAME A GREAT WIZARD...
BUT I DON'T REALLY RECOMMEND THIS MAGIC.
くるん
KURUN (SPIN)
?
......WHAT ARE YOU DOING, SWEET-HEART?
I'M PICKING UP MY TOY.
あせ
ASE (FRET)
あせ
ASE
TH— I'M AFRAID THAT'S NO TOY.
THOSE SHARDS ARE IMPORTANT—THEY KEEP A SCAAARY SPIRIT ALL SEALED UP.

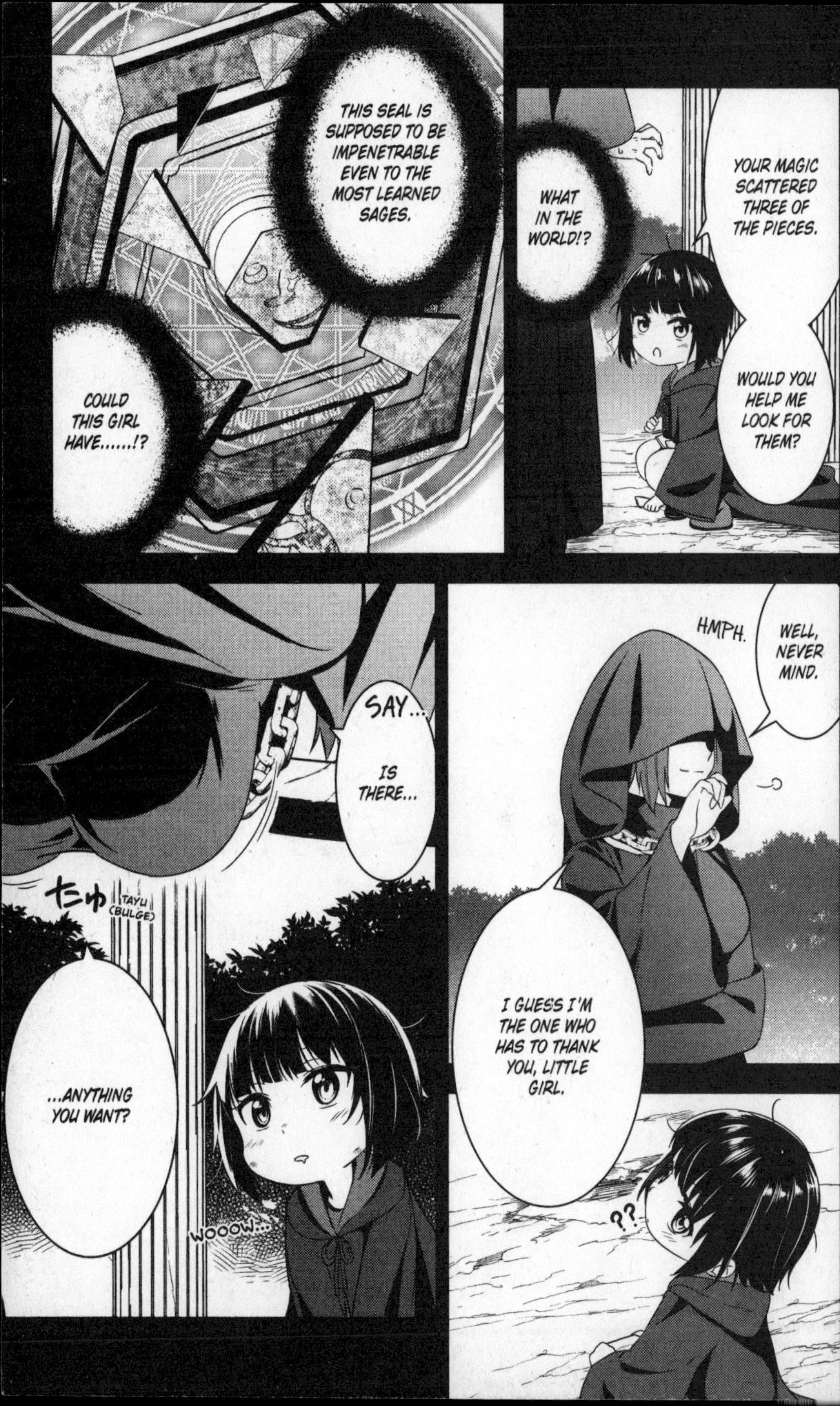
YOUR MAGIC SCATTERED THREE OF THE PIECES.
WOULD YOU HELP ME LOOK FOR THEM?
WHAT IN THE WORLD!?
THIS SEAL IS SUPPOSED TO BE IMPENETRABLE EVEN TO THE MOST LEARNED SAGES.
COULD THIS GIRL HAVE......!?
WELL, NEVER MIND.
HMPH.
I GUESS I'M THE ONE WHO HAS TO THANK YOU, LITTLE GIRL.
??
SAY...
IS THERE...
たゆ
TAYU (BULGE)
...ANYTHING YOU WANT?
WOOOW...

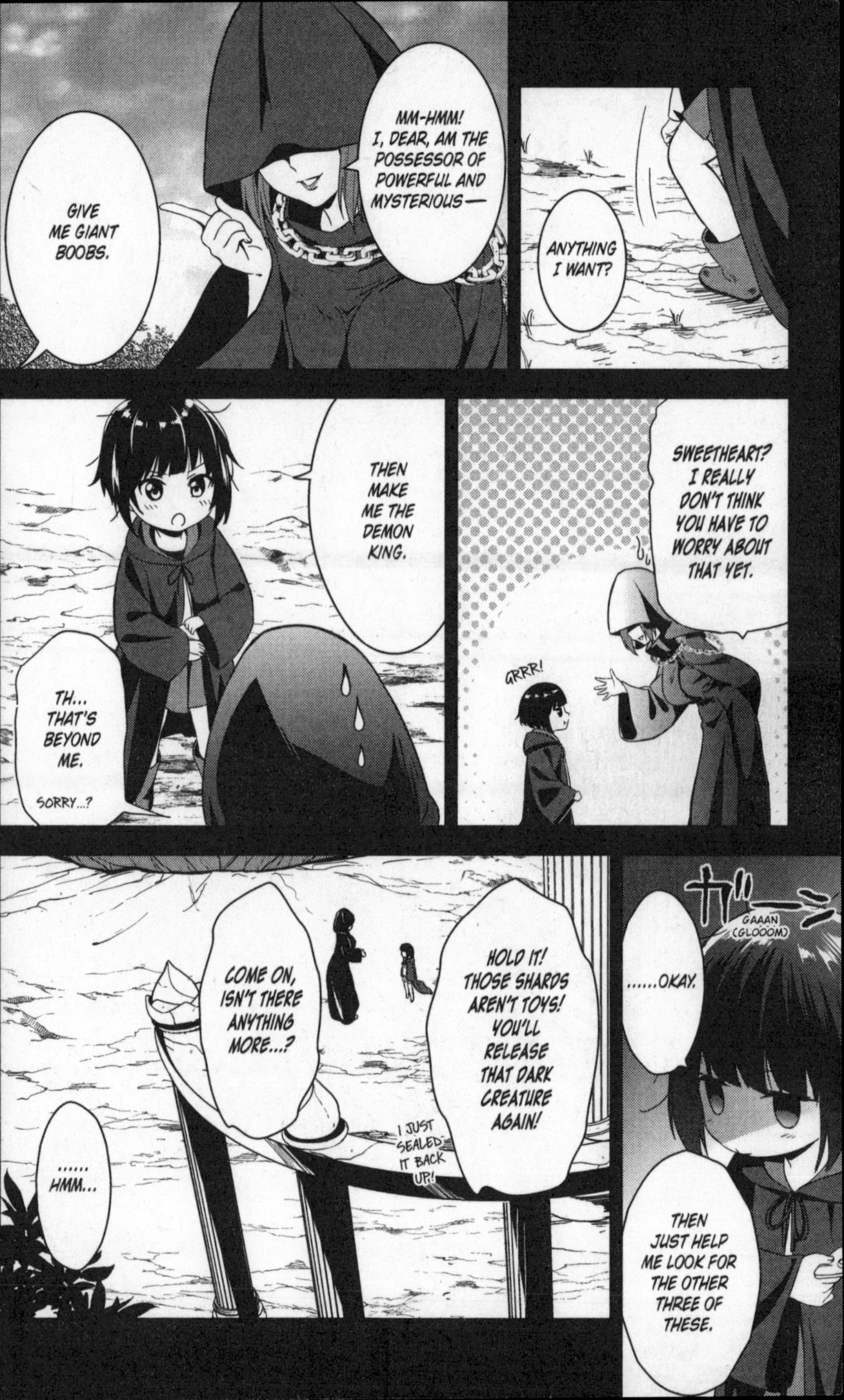
ANYTHING I WANT?
MM-HMM! I, DEAR, AM THE POSSESSOR OF POWERFUL AND MYSTERIOUS—
GIVE ME GIANT BOOBS.
SWEETHEART? I REALLY DON'T THINK YOU HAVE TO WORRY ABOUT THAT YET.
GRRR!
THEN MAKE ME THE DEMON KING.
TH... THAT'S BEYOND ME.
SORRY...?
ガーン
GAAAN (GLOOOM)
......OKAY.
THEN JUST HELP ME LOOK FOR THE OTHER THREE OF THESE.
HOLD IT! THOSE SHARDS AREN'T TOYS! YOU'LL RELEASE THAT DARK CREATURE AGAIN!
I JUST SEALED IT BACK UP!
COME ON, ISN'T THERE ANYTHING MORE...?
...... HMM...

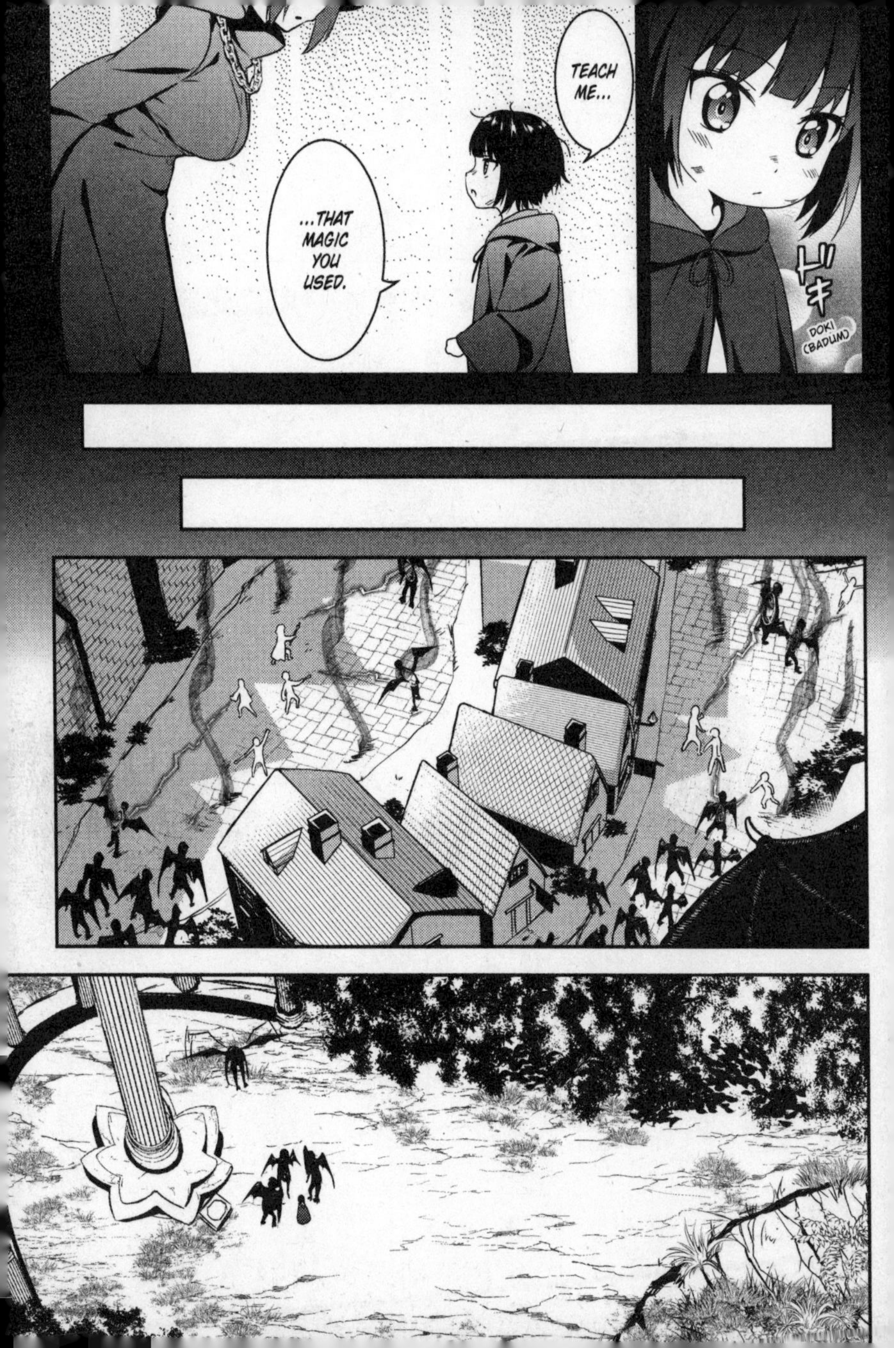
ドキ
DOKI (BADUM)
TEACH ME...
...THAT MAGIC YOU USED.

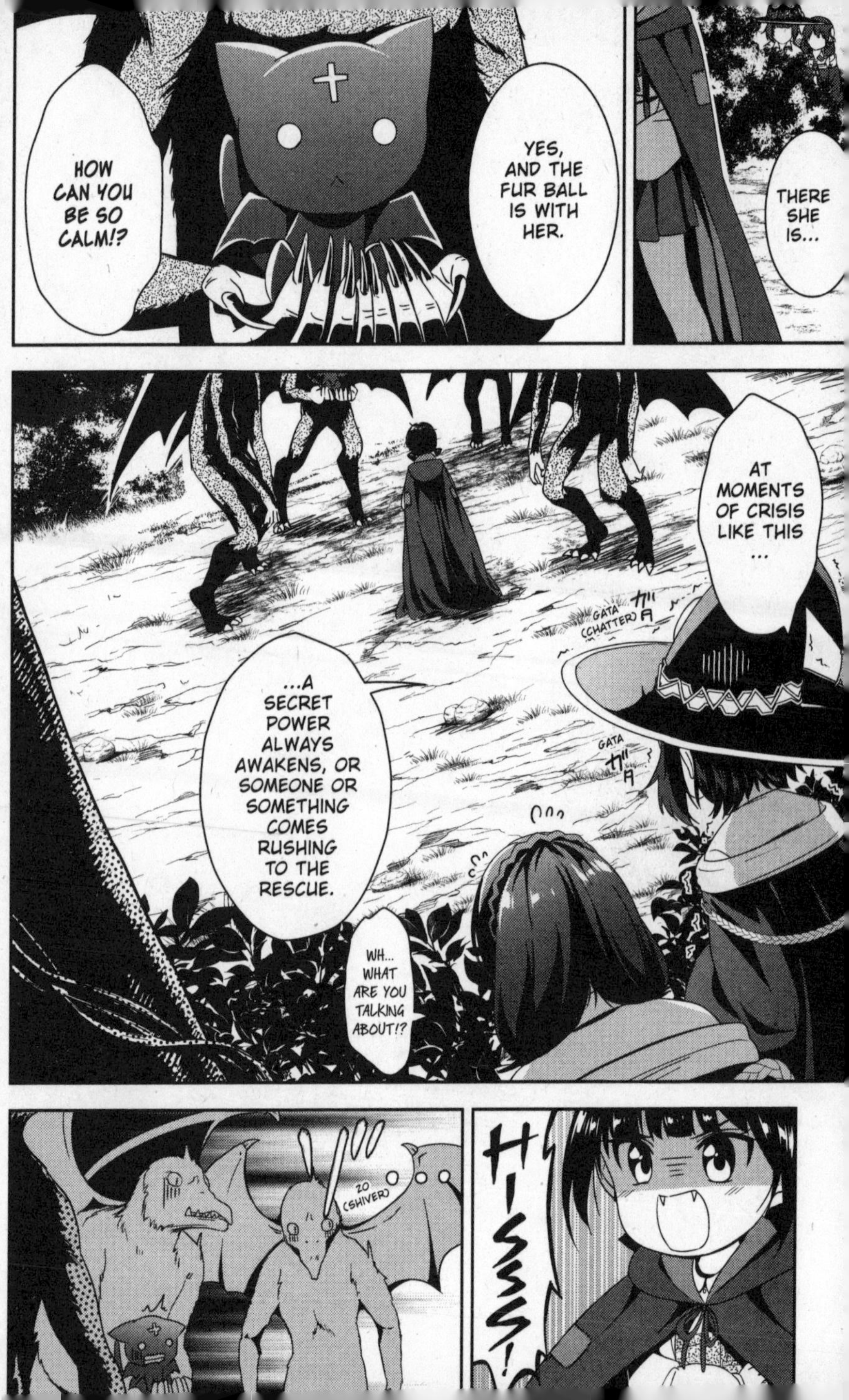
THERE SHE IS...
YES, AND THE FUR BALL IS WITH HER.
HOW CAN YOU BE SO CALM!?
AT MOMENTS OF CRISIS LIKE THIS ...
GATA (CHATTER)
GATA
...A SECRET POWER ALWAYS AWAKENS, OR SOMEONE OR SOMETHING COMES RUSHING TO THE RESCUE.
WH... WHAT ARE YOU TALKING ABOUT!?
HISSS!
ZO (SHIVER)

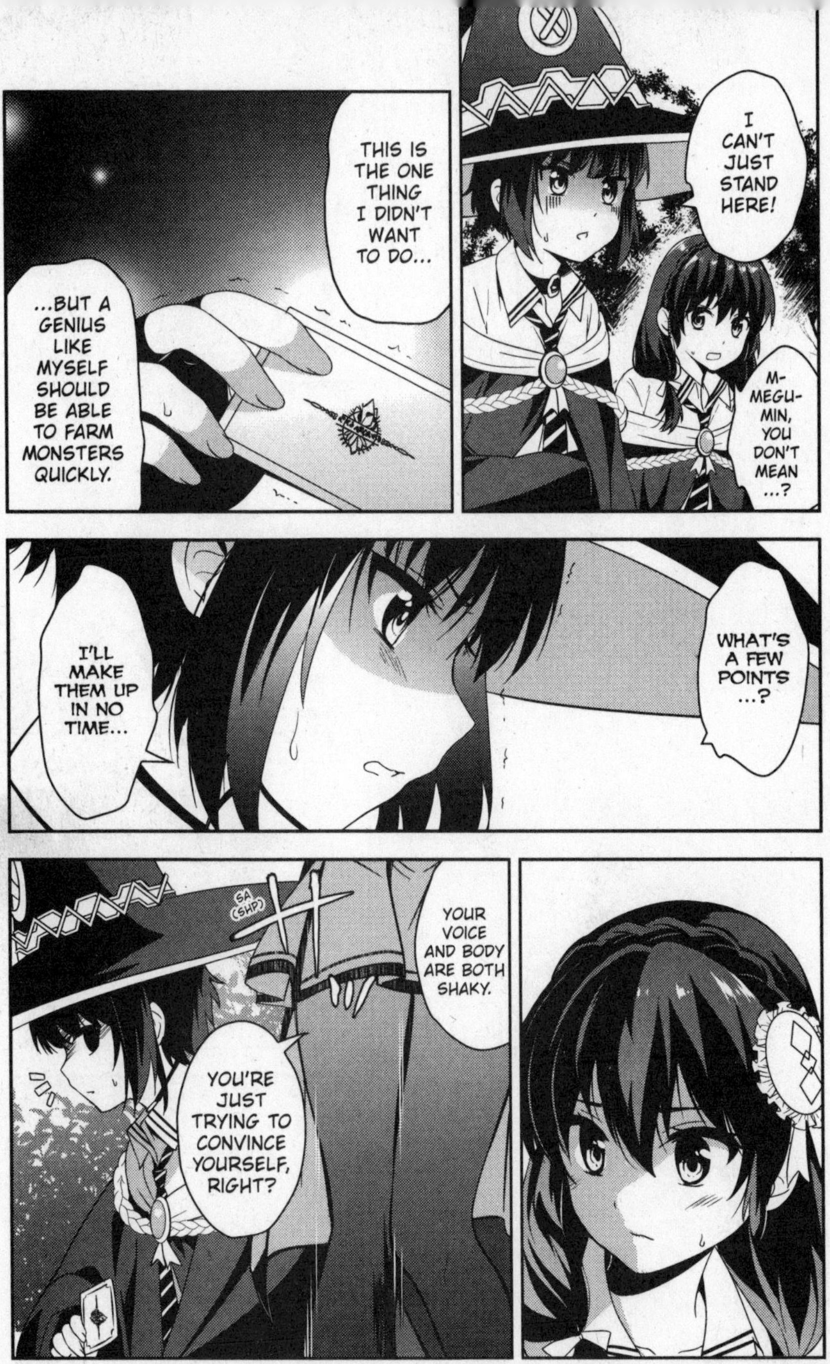
I CAN'T JUST STAND HERE!
M-MEGUMIN, YOU DON'T MEAN ...?
THIS IS THE ONE THING I DIDN'T WANT TO DO...
...BUT A GENIUS LIKE MYSELF SHOULD BE ABLE TO FARM MONSTERS QUICKLY.
WHAT'S A FEW POINTS ...?
I'LL MAKE THEM UP IN NO TIME...
SA (SHP)
YOUR VOICE AND BODY ARE BOTH SHAKY.
YOU'RE JUST TRYING TO CONVINCE YOURSELF, RIGHT?

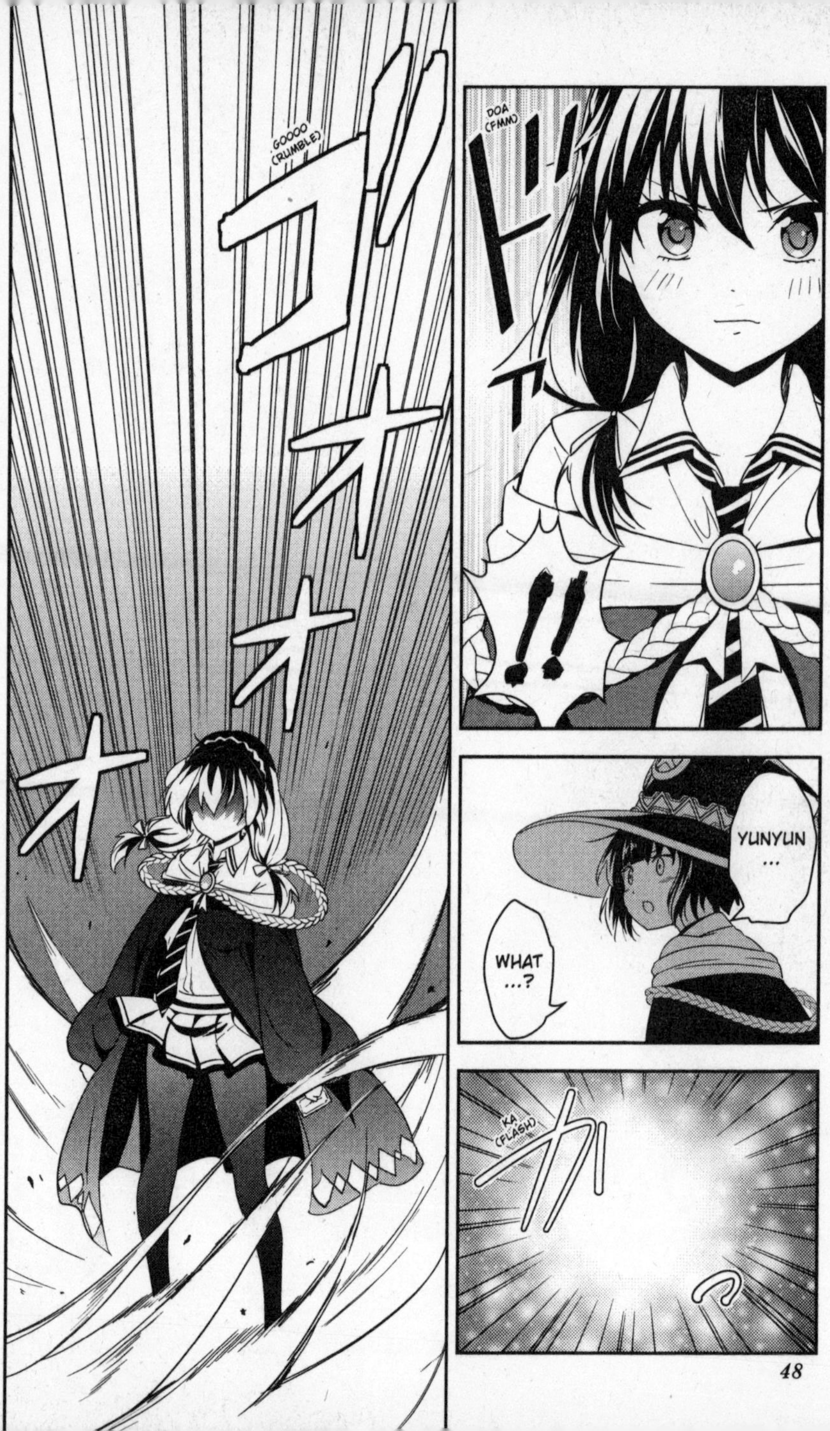
DOA (FMM)
!!
YUNYUN ...
WHAT ...?
KA (FLASH)
GOOOO (RUMBLE)

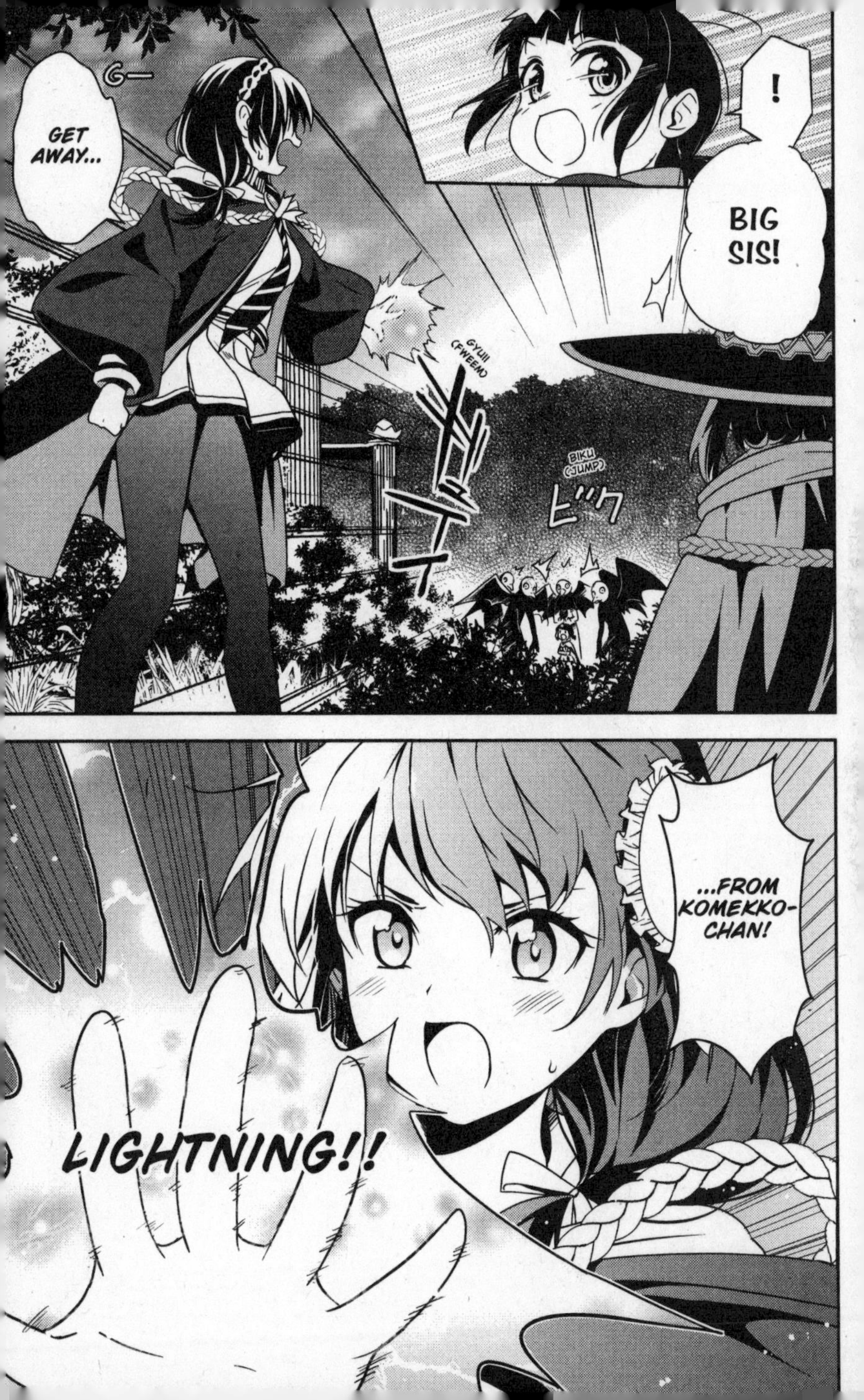
!
BIG SIS!
GYUII (FWEEM)
BIKU (JUMP)
G—
GET AWAY...
...FROM KOMEKKO-CHAN!
LIGHTNING!!

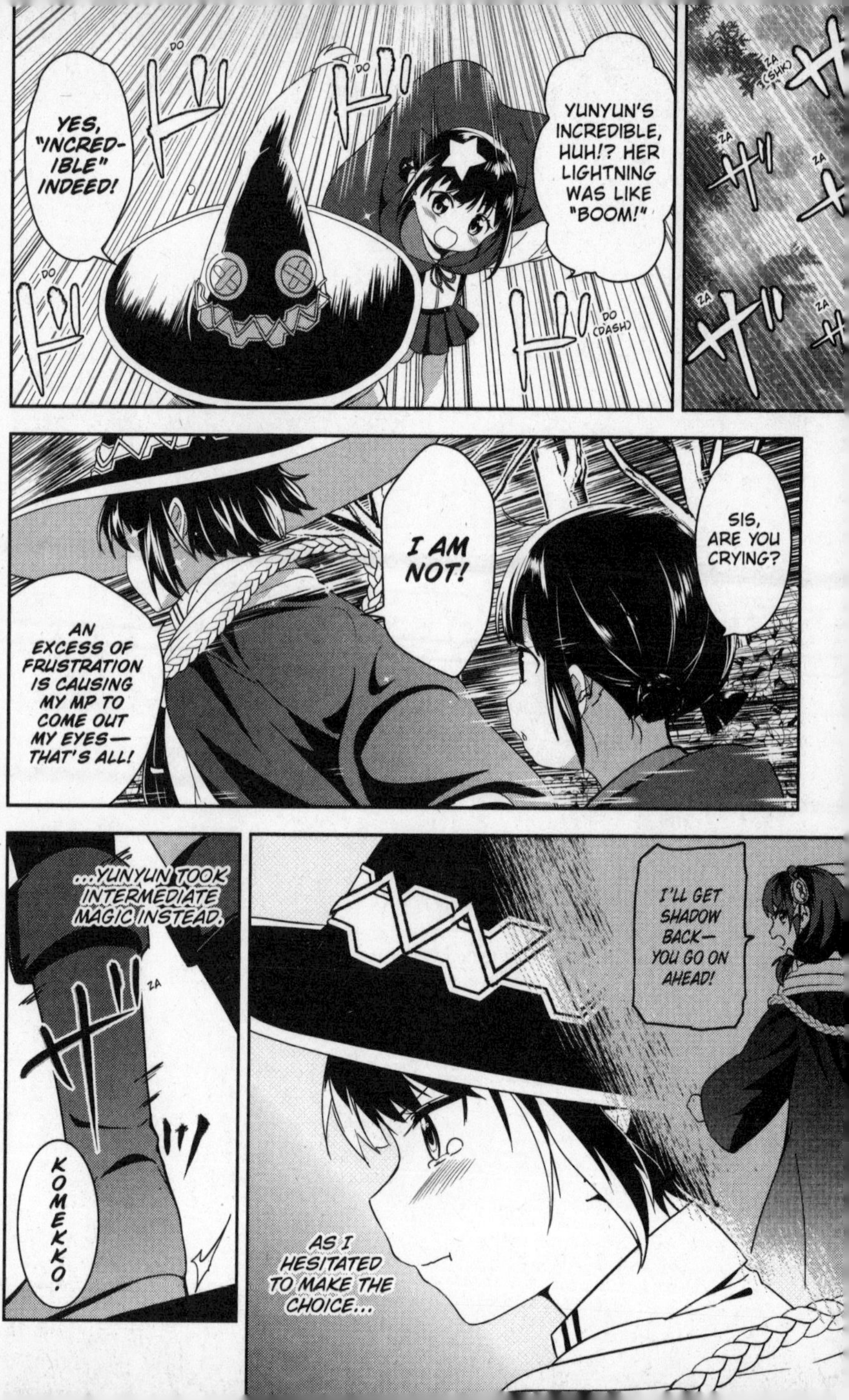
ZA (SHK)
ZA
ZA
ZA
ZA
YUNYUN'S INCREDIBLE, HUH!? HER LIGHTNING WAS LIKE "BOOM!"
DO
DO
YES, "INCREDIBLE" INDEED!
DO (DASH)
DO
SIS, ARE YOU CRYING?
I AM NOT!
AN EXCESS OF FRUSTRATION IS CAUSING MY MP TO COME OUT MY EYES—THAT'S ALL!
I'LL GET SHADOW BACK—YOU GO ON AHEAD!
AS I HESITATED TO MAKE THE CHOICE...
...YUNYUN TOOK INTERMEDIATE MAGIC INSTEAD.
ZA
KOMEKKO.

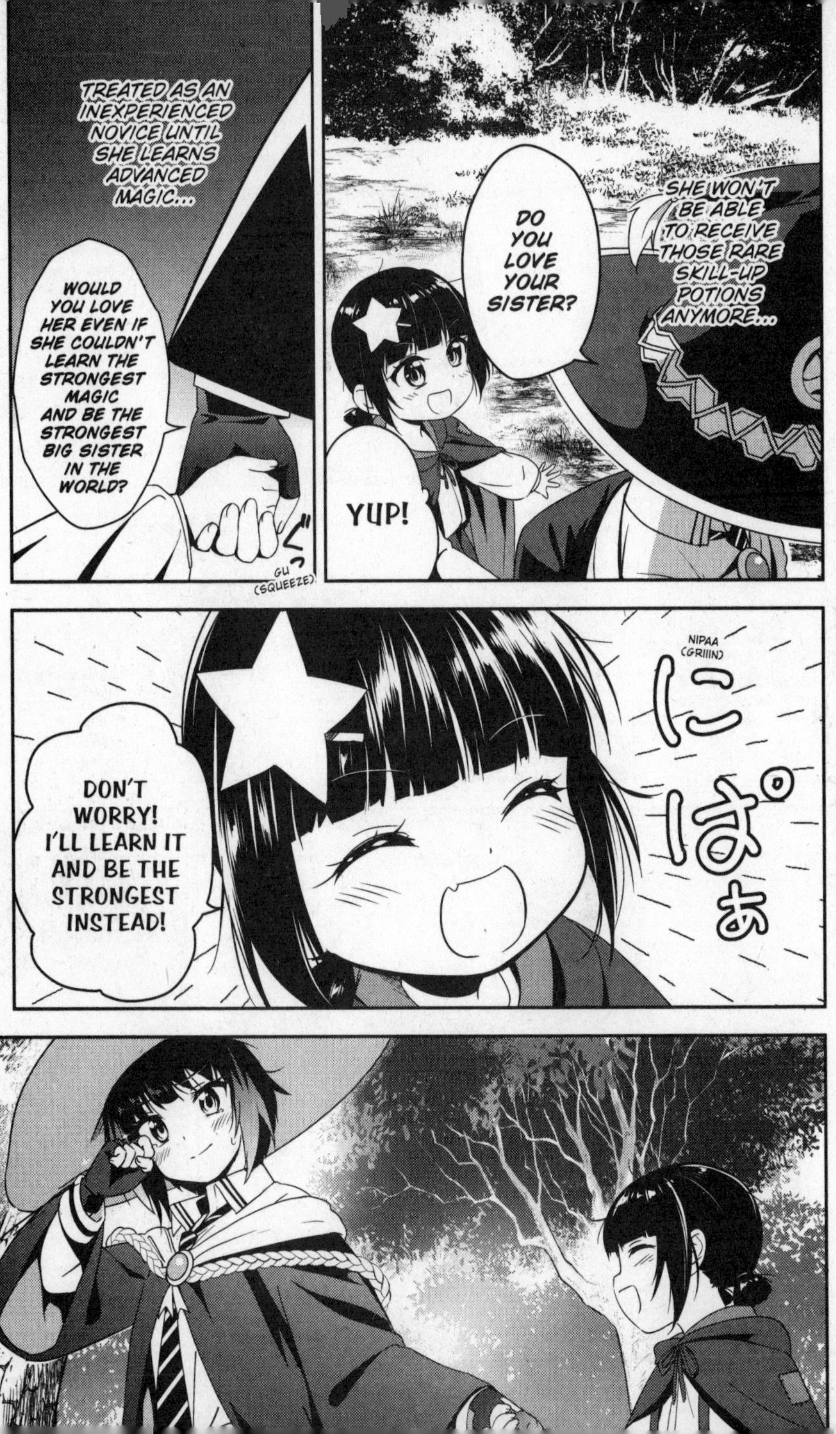
SHE WON'T BE ABLE TO RECEIVE THOSE RARE SKILL-UP POTIONS ANYMORE...
DO YOU LOVE YOUR SISTER?
YUP!
TREATED AS AN INEXPERIENCED NOVICE UNTIL SHE LEARNS ADVANCED MAGIC...
WOULD YOU LOVE HER EVEN IF SHE COULDN'T LEARN THE STRONGEST MAGIC AND BE THE STRONGEST BIG SISTER IN THE WORLD?
ぐっ
GU (SQUEEZE)
にぱぁ
NIPAA (GRIIIN)
DON'T WORRY! I'LL LEARN IT AND BE THE STRONGEST INSTEAD!

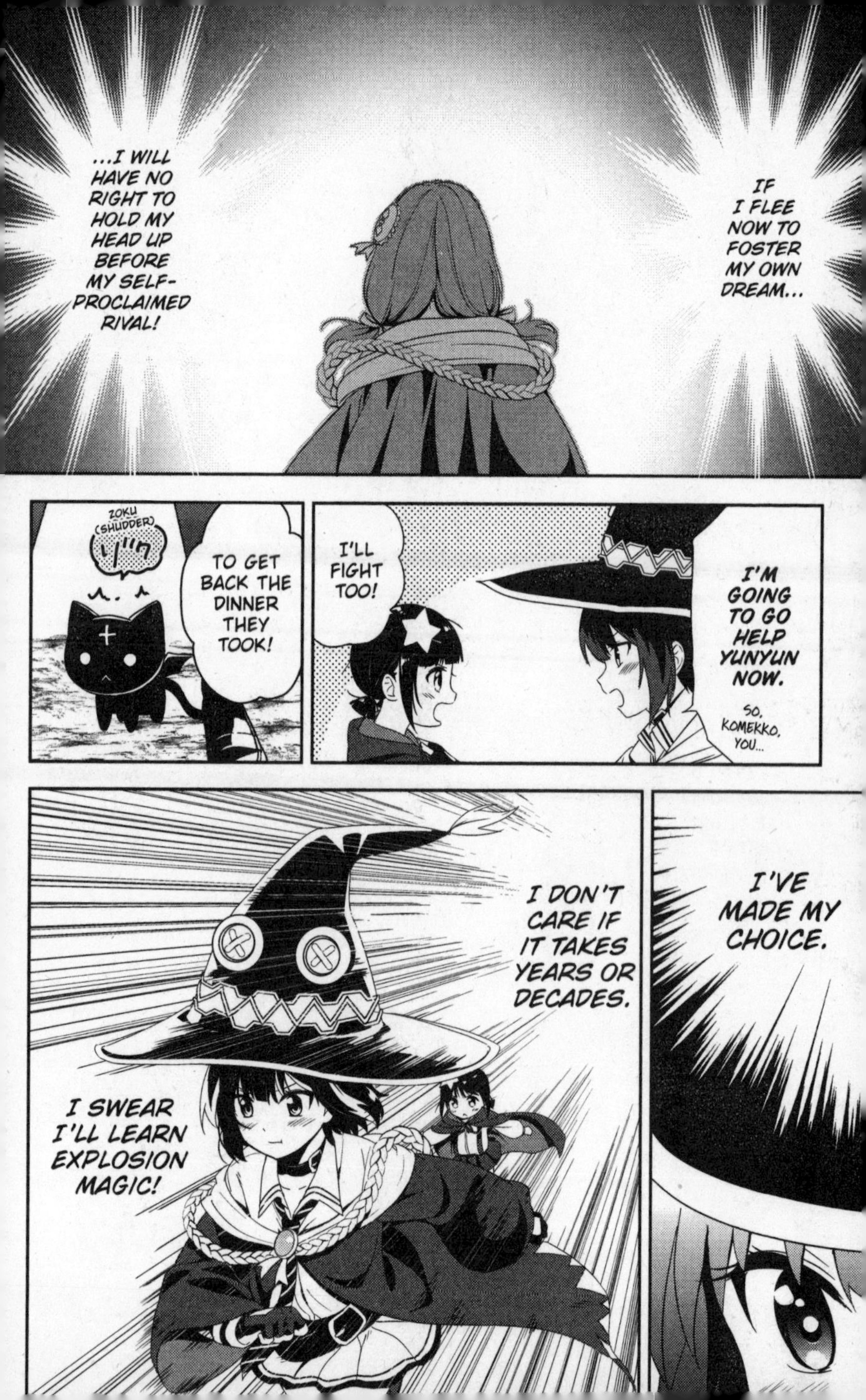
IF I FLEE NOW TO FOSTER MY OWN DREAM...
...I WILL HAVE NO RIGHT TO HOLD MY HEAD UP BEFORE MY SELF-PROCLAIMED RIVAL!
I'M GOING TO GO HELP YUNYUN NOW.
SO, KOMEKKO, YOU...
I'LL FIGHT TOO!
TO GET BACK THE DINNER THEY TOOK!
ZOKU (SHUDDER)
I'VE MADE MY CHOICE.
I DON'T CARE IF IT TAKES YEARS OR DECADES.
I SWEAR I'LL LEARN EXPLOSION MAGIC!

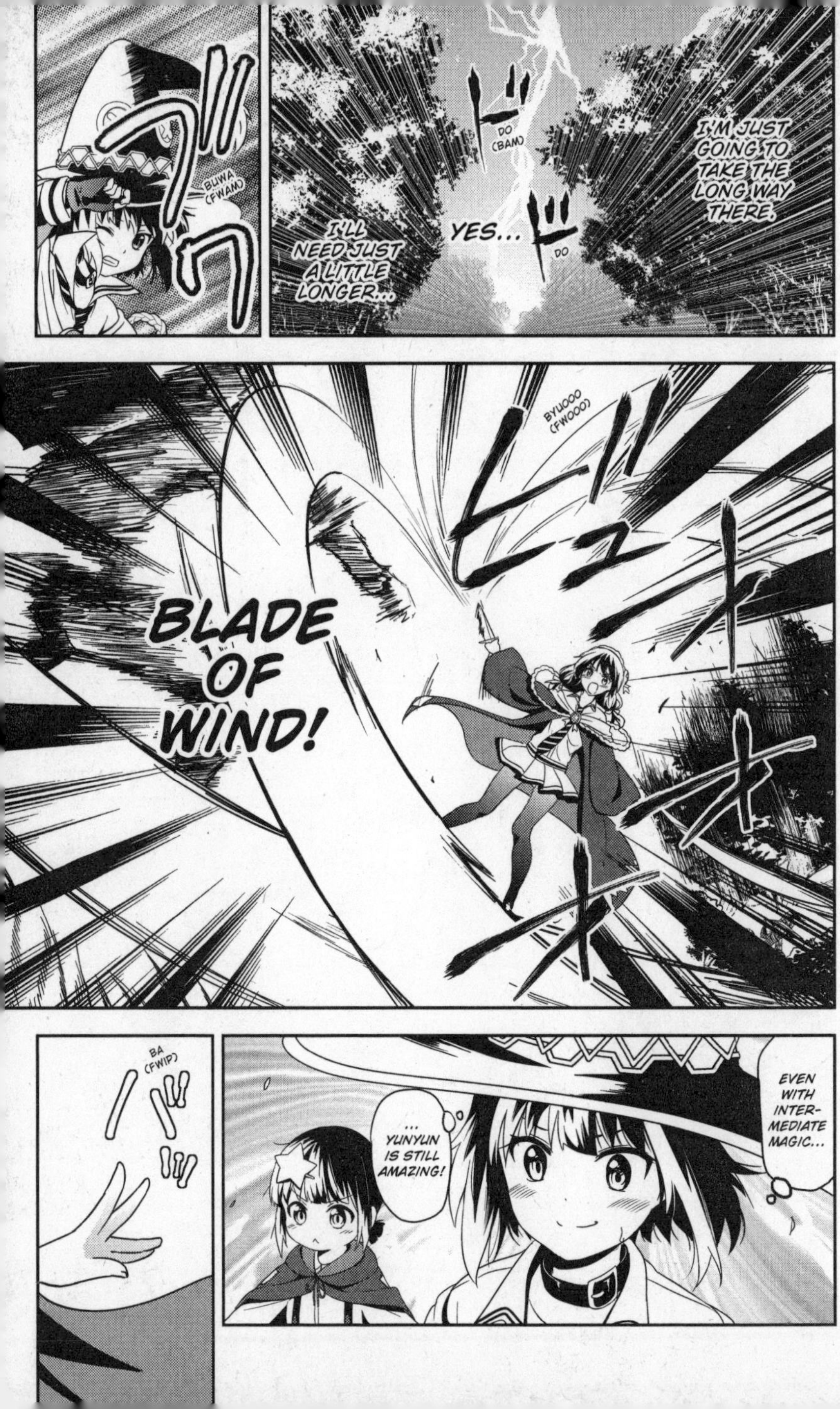
I'M JUST GOING TO TAKE THE LONG WAY THERE.
DO (BAM)
YES...
DO
I'LL NEED JUST A LITTLE LONGER...
BUWA (FWAM)
BYUOOO (FWOOO)
BLADE OF WIND!
EVEN WITH INTER-MEDIATE MAGIC...
... YUNYUN IS STILL AMAZING!
BA (FWIP)

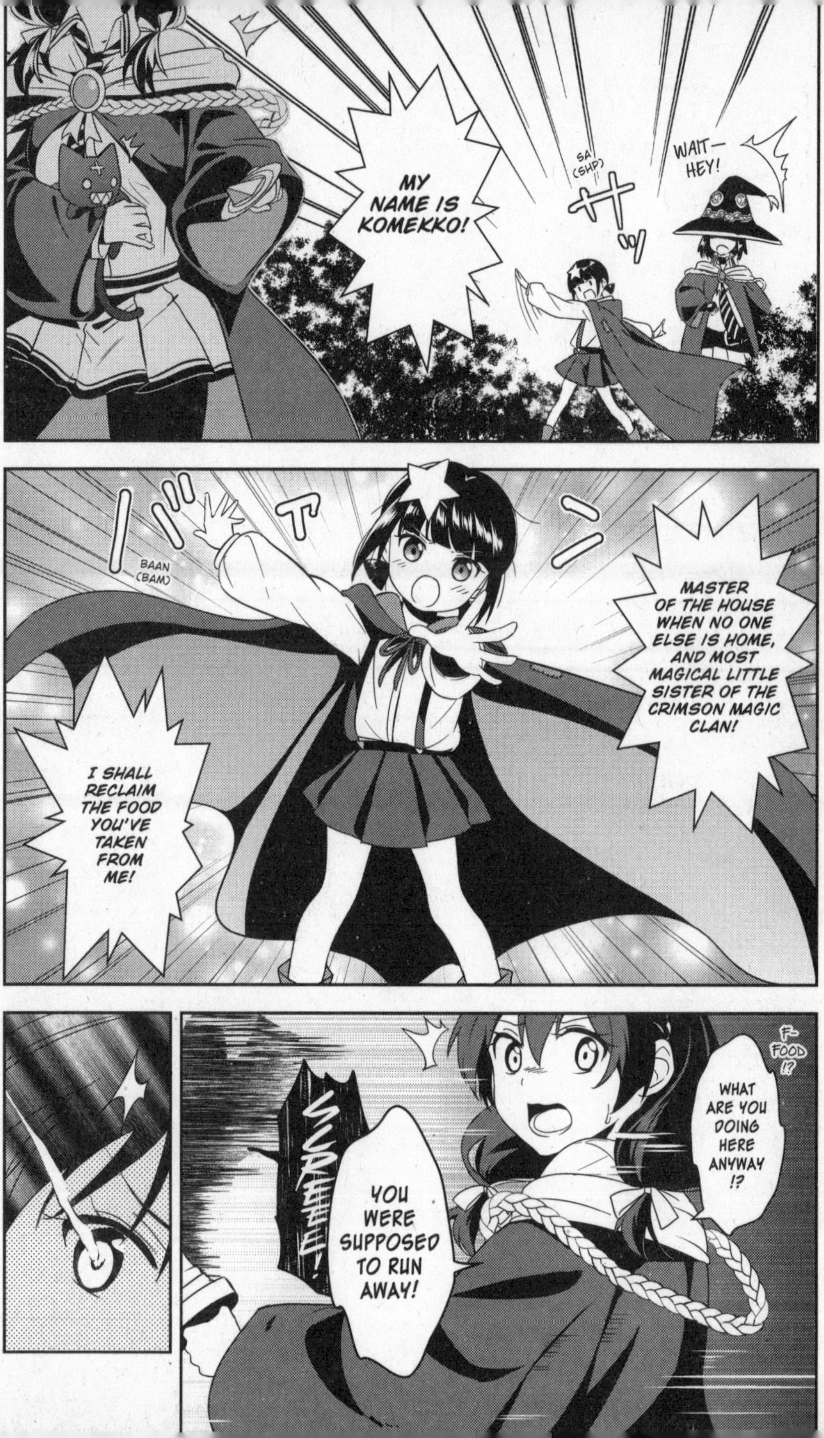
WAIT— HEY!
SA (SHP)
MY NAME IS KOMEKKO!
MASTER OF THE HOUSE WHEN NO ONE ELSE IS HOME, AND MOST MAGICAL LITTLE SISTER OF THE CRIMSON MAGIC CLAN!
BAAN (BAM)
I SHALL RECLAIM THE FOOD YOU'VE TAKEN FROM ME!
F-FOOD!?
WHAT ARE YOU DOING HERE ANYWAY!?
YOU WERE SUPPOSED TO RUN AWAY!
SCREEEE!

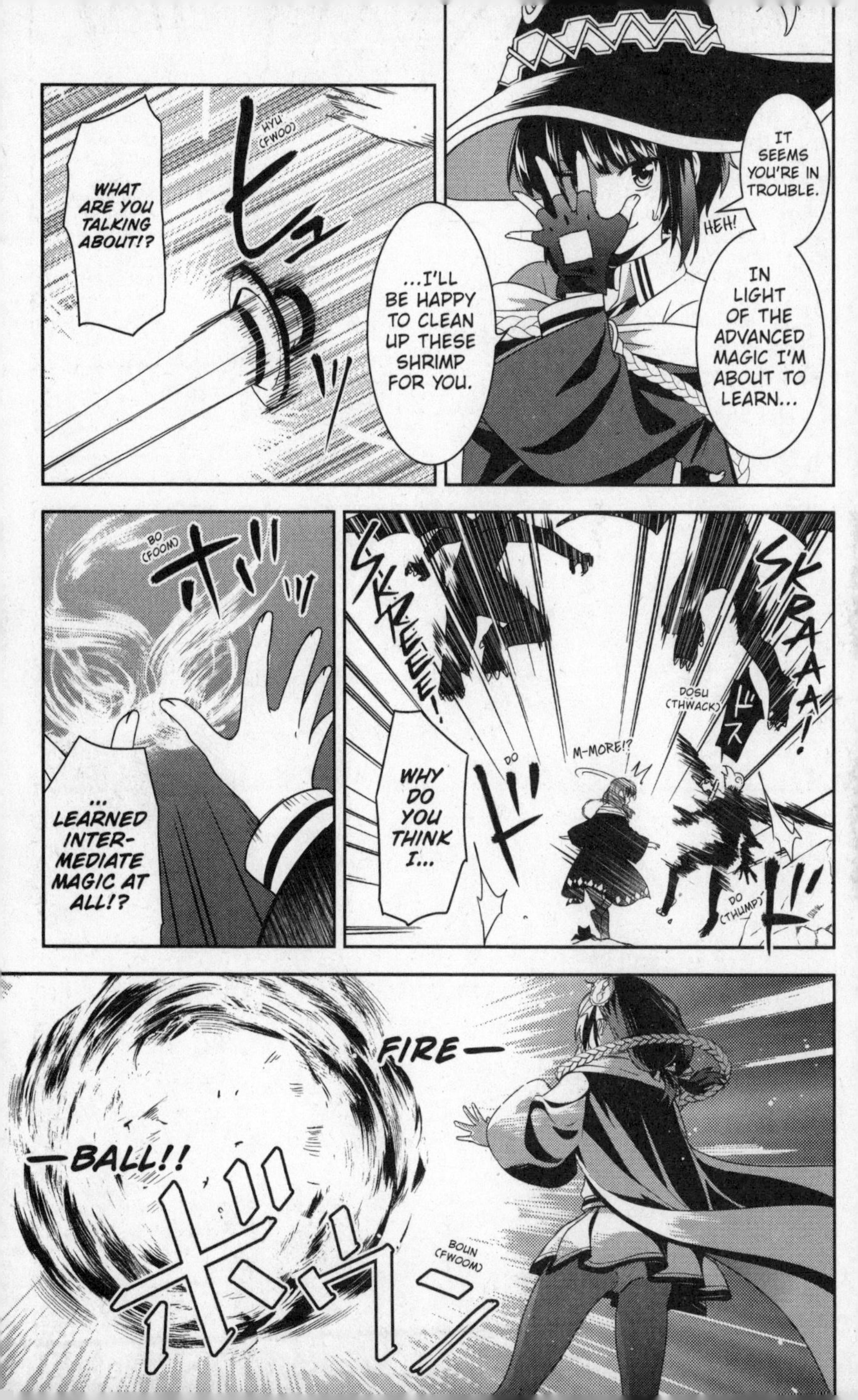
IT SEEMS YOU'RE IN TROUBLE.
HEH!
IN LIGHT OF THE ADVANCED MAGIC I'M ABOUT TO LEARN...
...I'LL BE HAPPY TO CLEAN UP THESE SHRIMP FOR YOU.
HYU (FWOO)
WHAT ARE YOU TALKING ABOUT!?
SKRAAA!
SKREEEE!
DOSU (THWACK)
M-MORE!?
DO
DO (THUMP)
WHY DO YOU THINK I...
BO (FOOM)
...LEARNED INTER-MEDIATE MAGIC AT ALL!?
FIRE—
—BALL!!
BOUN (FWOOM)

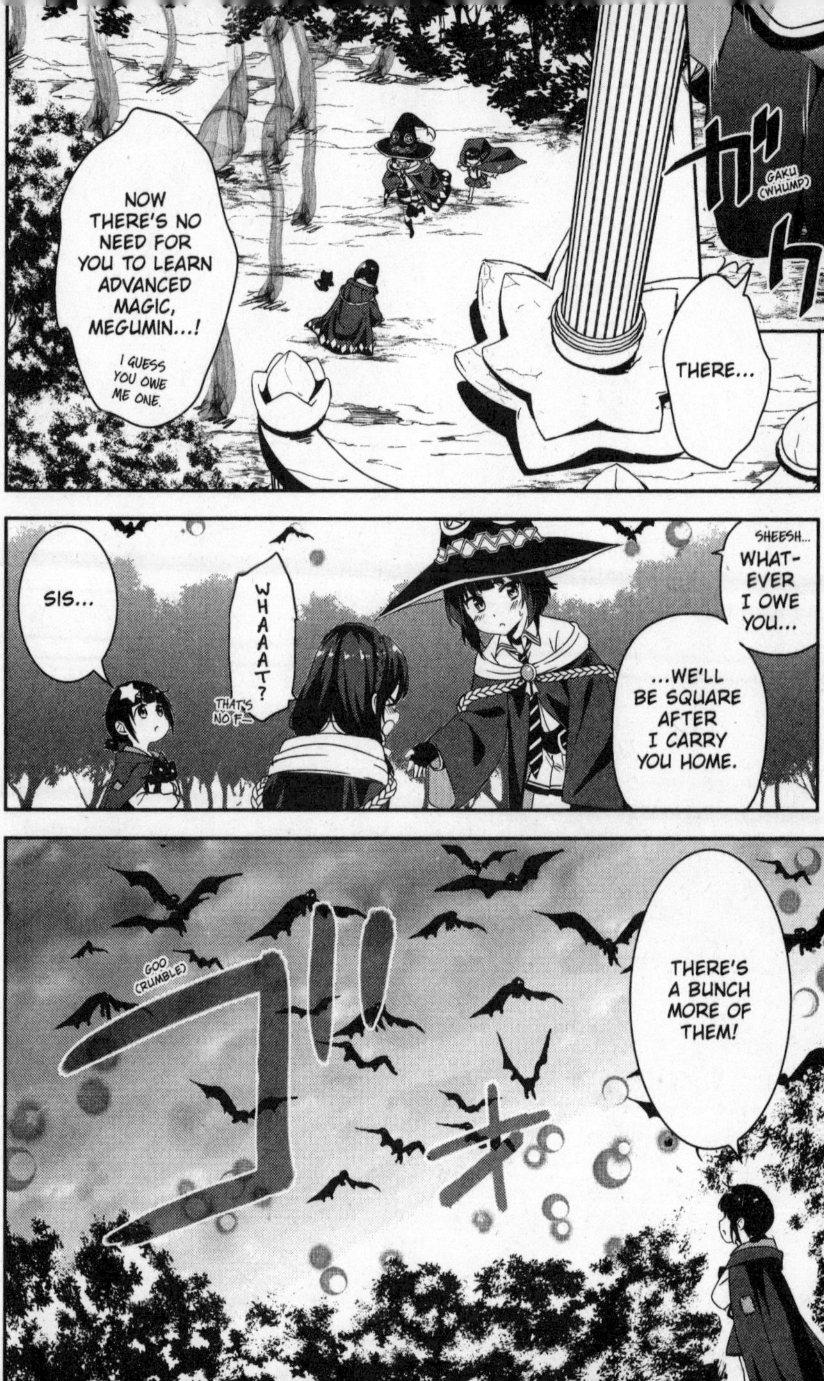
GAKU (WHUMP)
THERE...
NOW THERE'S NO NEED FOR YOU TO LEARN ADVANCED MAGIC, MEGUMIN...!
I GUESS YOU OWE ME ONE.
SHEESH... WHAT-EVER I OWE YOU...
...WE'LL BE SQUARE AFTER I CARRY YOU HOME.
WHAAAT?
THAT'S NO F—
SIS...
THERE'S A BUNCH MORE OF THEM!
GOO (RUMBLE)

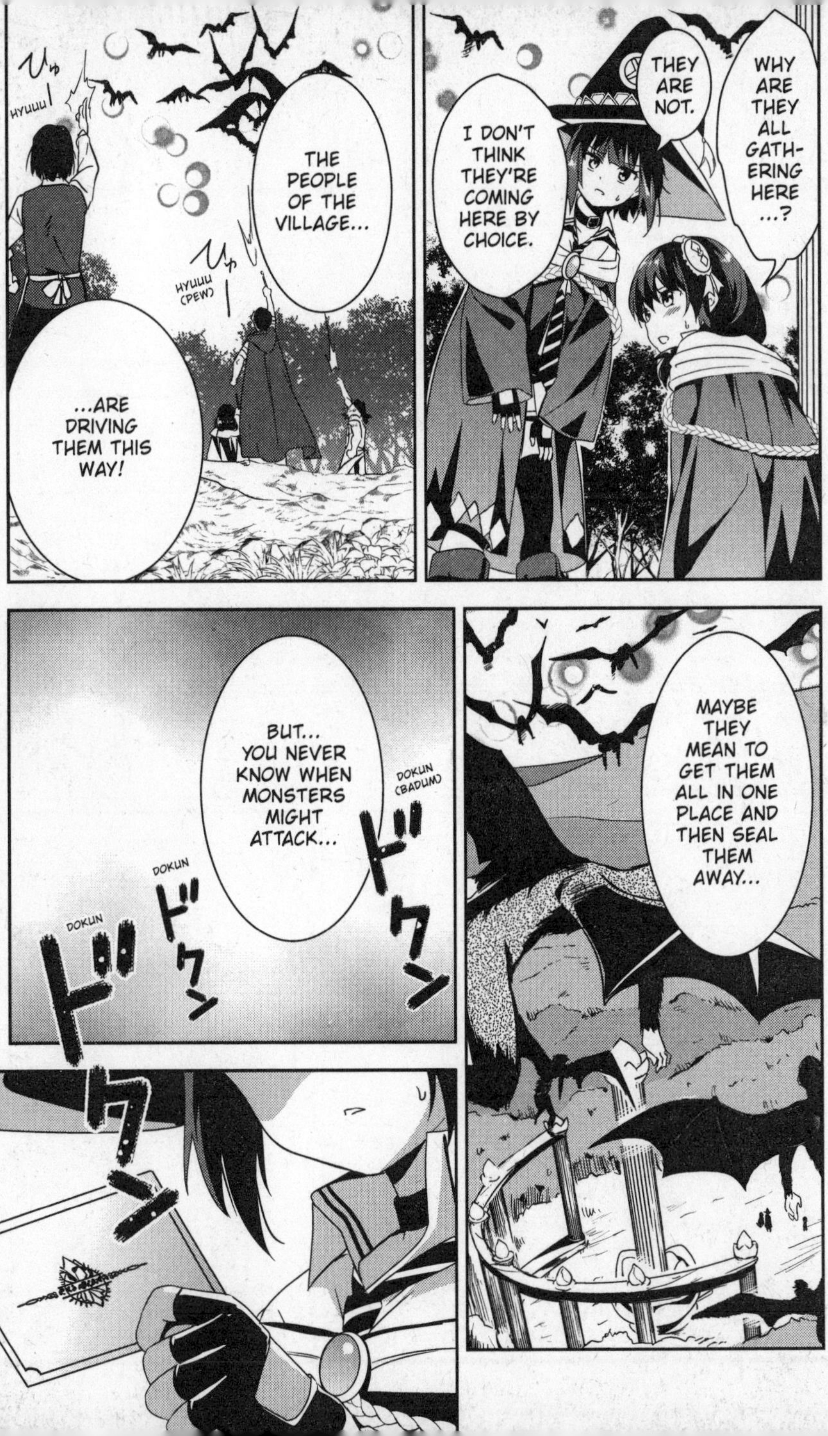
WHY ARE THEY ALL GATHERING HERE...?
THEY ARE NOT.
I DON'T THINK THEY'RE COMING HERE BY CHOICE.
THE PEOPLE OF THE VILLAGE...
ひゅ HYUUU
ひゅ HYUUU (PEW)
...ARE DRIVING THEM THIS WAY!
MAYBE THEY MEAN TO GET THEM ALL IN ONE PLACE AND THEN SEAL THEM AWAY...
BUT... YOU NEVER KNOW WHEN MONSTERS MIGHT ATTACK...
ドクン DOKUN (BADUM)
ドクン DOKUN
ドクン DOKUN

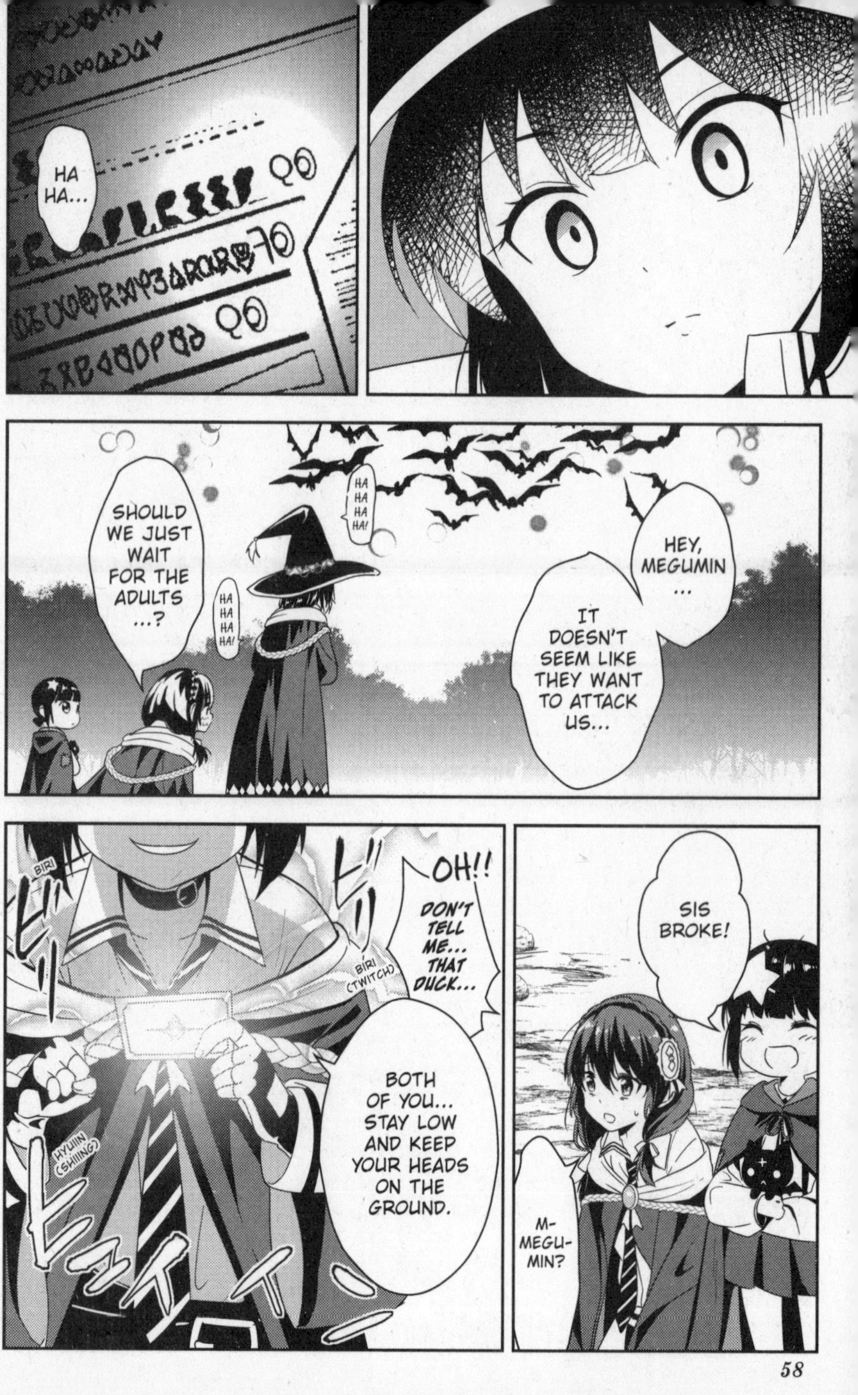
HA HA...
HEY, MEGUMIN...
IT DOESN'T SEEM LIKE THEY WANT TO ATTACK US...
HA HA HA HA!
SHOULD WE JUST WAIT FOR THE ADULTS...?
HA HA HA HA HA!
SIS BROKE!
M-MEGUMIN?
OH!!
DON'T TELL ME... THAT DUCK...
BIRI (TWITCH)
BIRI
BOTH OF YOU... STAY LOW AND KEEP YOUR HEADS ON THE GROUND.
HYUIIN (SHIING)

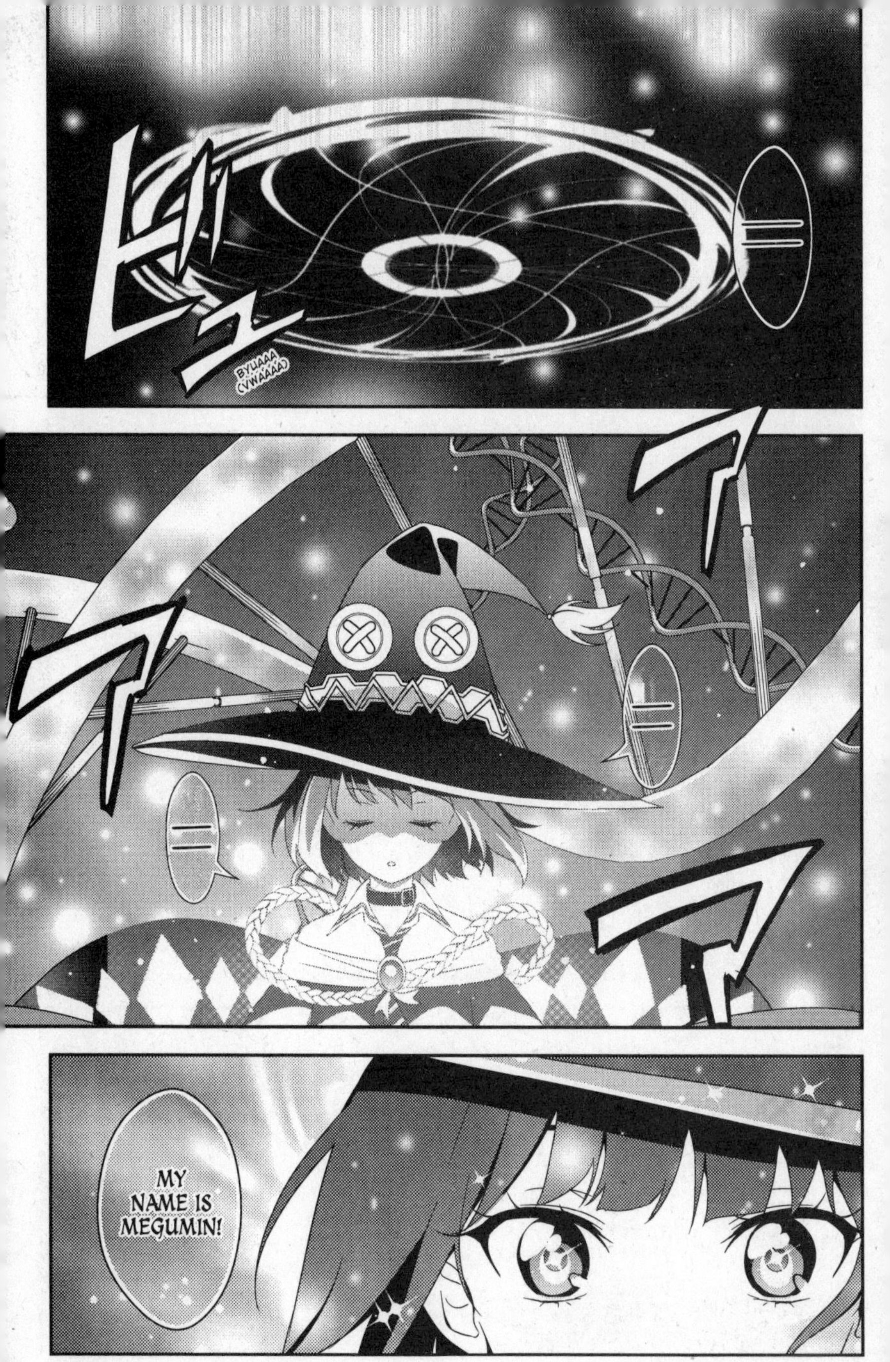
BYUAAA (VWAAAA)
MY NAME IS MEGUMIN!

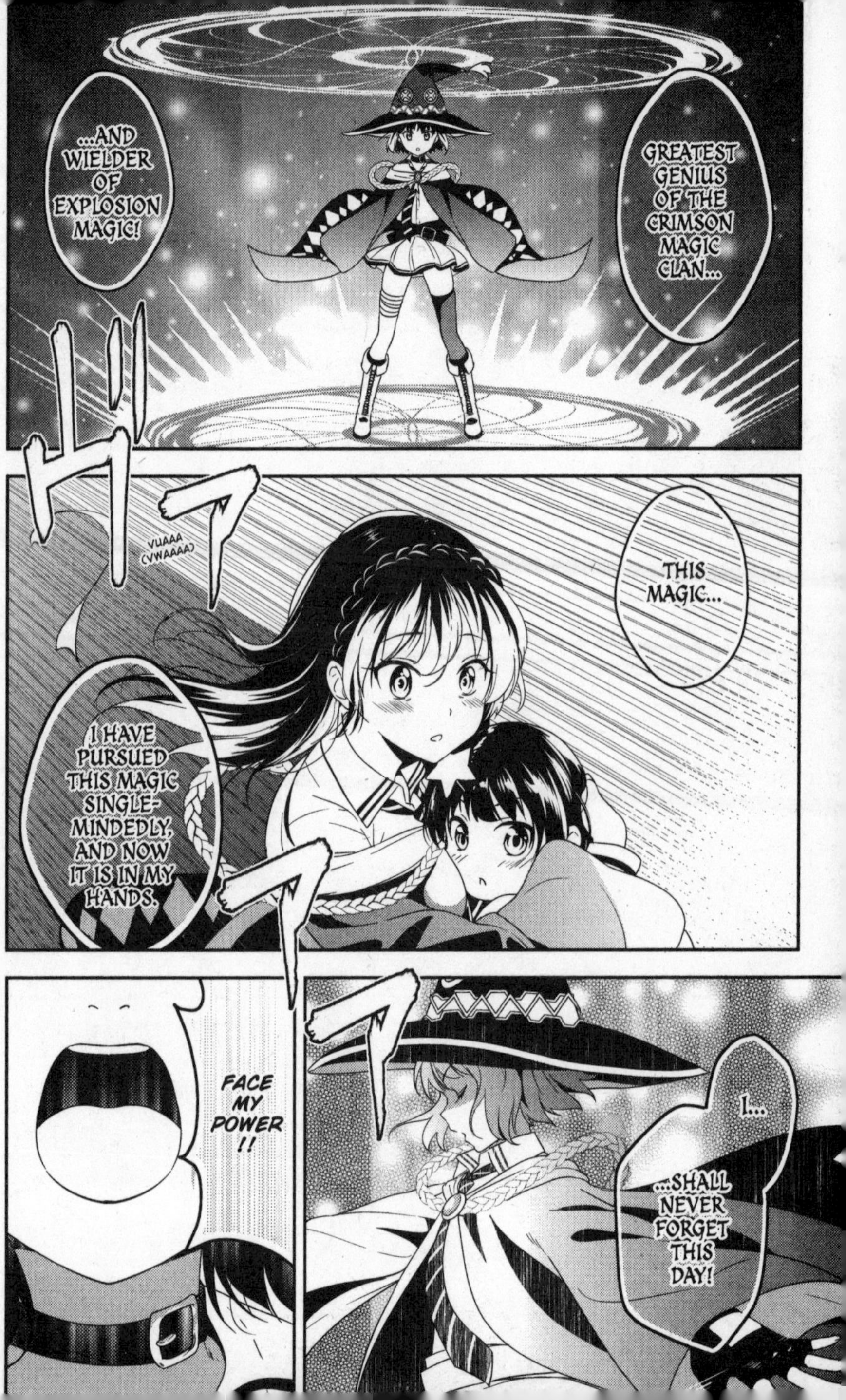
GREATEST GENIUS OF THE CRIMSON MAGIC CLAN...
...AND WIELDER OF EXPLOSION MAGIC!
VUAAA (VWAAAA)
THIS MAGIC...
I HAVE PURSUED THIS MAGIC SINGLE-MINDEDLY, AND NOW IT IS IN MY HANDS.
I...
...SHALL NEVER FORGET THIS DAY!
FACE MY POWER!!

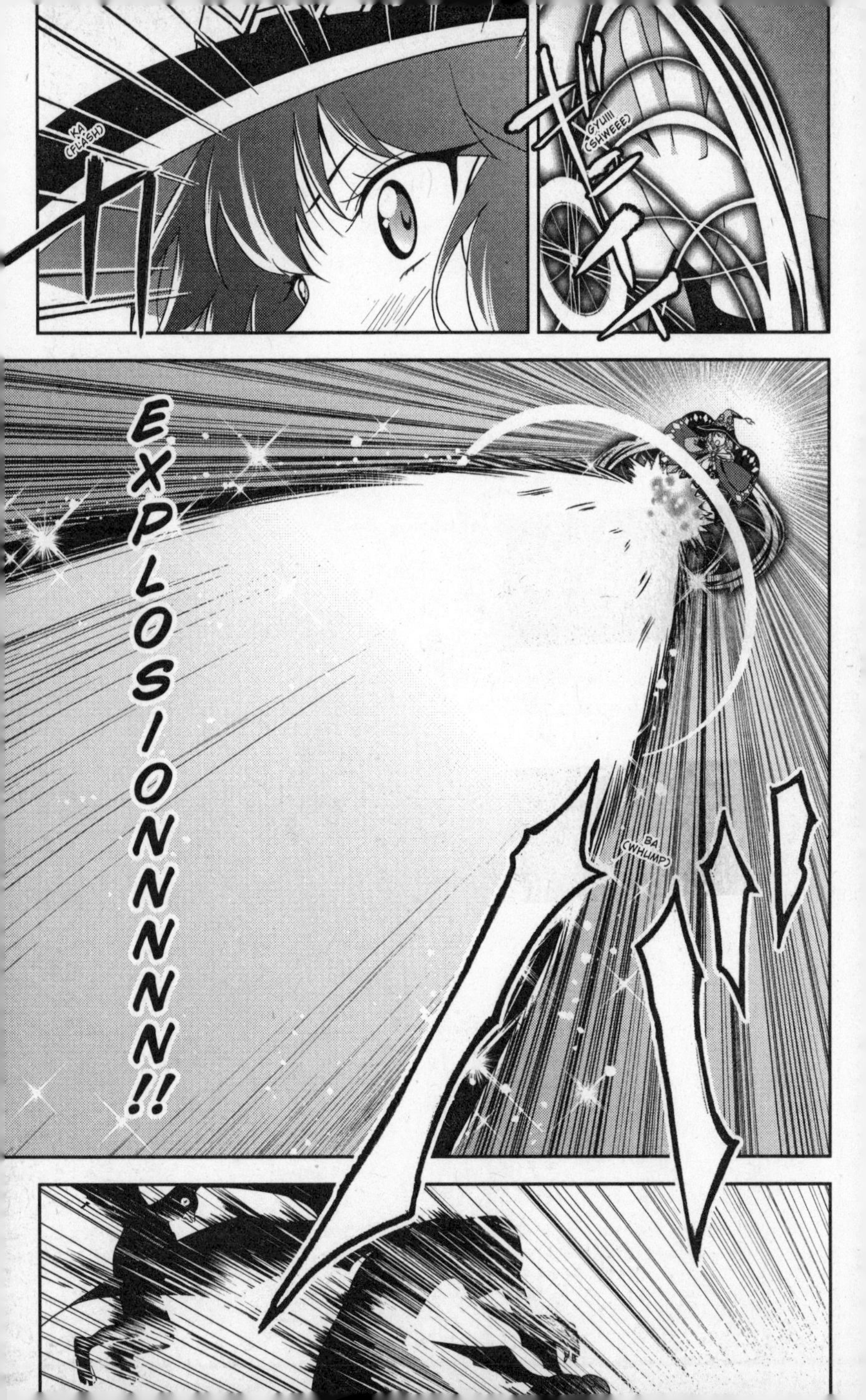
GYUIII (SHWEEE)
KA (FLASH)
EXPLOSIONNNNN!!
BA (WHUMP)

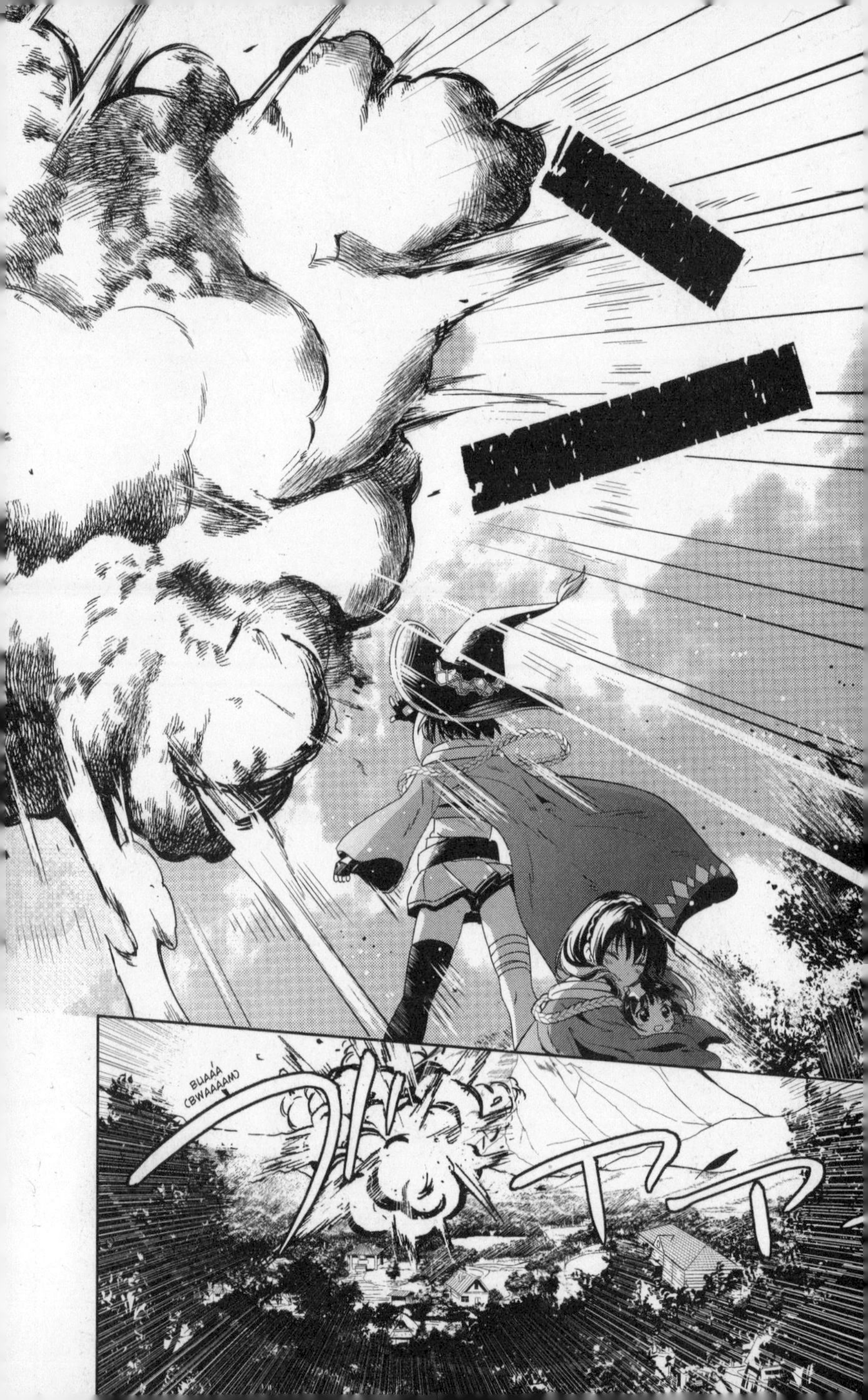
BUAAA
(BWAAAAM)

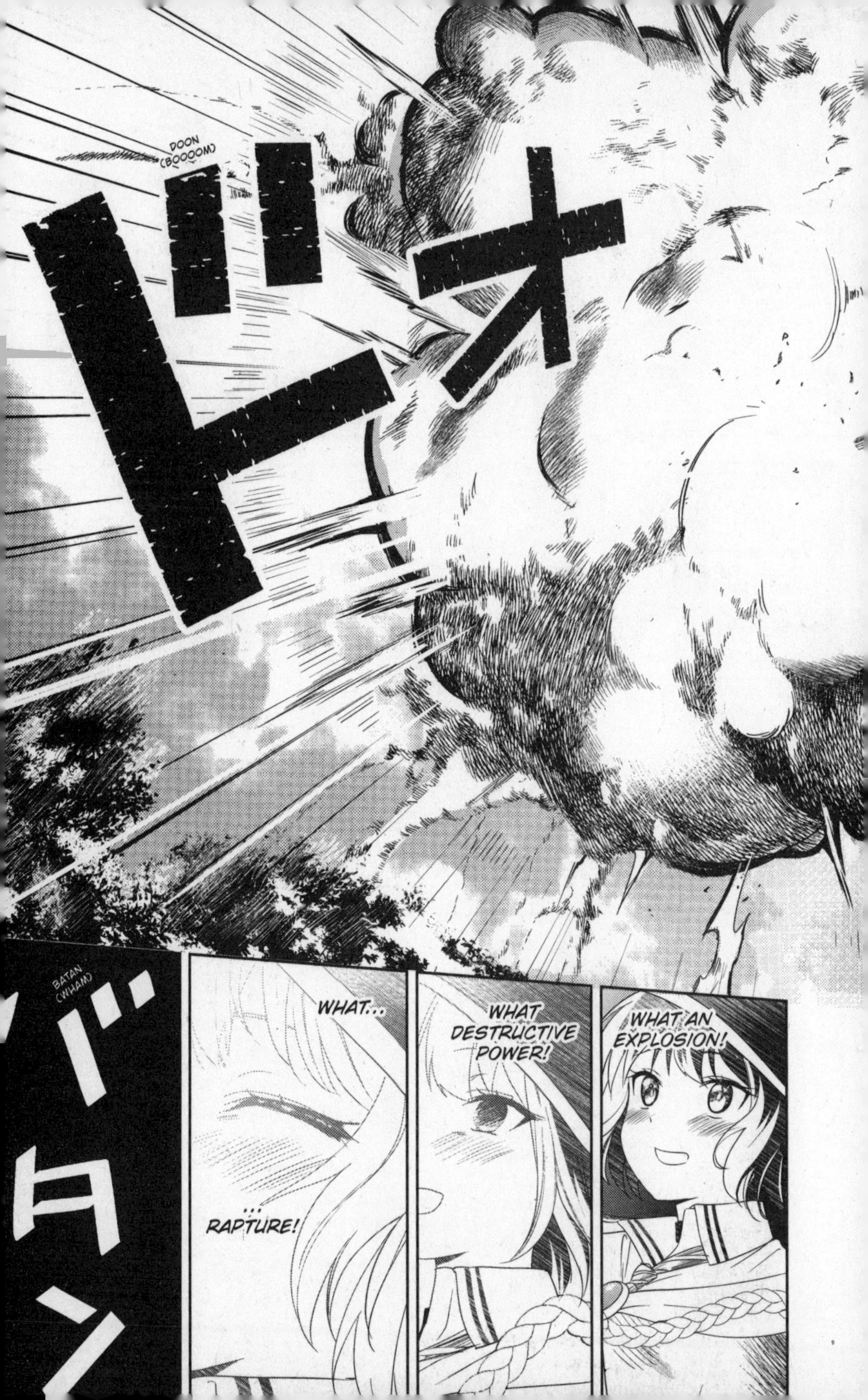
DOON (BOOOOM)
WHAT AN EXPLOSION!
WHAT DESTRUCTIVE POWER!
WHAT...
... RAPTURE!
BATAN (WHAM)
バタン

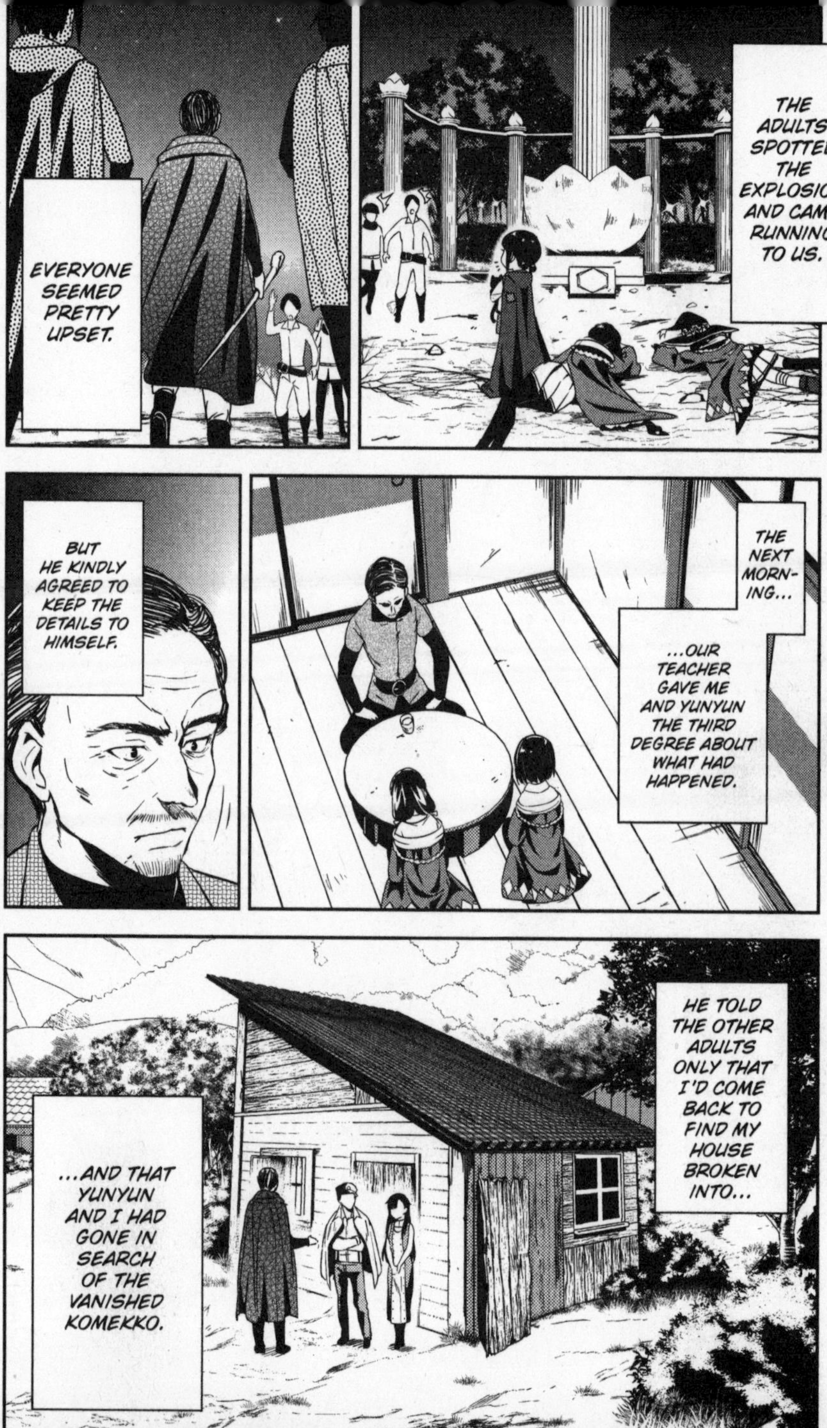
THE ADULTS SPOTTED THE EXPLOSION AND CAME RUNNING TO US.
EVERYONE SEEMED PRETTY UPSET.
THE NEXT MORNING...
...OUR TEACHER GAVE ME AND YUNYUN THE THIRD DEGREE ABOUT WHAT HAD HAPPENED.
BUT HE KINDLY AGREED TO KEEP THE DETAILS TO HIMSELF.
HE TOLD THE OTHER ADULTS ONLY THAT I'D COME BACK TO FIND MY HOUSE BROKEN INTO...
...AND THAT YUNYUN AND I HAD GONE IN SEARCH OF THE VANISHED KOMEKKO.

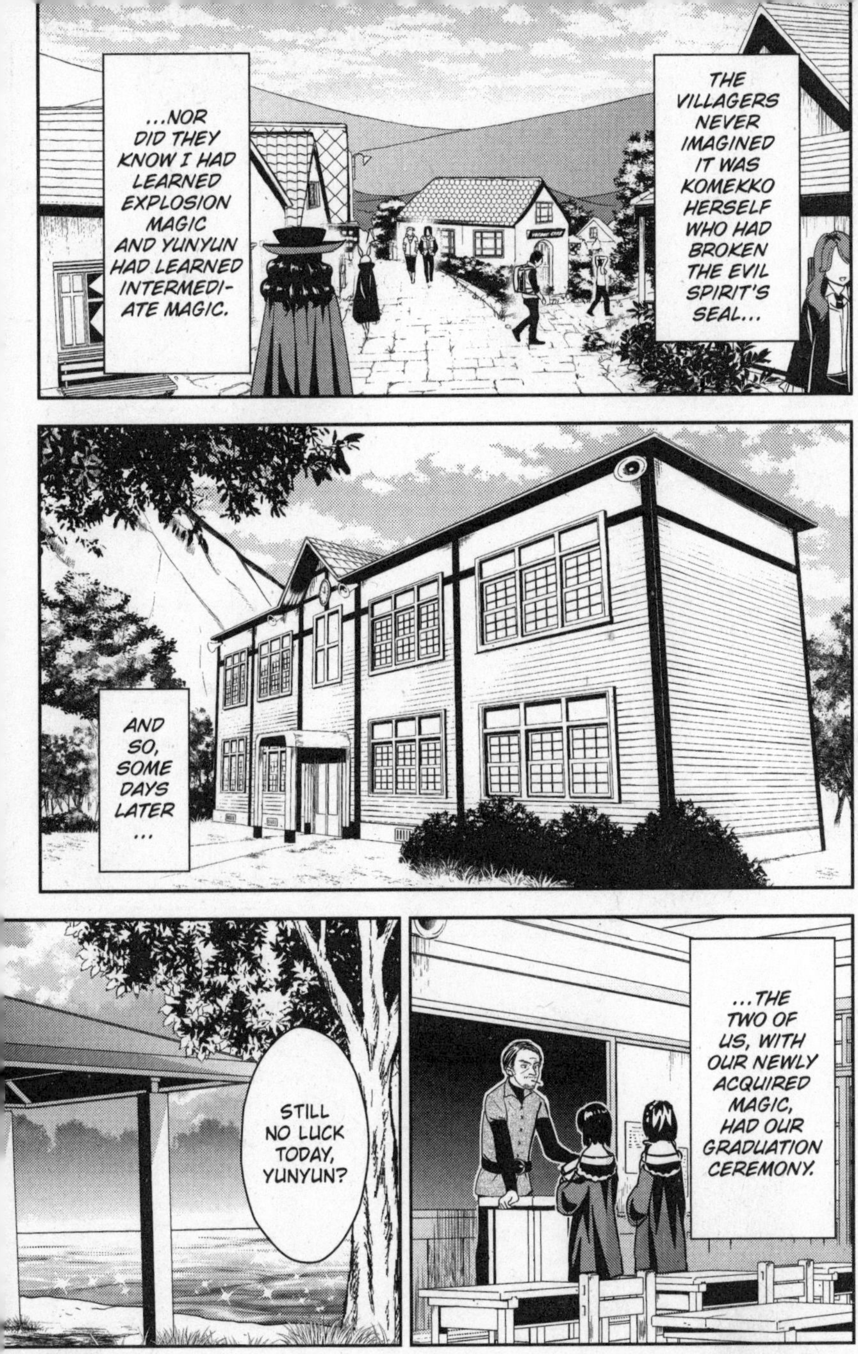
THE VILLAGERS NEVER IMAGINED IT WAS KOMEKKO HERSELF WHO HAD BROKEN THE EVIL SPIRIT'S SEAL...
...NOR DID THEY KNOW I HAD LEARNED EXPLOSION MAGIC AND YUNYUN HAD LEARNED INTERMEDIATE MAGIC.
AND SO, SOME DAYS LATER...
...THE TWO OF US, WITH OUR NEWLY ACQUIRED MAGIC, HAD OUR GRADUATION CEREMONY.
STILL NO LUCK TODAY, YUNYUN?

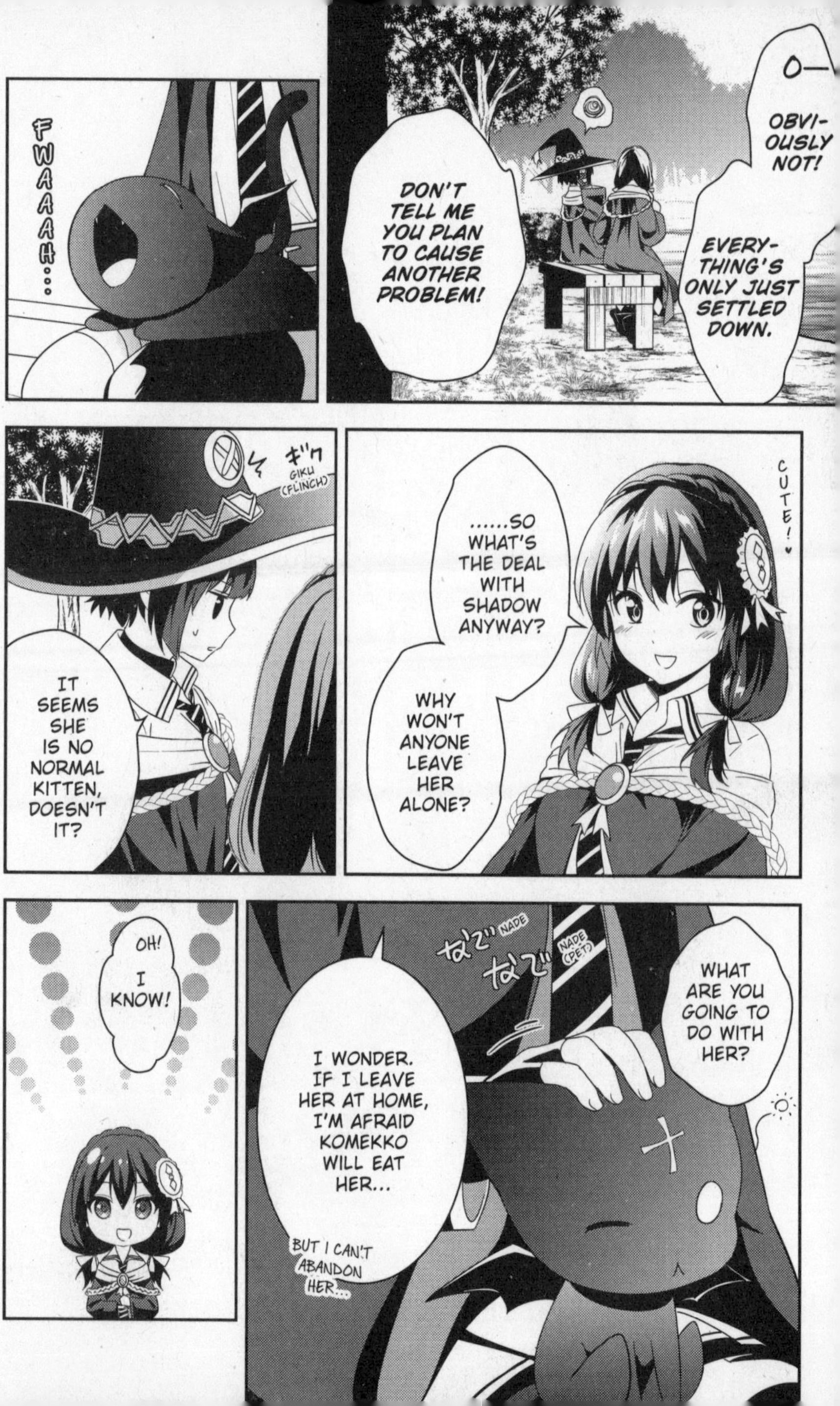
O—
OBVIOUSLY NOT!
EVERYTHING'S ONLY JUST SETTLED DOWN.
DON'T TELL ME YOU PLAN TO CAUSE ANOTHER PROBLEM!
FWAAAAH...
CUTE!
......SO WHAT'S THE DEAL WITH SHADOW ANYWAY?
WHY WON'T ANYONE LEAVE HER ALONE?
ギク GIKU (FLINCH)
IT SEEMS SHE IS NO NORMAL KITTEN, DOESN'T IT?
WHAT ARE YOU GOING TO DO WITH HER?
なで NADE
なで NADE (PET)
I WONDER. IF I LEAVE HER AT HOME, I'M AFRAID KOMEKKO WILL EAT HER...
BUT I CAN'T ABANDON HER...
OH! I KNOW!

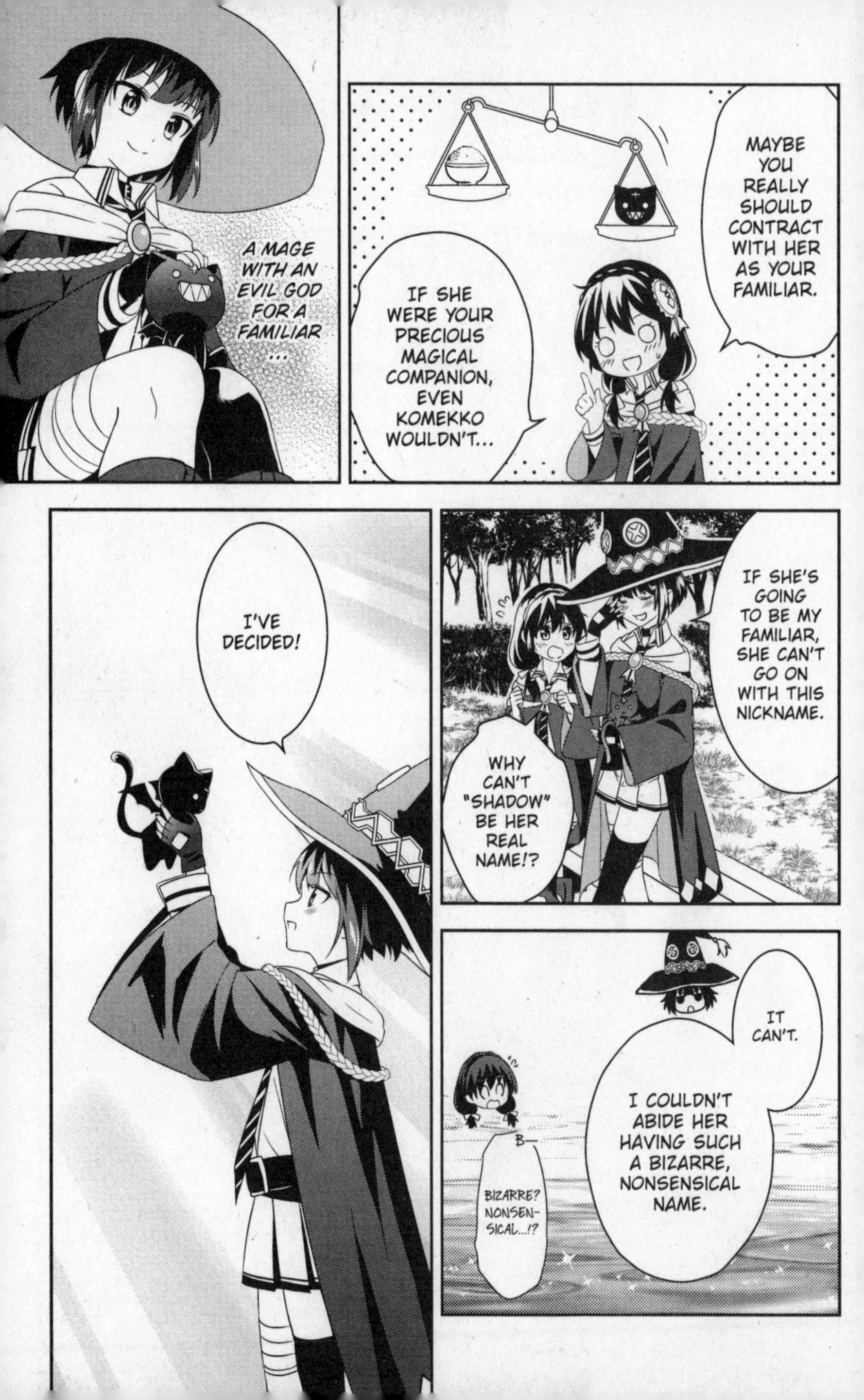
MAYBE YOU REALLY SHOULD CONTRACT WITH HER AS YOUR FAMILIAR.
IF SHE WERE YOUR PRECIOUS MAGICAL COMPANION, EVEN KOMEKKO WOULDN'T...
A MAGE WITH AN EVIL GOD FOR A FAMILIAR...
IF SHE'S GOING TO BE MY FAMILIAR, SHE CAN'T GO ON WITH THIS NICKNAME.
WHY CAN'T "SHADOW" BE HER REAL NAME!?
IT CAN'T.
I COULDN'T ABIDE HER HAVING SUCH A BIZARRE, NONSENSICAL NAME.
B—
BIZARRE? NONSENSICAL...!?
I'VE DECIDED!

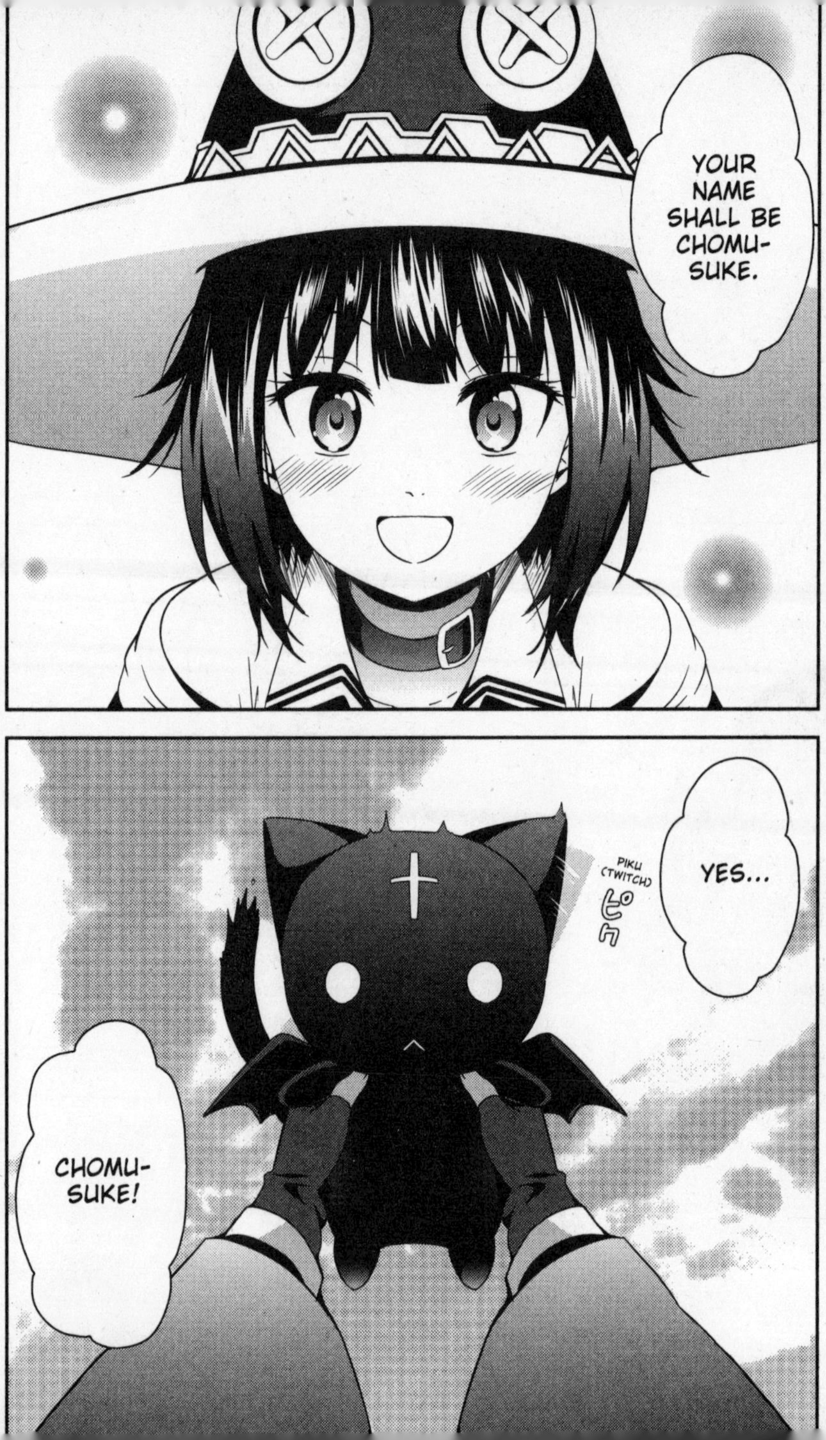
YOUR NAME SHALL BE CHOMU-SUKE.
YES...
PIKU (TWITCH)
ピク
CHOMU-SUKE!

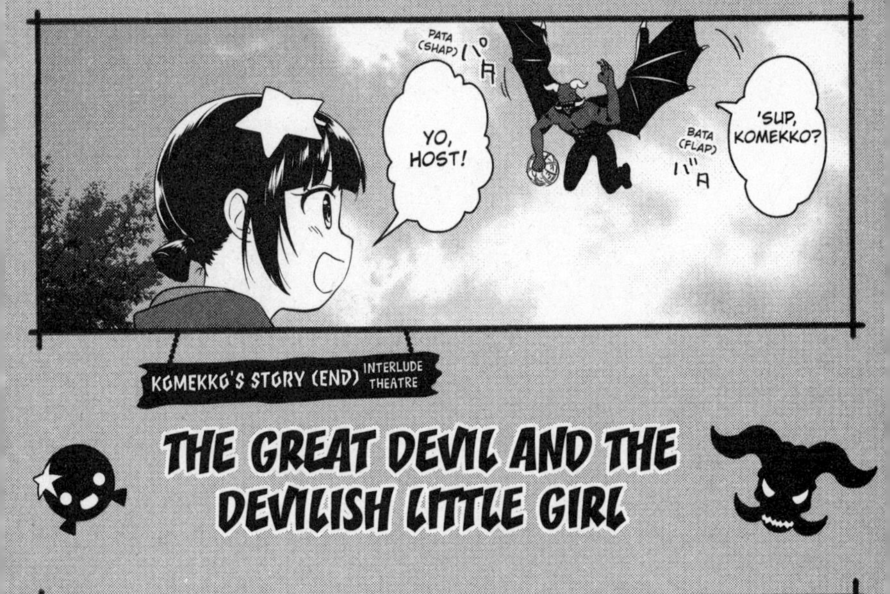
'SUP, KOMEKKO?
BATA (FLAP)
PATA (SHAP)
YO, HOST!

KOMEKKO'S STORY (END) INTERLUDE THEATRE

THE GREAT DEVIL AND THE DEVILISH LITTLE GIRL

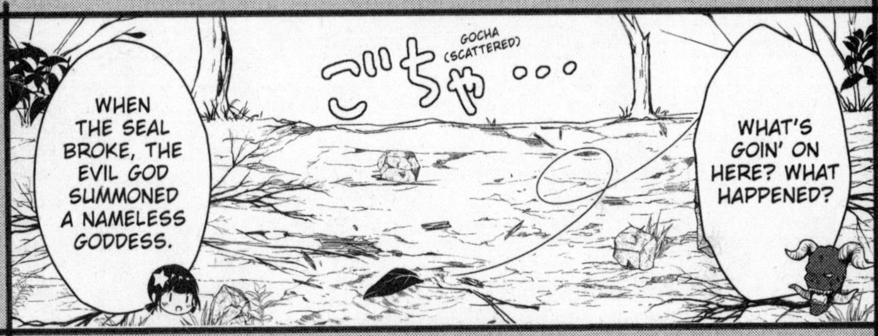
WHAT'S GOIN' ON HERE? WHAT HAPPENED?
GOCHA (SCATTERED)
WHEN THE SEAL BROKE, THE EVIL GOD SUMMONED A NAMELESS GODDESS.

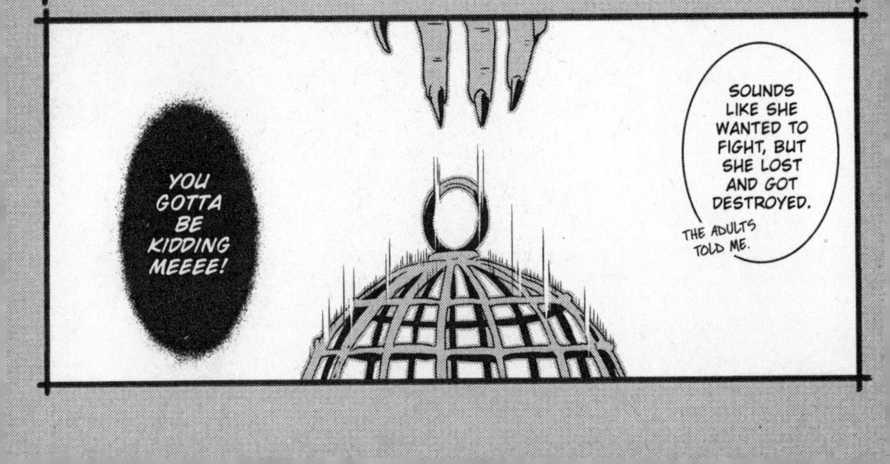
SOUNDS LIKE SHE WANTED TO FIGHT, BUT SHE LOST AND GOT DESTROYED.
THE ADULTS TOLD ME.
YOU GOTTA BE KIDDING MEEEE!

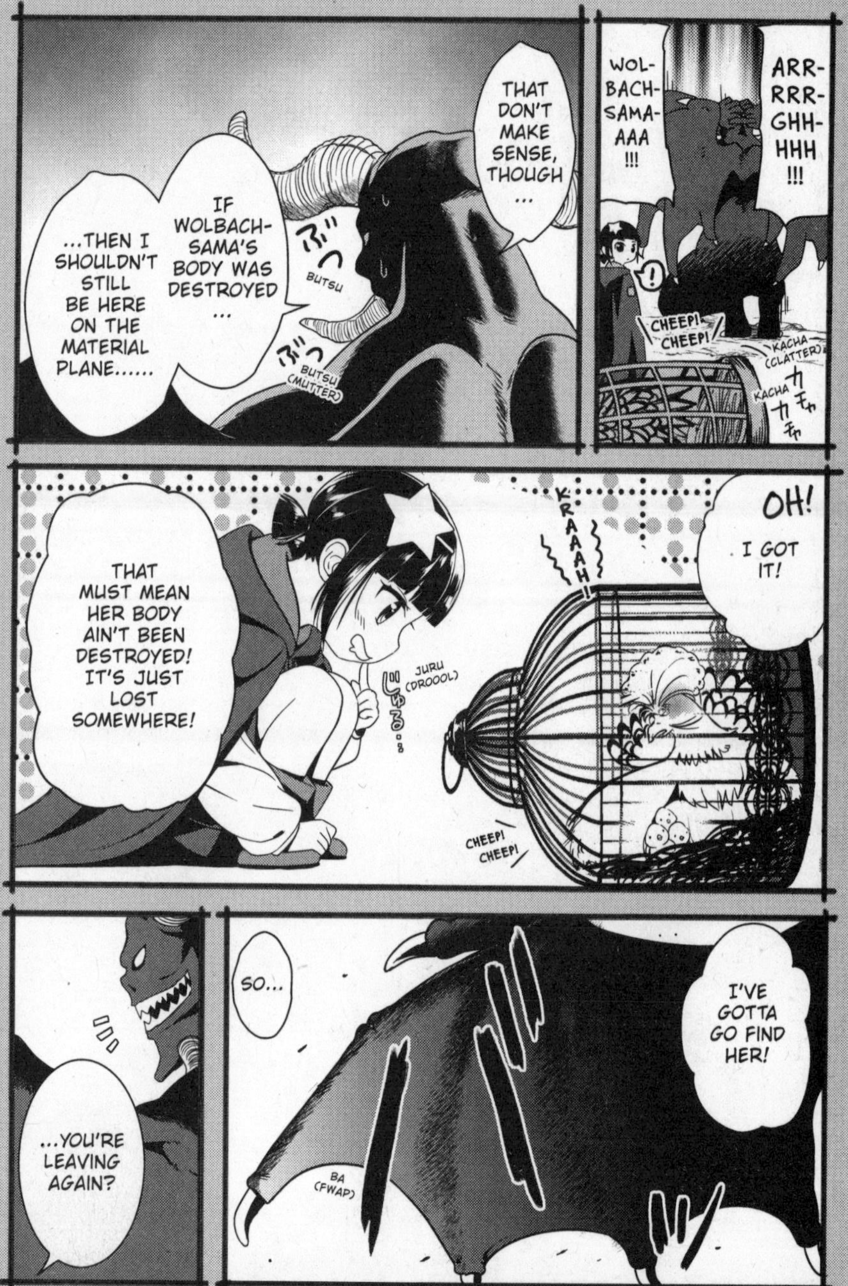
ARR-RRR-GHH-HHH!!!
WOL-BACH-SAMA-AAA!!!
!
CHEEP! CHEEP!
KACHA (CLATTER)
KACHA
カチャ
カチャ
THAT DON'T MAKE SENSE, THOUGH...
ぶつ
BUTSU
ぶつ
BUTSU (MUTTER)
IF WOLBACH-SAMA'S BODY WAS DESTROYED...
...THEN I SHOULDN'T STILL BE HERE ON THE MATERIAL PLANE......
OH!
I GOT IT!
KRAAAH!
THAT MUST MEAN HER BODY AIN'T BEEN DESTROYED! IT'S JUST LOST SOMEWHERE!
JURU (DROOOL)
じゅる..
CHEEP! CHEEP!
I'VE GOTTA GO FIND HER!
SO...
BA (FWAP)
...YOU'RE LEAVING AGAIN?

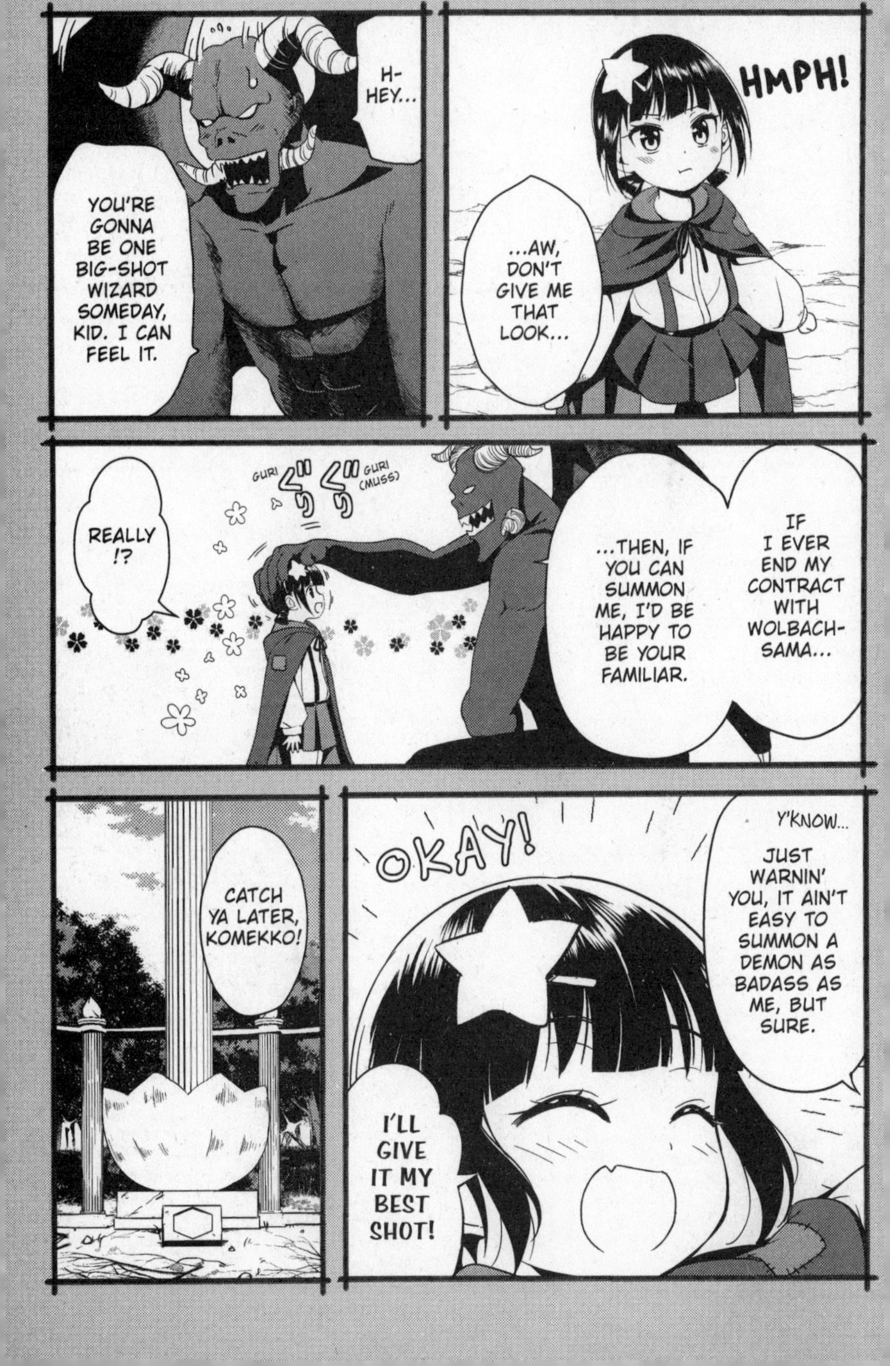
HMPH!
...AW, DON'T GIVE ME THAT LOOK...
H-HEY...
YOU'RE GONNA BE ONE BIG-SHOT WIZARD SOMEDAY, KID. I CAN FEEL IT.
IF I EVER END MY CONTRACT WITH WOLBACH-SAMA...
...THEN, IF YOU CAN SUMMON ME, I'D BE HAPPY TO BE YOUR FAMILIAR.
ぐりぐり
GURI GURI (MUSS)
REALLY!?
Y'KNOW...
JUST WARNIN' YOU, IT AIN'T EASY TO SUMMON A DEMON AS BADASS AS ME, BUT SURE.
OKAY!
I'LL GIVE IT MY BEST SHOT!
CATCH YA LATER, KOMEKKO!

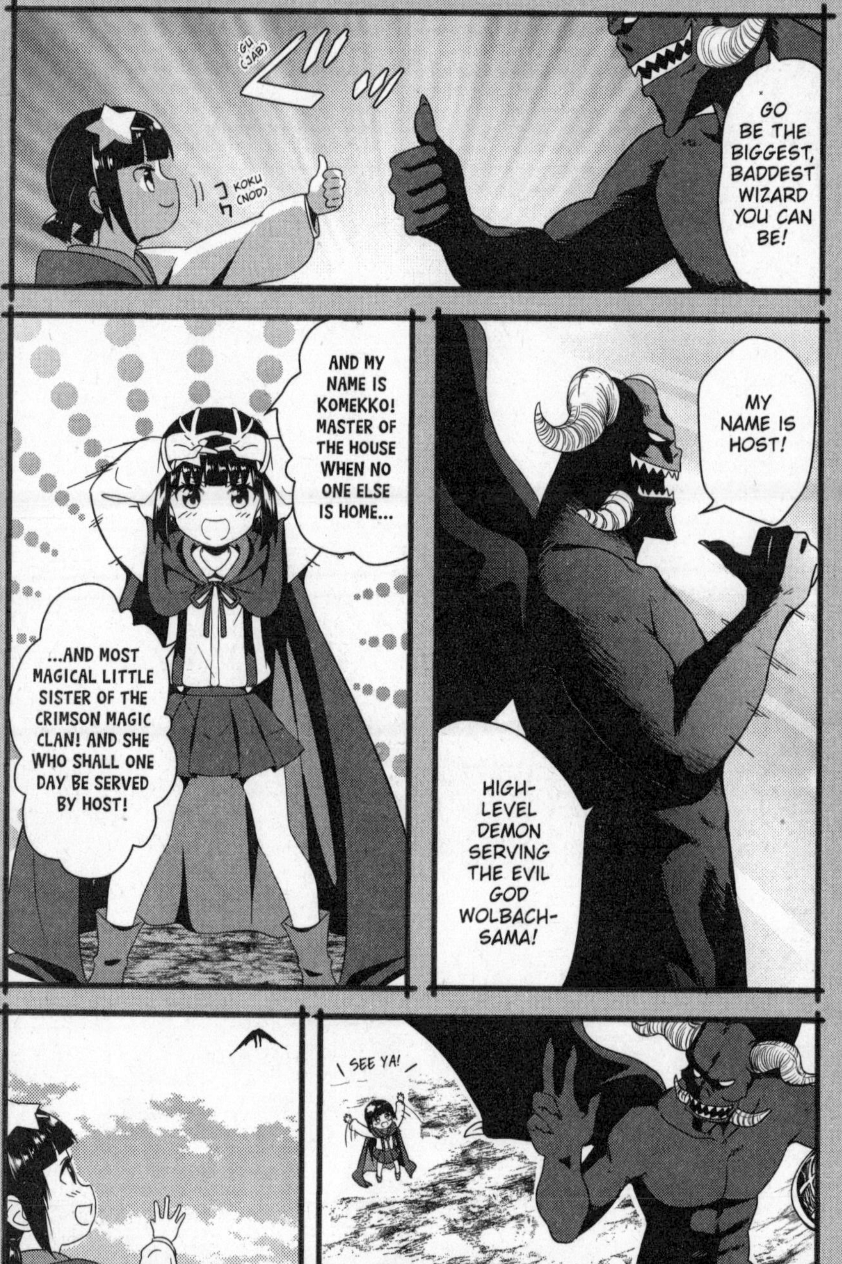
GO BE THE BIGGEST, BADDEST WIZARD YOU CAN BE!
GU (JAB)
KOKU (NOD)
MY NAME IS HOST!
HIGH-LEVEL DEMON SERVING THE EVIL GOD WOLBACH-SAMA!
AND MY NAME IS KOMEKKO! MASTER OF THE HOUSE WHEN NO ONE ELSE IS HOME...
...AND MOST MAGICAL LITTLE SISTER OF THE CRIMSON MAGIC CLAN! AND SHE WHO SHALL ONE DAY BE SERVED BY HOST!
SEE YA!

KONOSUBA: AN EXPLOSION ON THIS WONDERFUL WORLD!

KONOSUBA: AN EXPLOSION ON THIS WONDERFUL WORLD!

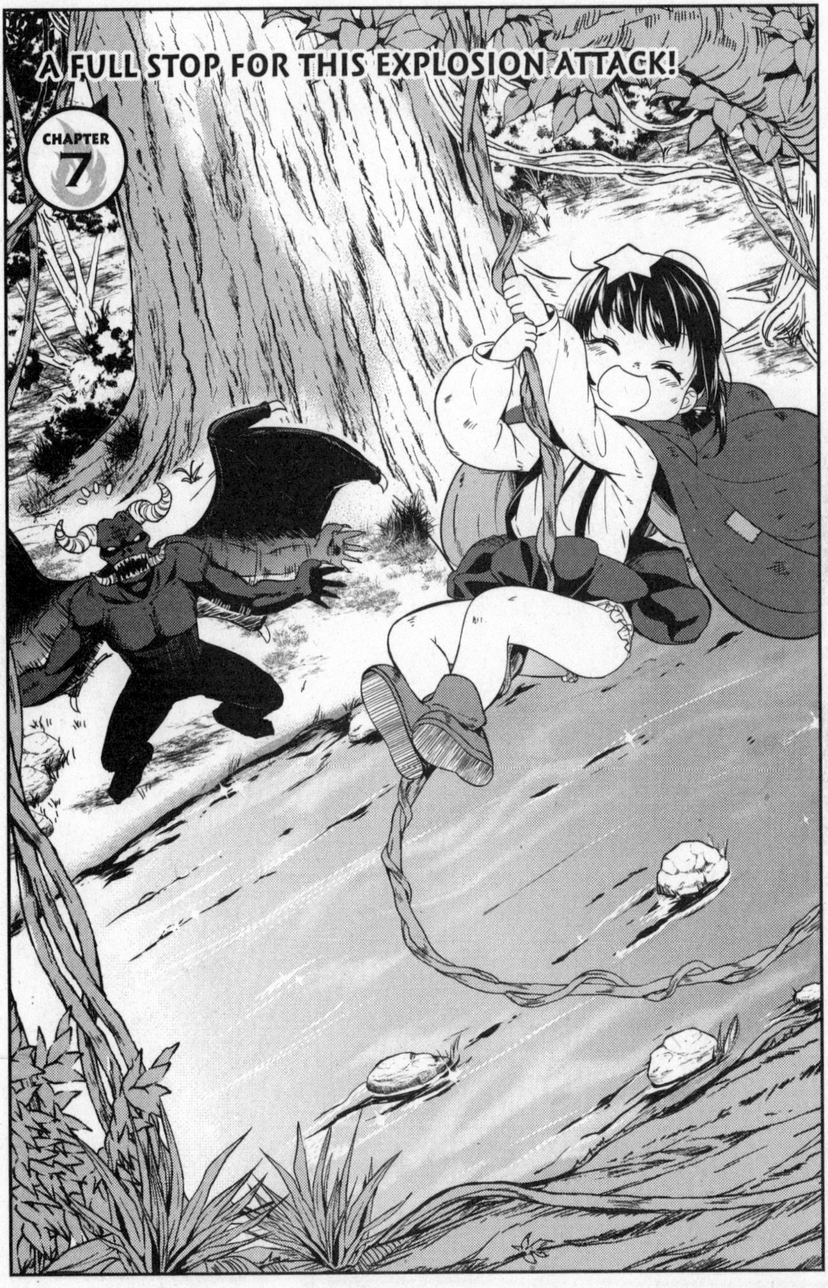
A FULL STOP FOR THIS EXPLOSION ATTACK!
CHAPTER
7

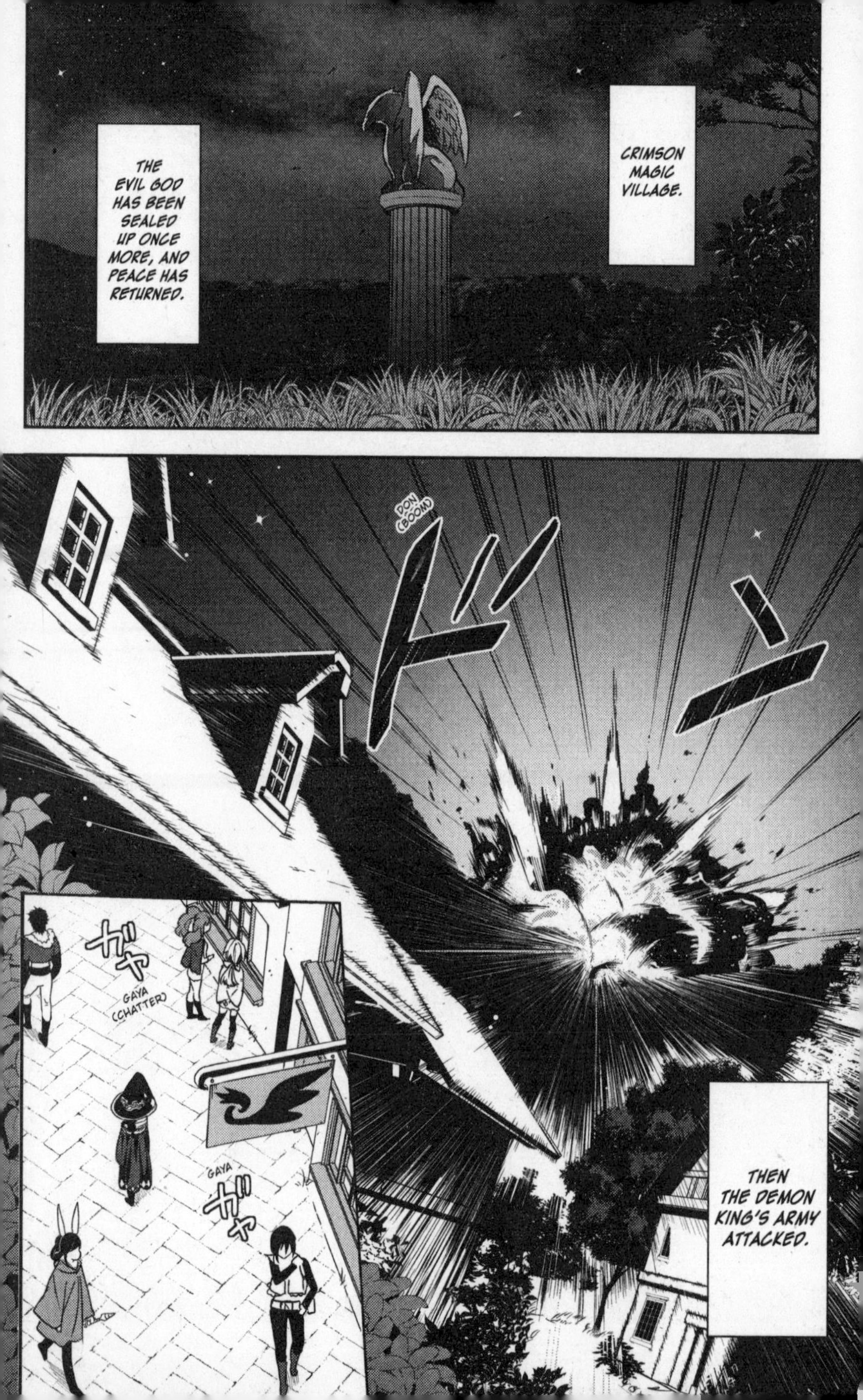
CRIMSON MAGIC VILLAGE.
THE EVIL GOD HAS BEEN SEALED UP ONCE MORE, AND PEACE HAS RETURNED.
ドン
DON (BOOM)
THEN THE DEMON KING'S ARMY ATTACKED.
ガヤ
GAYA (CHATTER)
ガヤ
GAYA

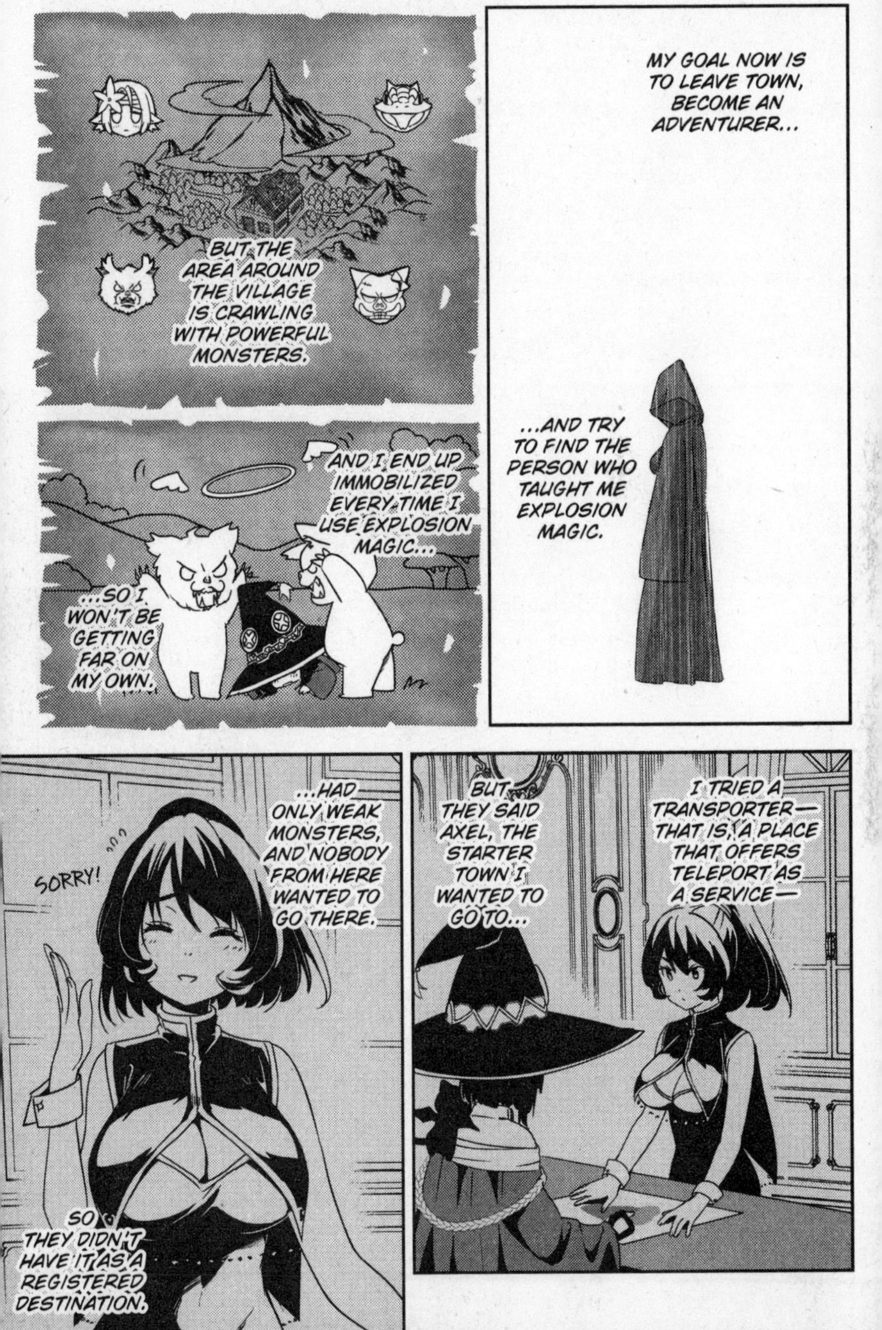
MY GOAL NOW IS TO LEAVE TOWN, BECOME AN ADVENTURER...
...AND TRY TO FIND THE PERSON WHO TAUGHT ME EXPLOSION MAGIC.
BUT THE AREA AROUND THE VILLAGE IS CRAWLING WITH POWERFUL MONSTERS.
AND I END UP IMMOBILIZED EVERY TIME I USE EXPLOSION MAGIC...
...SO I WON'T BE GETTING FAR ON MY OWN.
I TRIED A TRANSPORTER—THAT IS, A PLACE THAT OFFERS TELEPORT AS A SERVICE—
BUT THEY SAID AXEL, THE STARTER TOWN I WANTED TO GO TO...
...HAD ONLY WEAK MONSTERS, AND NOBODY FROM HERE WANTED TO GO THERE.
SORRY!
SO THEY DIDN'T HAVE IT AS A REGISTERED DESTINATION.

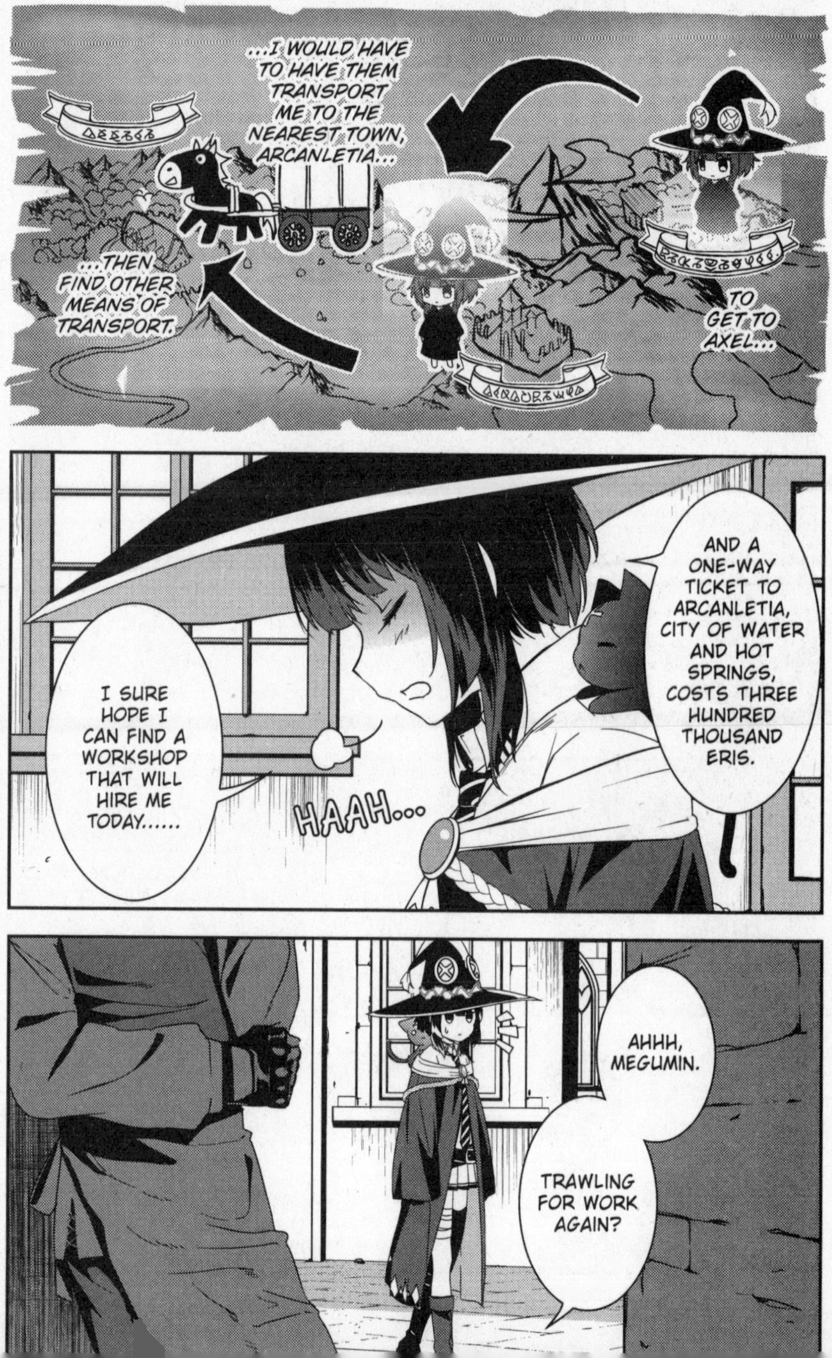
TO GET TO AXEL...
...I WOULD HAVE TO HAVE THEM TRANSPORT ME TO THE NEAREST TOWN, ARCANLETIA...
...THEN FIND OTHER MEANS OF TRANSPORT.
AND A ONE-WAY TICKET TO ARCANLETIA, CITY OF WATER AND HOT SPRINGS, COSTS THREE HUNDRED THOUSAND ERIS.
HAAAH...
I SURE HOPE I CAN FIND A WORKSHOP THAT WILL HIRE ME TODAY......
AHHH, MEGUMIN.
TRAWLING FOR WORK AGAIN?

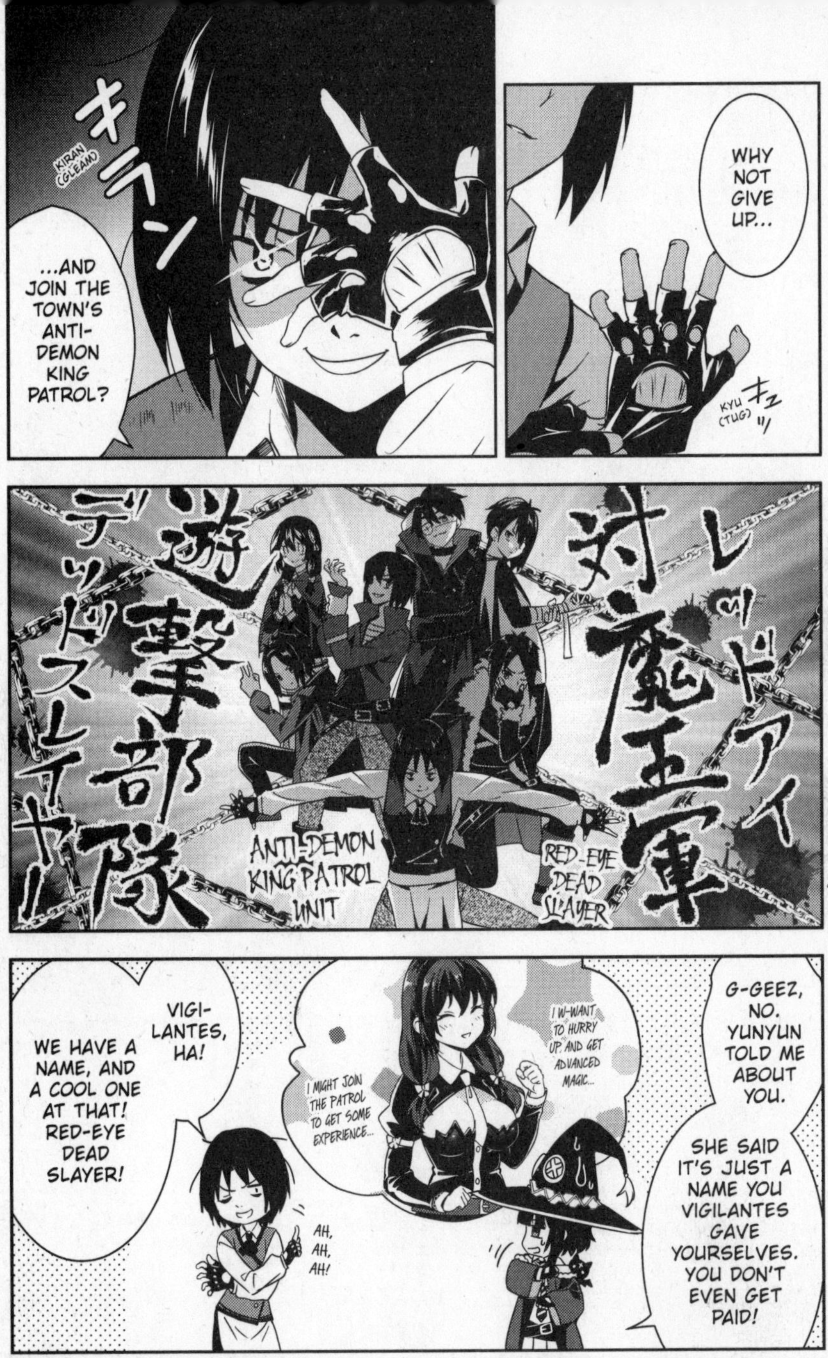
WHY NOT GIVE UP...
KYU (TUG)
KIRAN (GLEAM)
...AND JOIN THE TOWN'S ANTI-DEMON KING PATROL?
レッドアイ
対魔王軍
遊撃部隊
デッドスレイヤー!
RED-EYE DEAD SLAYER
ANTI-DEMON KING PATROL UNIT
G-GEEZ, NO. YUNYUN TOLD ME ABOUT YOU.
SHE SAID IT'S JUST A NAME YOU VIGILANTES GAVE YOURSELVES. YOU DON'T EVEN GET PAID!
I W-WANT TO HURRY UP AND GET ADVANCED MAGIC...
I MIGHT JOIN THE PATROL TO GET SOME EXPERIENCE...
VIGI-LANTES, HA!
AH, AH, AH!
WE HAVE A NAME, AND A COOL ONE AT THAT! RED-EYE DEAD SLAYER!

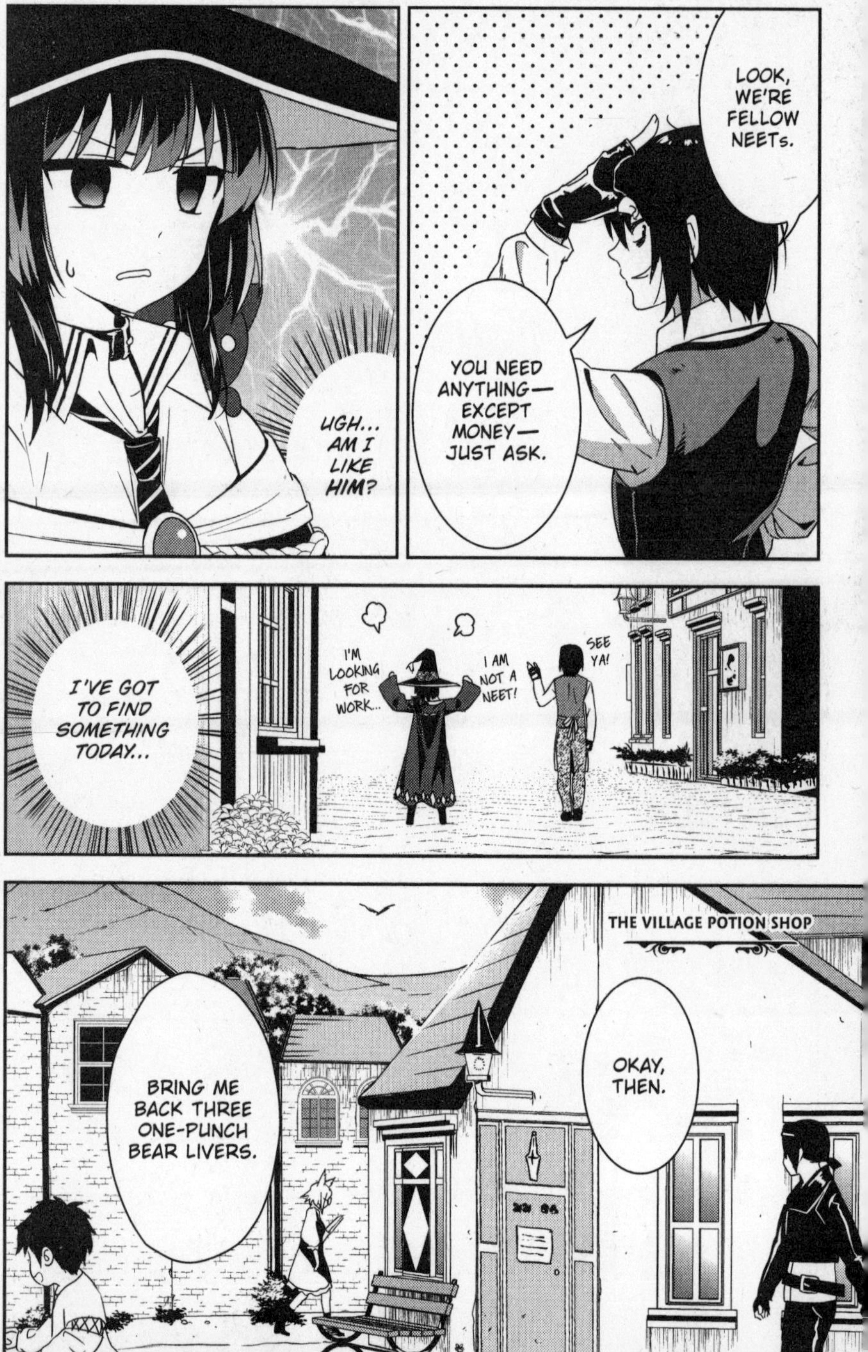
LOOK, WE'RE FELLOW NEETs.
YOU NEED ANYTHING—EXCEPT MONEY—JUST ASK.
UGH... AM I LIKE HIM?
SEE YA!
I AM NOT A NEET!
I'M LOOKING FOR WORK...
I'VE GOT TO FIND SOMETHING TODAY...
THE VILLAGE POTION SHOP
OKAY, THEN.
BRING ME BACK THREE ONE-PUNCH BEAR LIVERS.

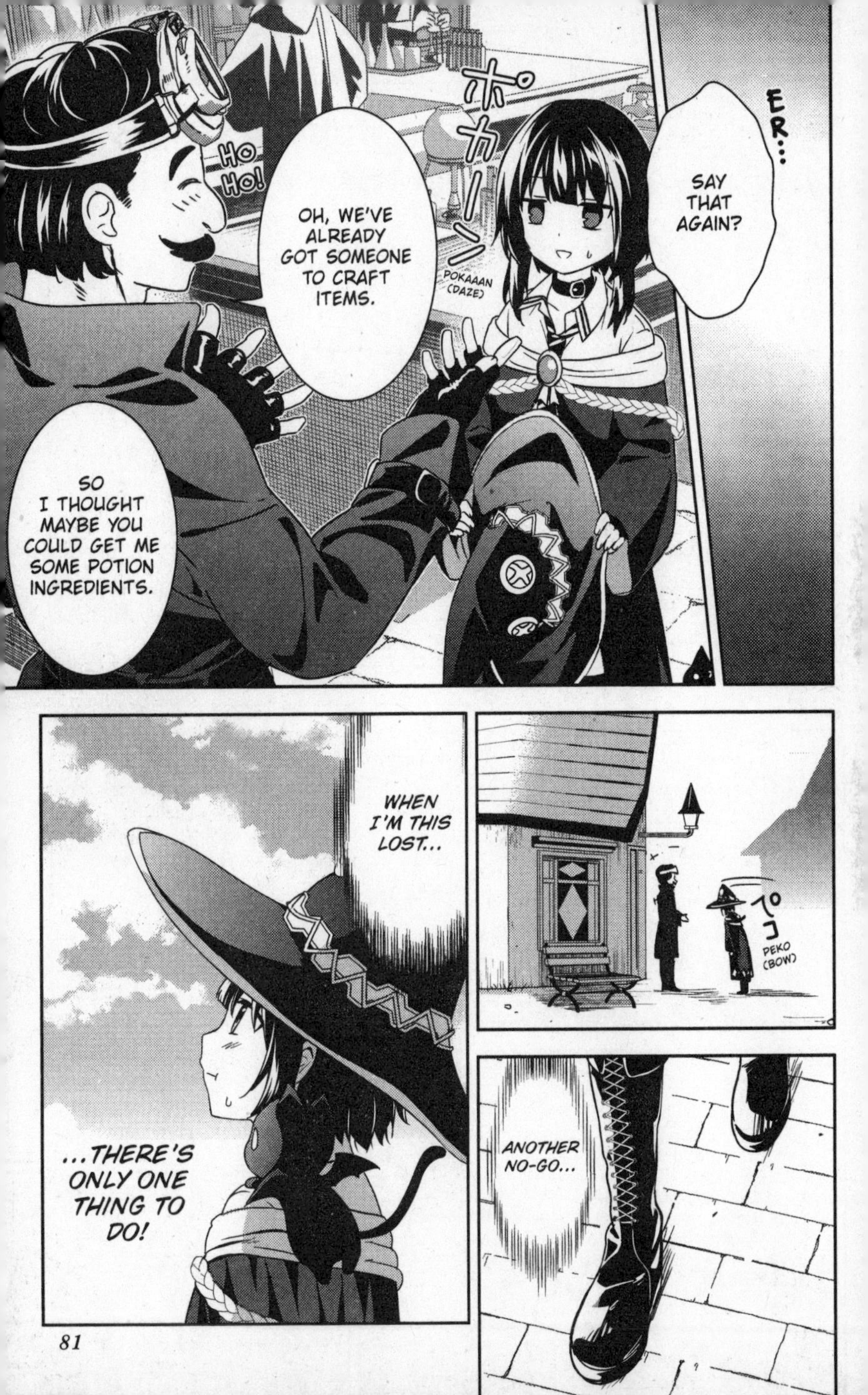
ER...
SAY THAT AGAIN?
POKAAAN (DAZE)
OH, WE'VE ALREADY GOT SOMEONE TO CRAFT ITEMS.
HO HO!
SO I THOUGHT MAYBE YOU COULD GET ME SOME POTION INGREDIENTS.
PEKO (BOW)
ANOTHER NO-GO...
WHEN I'M THIS LOST...
...THERE'S ONLY ONE THING TO DO!

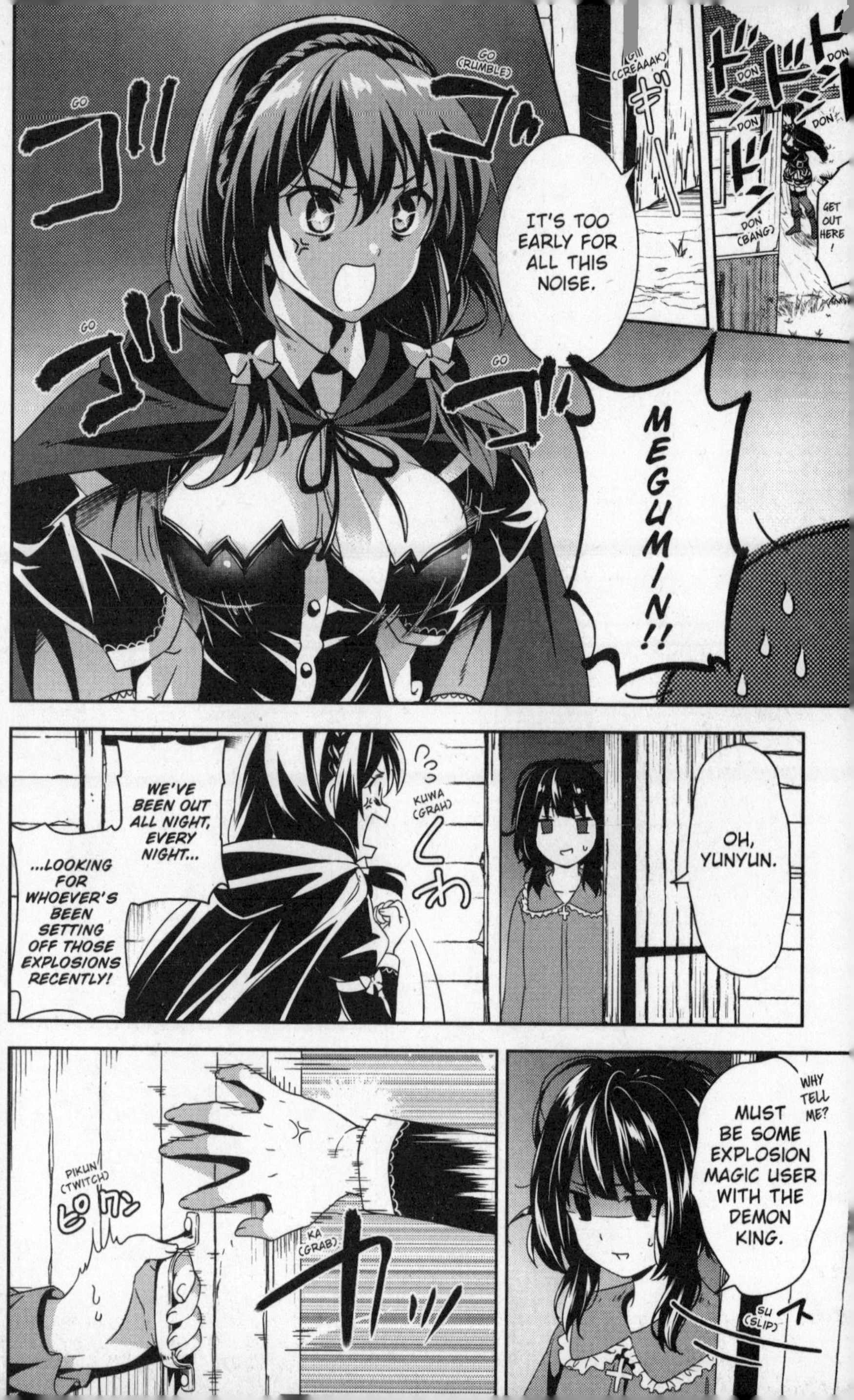

DON DON
DON
DON
DON (BANG)
GET OUT HERE!
GII (CREAAAK)
IT'S TOO EARLY FOR ALL THIS NOISE.
GO (RUMBLE)
GO
GO
GO
MEGUMIN!!
OH, YUNYUN.
KUWA (GRAH)
WE'VE BEEN OUT ALL NIGHT, EVERY NIGHT...
...LOOKING FOR WHOEVER'S BEEN SETTING OFF THOSE EXPLOSIONS RECENTLY!
WHY TELL ME?
MUST BE SOME EXPLOSION MAGIC USER WITH THE DEMON KING.
SU (SLIP)
KA (GRAB)
PIKUN (TWITCH)

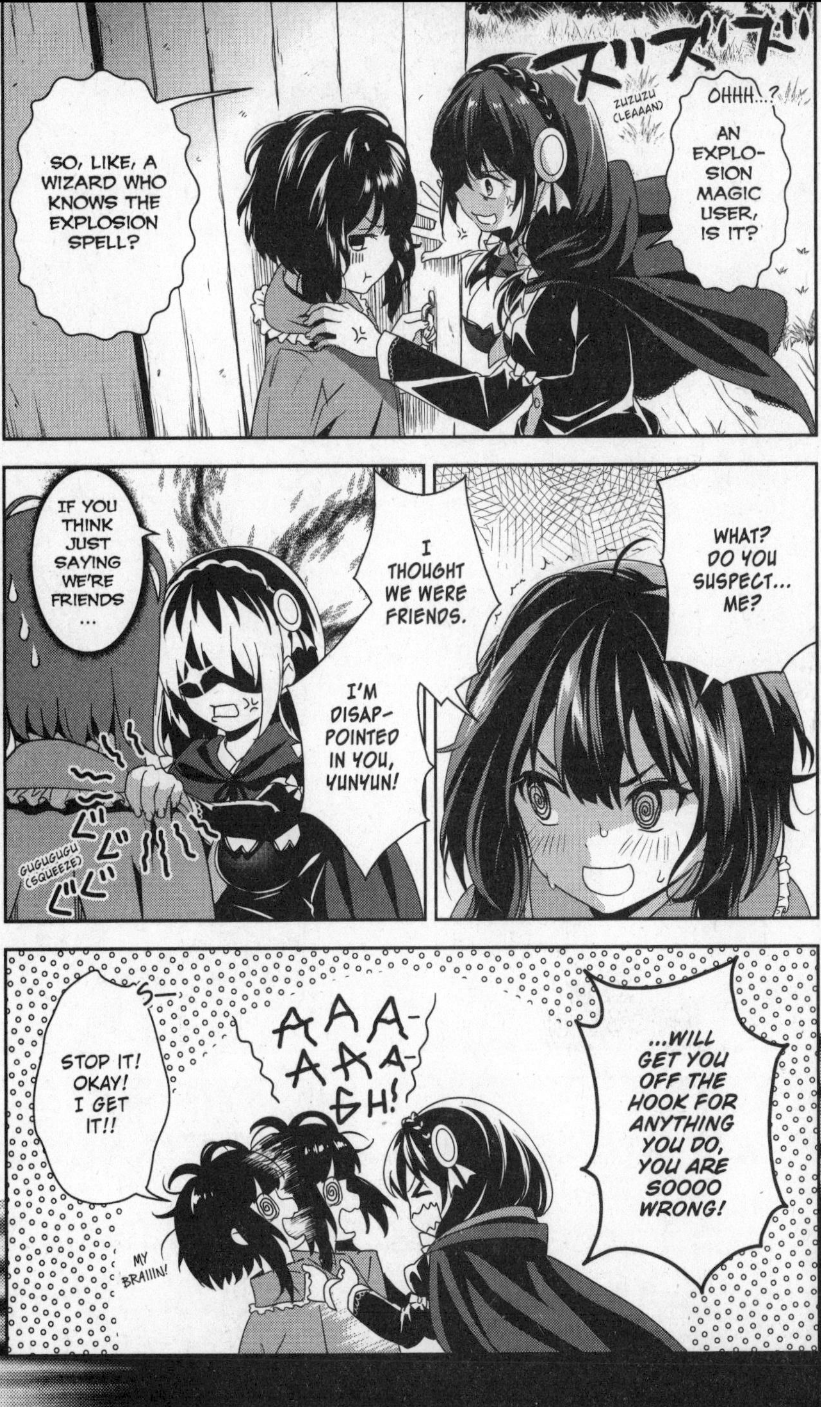
ズズズ
ZUZUZU (LEAAAN)
OHHH...?
AN EXPLOSION MAGIC USER, IS IT?
SO, LIKE, A WIZARD WHO KNOWS THE EXPLOSION SPELL?
WHAT? DO YOU SUSPECT... ME?
I THOUGHT WE WERE FRIENDS.
I'M DISAPPOINTED IN YOU, YUNYUN!
IF YOU THINK JUST SAYING WE'RE FRIENDS ...
GUGUGUGU (SQUEEZE)
...WILL GET YOU OFF THE HOOK FOR ANYTHING YOU DO, YOU ARE SOOOO WRONG!
AAA-AAAGH!
S— STOP IT! OKAY! I GET IT!!
MY BRAIIIN!

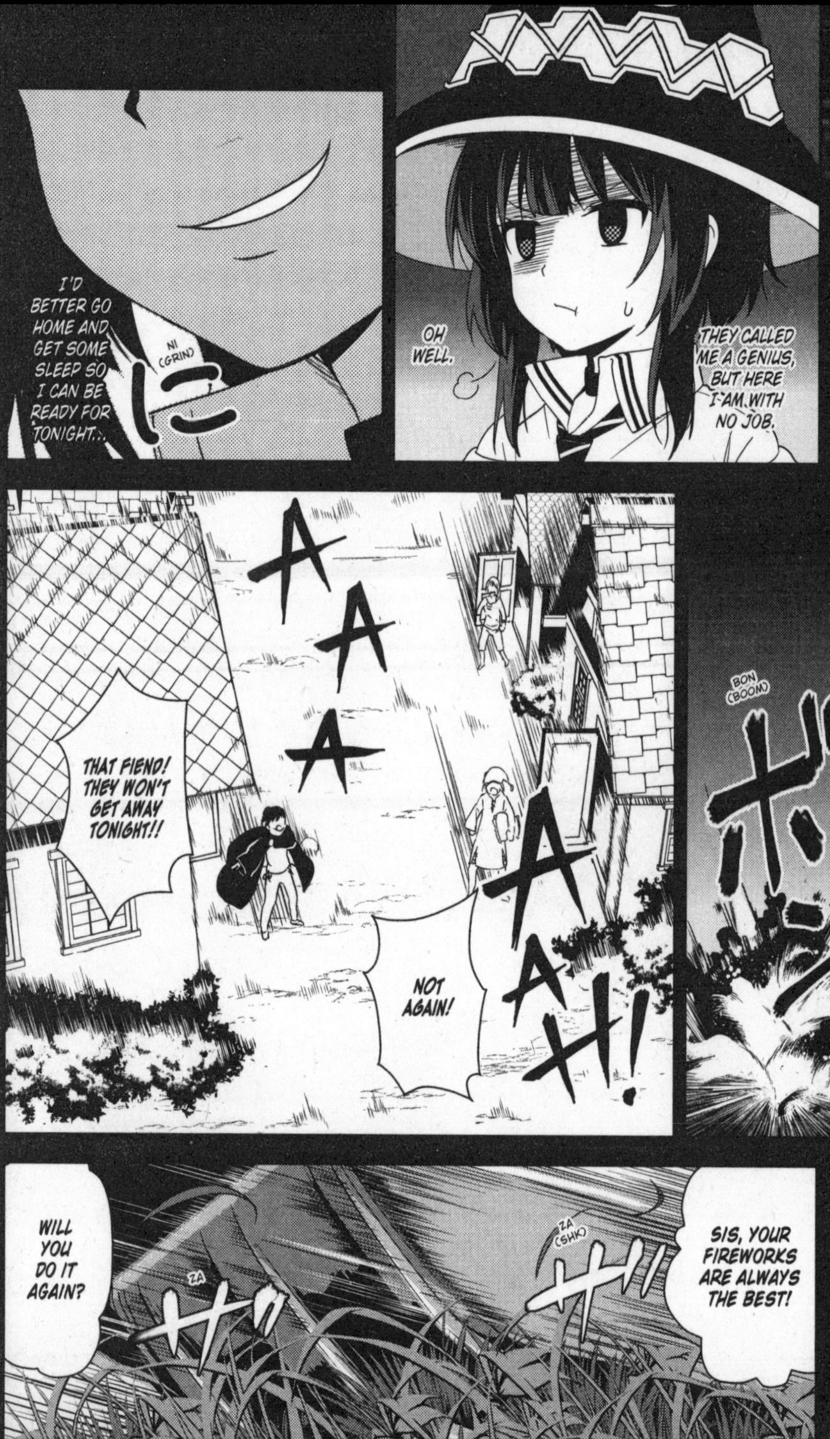
THEY CALLED ME A GENIUS, BUT HERE I AM WITH NO JOB.
OH WELL.
NI (GRIN)
I'D BETTER GO HOME AND GET SOME SLEEP SO I CAN BE READY FOR TONIGHT...
BON (BOOM)
AAAAAAH!
NOT AGAIN!
THAT FIEND! THEY WON'T GET AWAY TONIGHT!!
SIS, YOUR FIREWORKS ARE ALWAYS THE BEST!
ZA (SHK)
ZA
WILL YOU DO IT AGAIN?

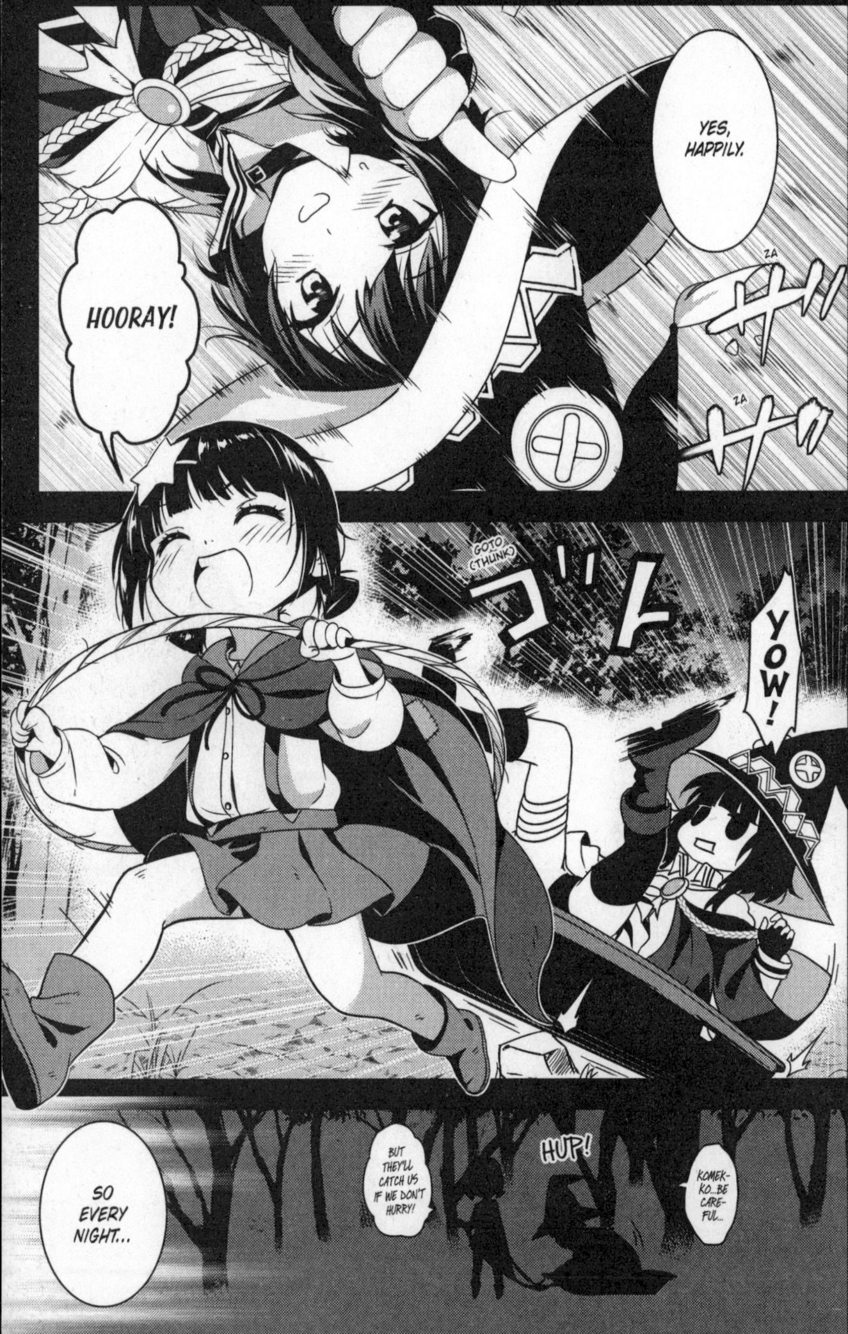
YES, HAPPILY.
ZA
ZA
HOORAY!
YOW!
GOTO (THUNK)
KOMEK-KO...BE CARE-FUL...
HUP!
BUT THEY'LL CATCH US IF WE DON'T HURRY!
SO EVERY NIGHT...

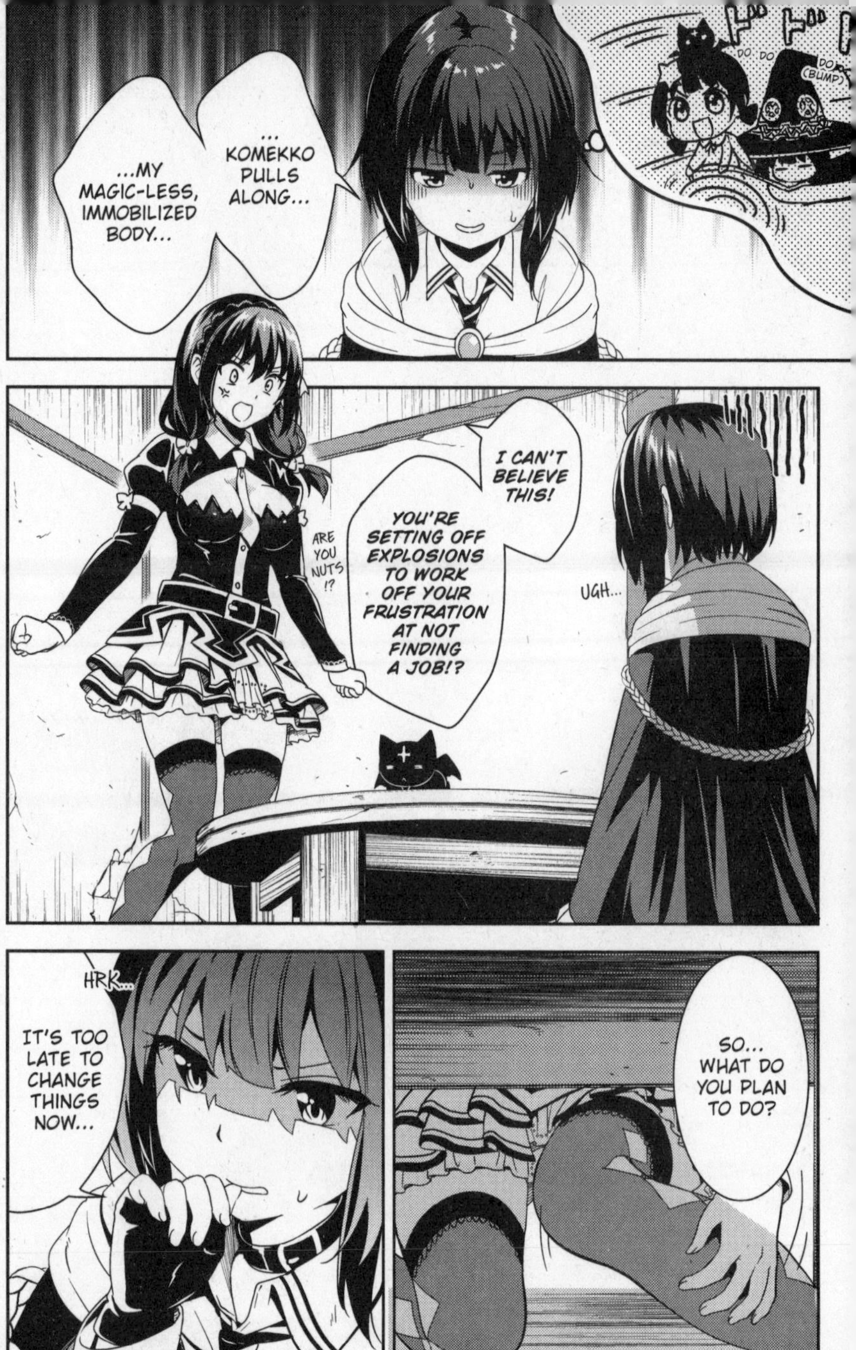
DO DO DO (BUMP)
...KOMEKKO PULLS ALONG...
...MY MAGIC-LESS, IMMOBILIZED BODY...
UGH...
I CAN'T BELIEVE THIS!
YOU'RE SETTING OFF EXPLOSIONS TO WORK OFF YOUR FRUSTRATION AT NOT FINDING A JOB!?
ARE YOU NUTS!?
SO... WHAT DO YOU PLAN TO DO?
HRK...
IT'S TOO LATE TO CHANGE THINGS NOW...

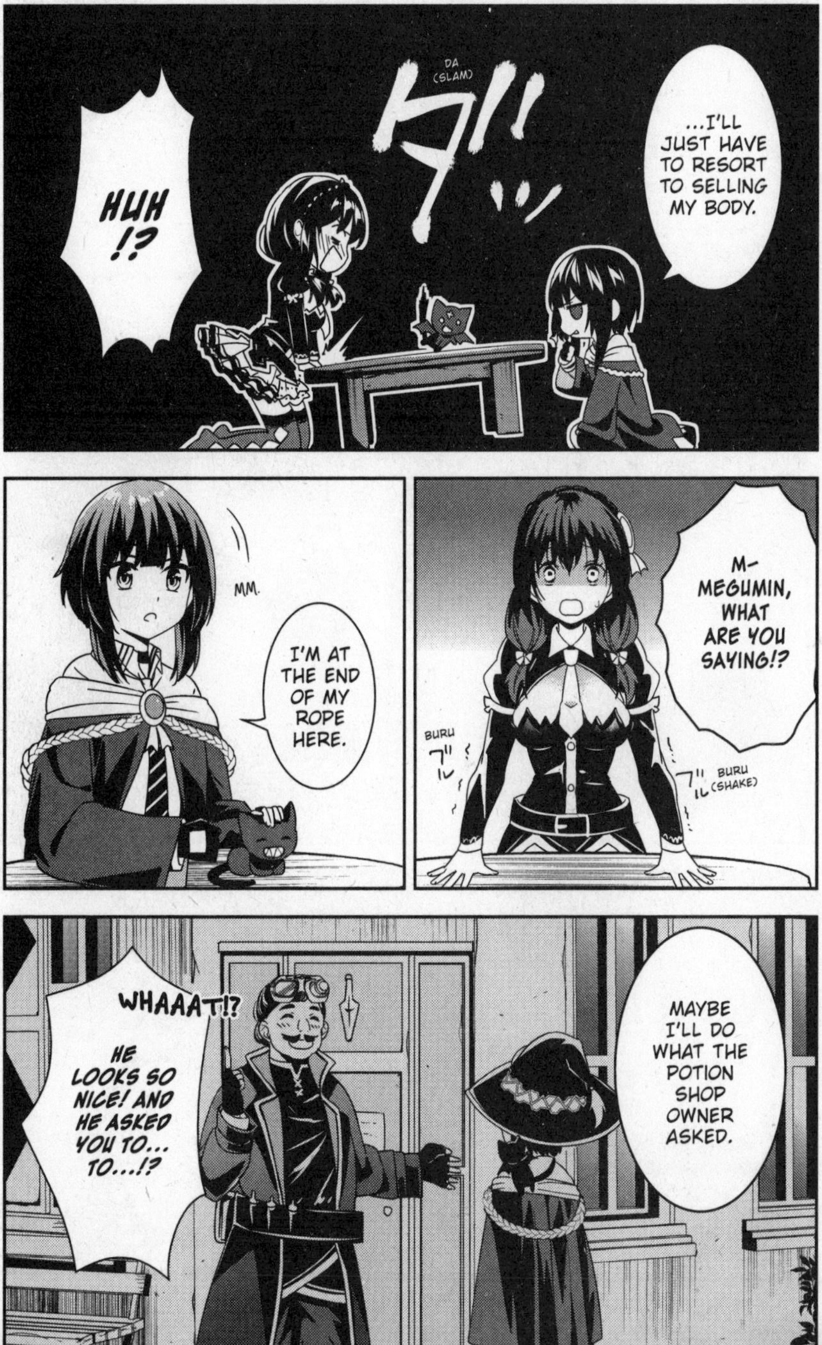
...I'LL JUST HAVE TO RESORT TO SELLING MY BODY.
DA (SLAM)
HUH!?
M-MEGUMIN, WHAT ARE YOU SAYING!?
BURU (SHAKE)
BURU
MM.
I'M AT THE END OF MY ROPE HERE.
MAYBE I'LL DO WHAT THE POTION SHOP OWNER ASKED.
WHAAAT!?
HE LOOKS SO NICE! AND HE ASKED YOU TO... TO...!?

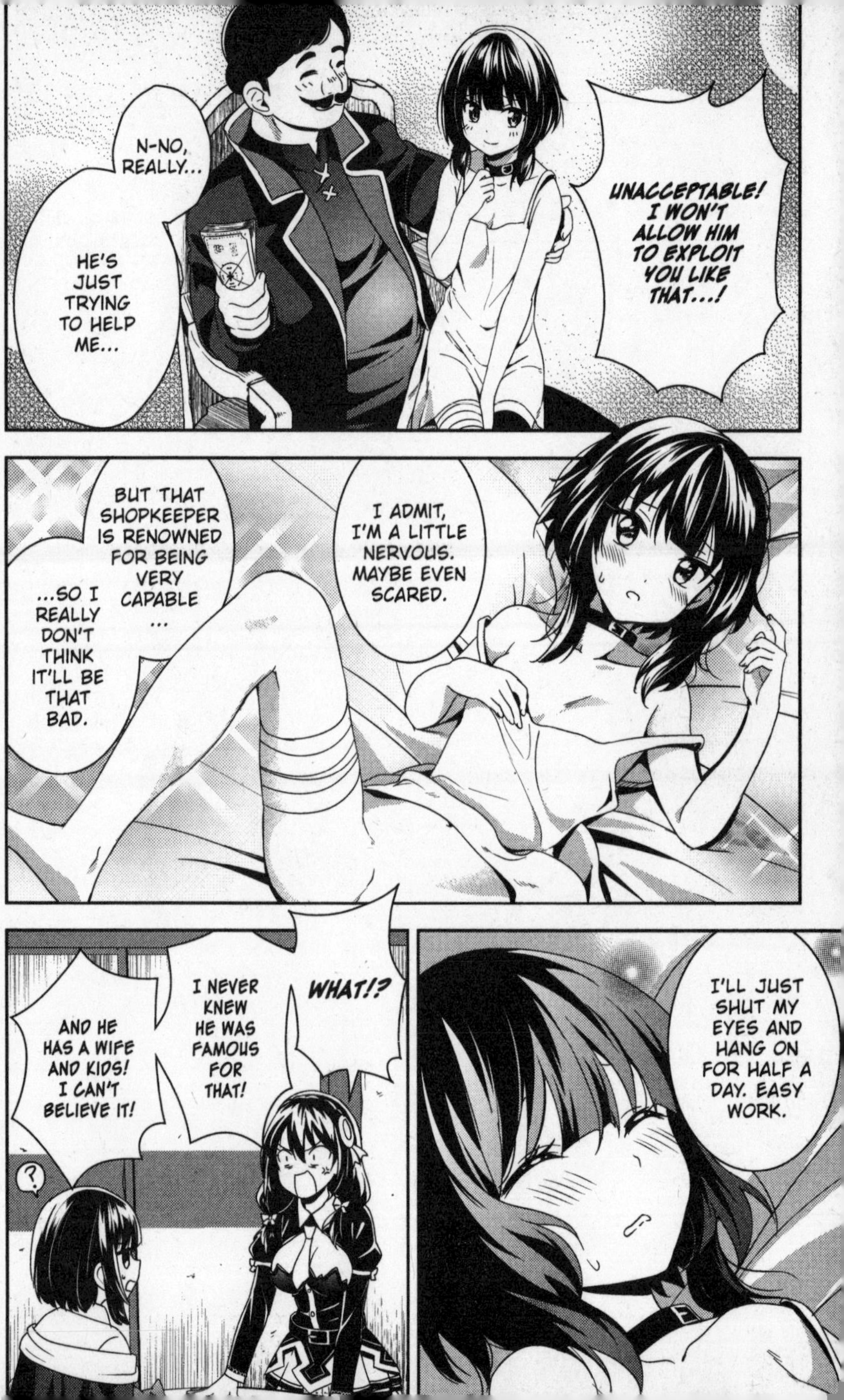
UNACCEPTABLE! I WON'T ALLOW HIM TO EXPLOIT YOU LIKE THAT...!
N-NO, REALLY...
HE'S JUST TRYING TO HELP ME...
I ADMIT, I'M A LITTLE NERVOUS. MAYBE EVEN SCARED.
BUT THAT SHOPKEEPER IS RENOWNED FOR BEING VERY CAPABLE...
...SO I REALLY DON'T THINK IT'LL BE THAT BAD.
I'LL JUST SHUT MY EYES AND HANG ON FOR HALF A DAY. EASY WORK.
WHAT!?
I NEVER KNEW HE WAS FAMOUS FOR THAT!
AND HE HAS A WIFE AND KIDS! I CAN'T BELIEVE IT!
?

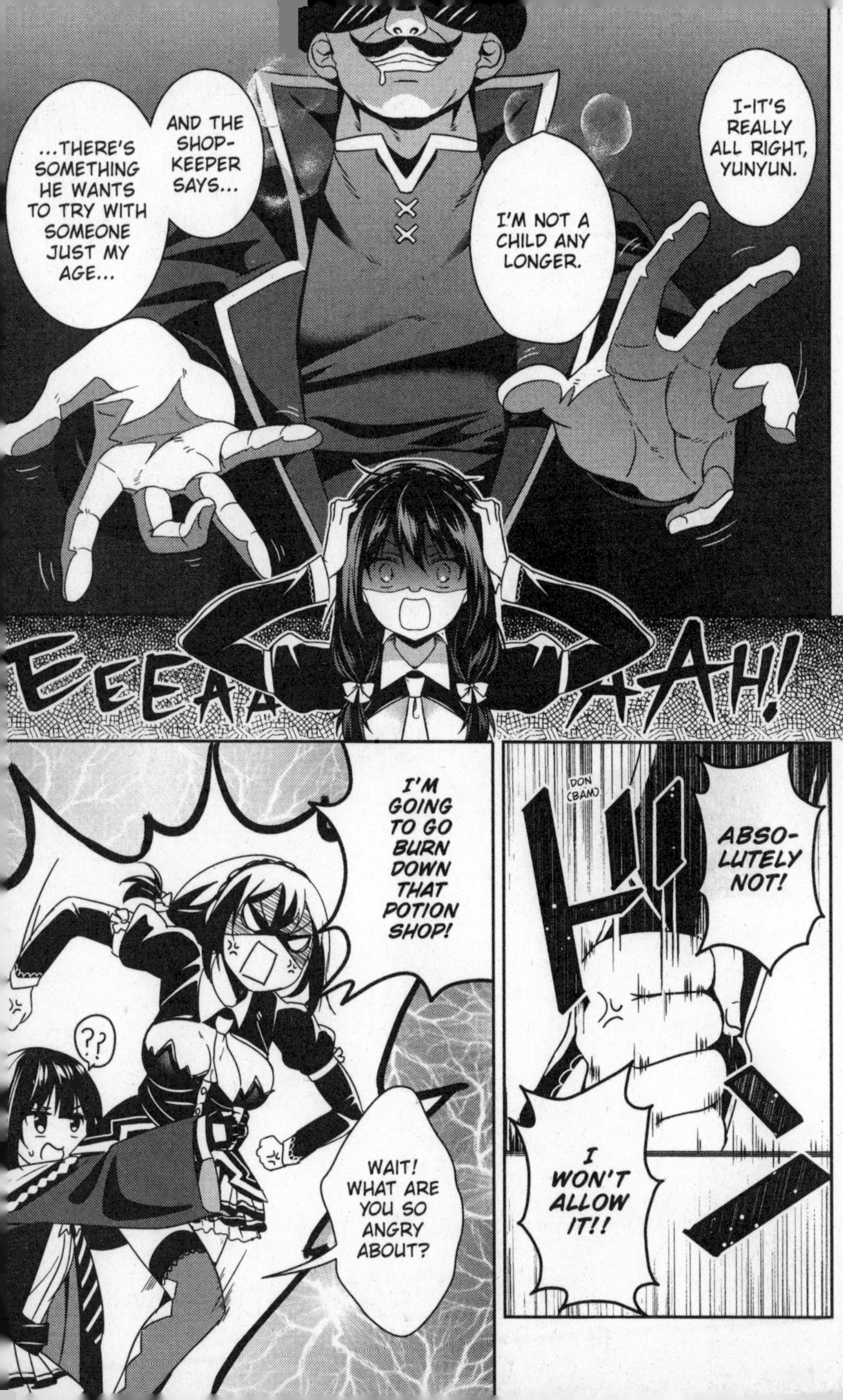
I-IT'S REALLY ALL RIGHT, YUNYUN.
I'M NOT A CHILD ANY LONGER.
AND THE SHOP-KEEPER SAYS...
...THERE'S SOMETHING HE WANTS TO TRY WITH SOMEONE JUST MY AGE...
EEEAA
AAH!
DON (BAM)
ABSO-LUTELY NOT!
I WON'T ALLOW IT!!
I'M GOING TO GO BURN DOWN THAT POTION SHOP!
??
WAIT! WHAT ARE YOU SO ANGRY ABOUT?

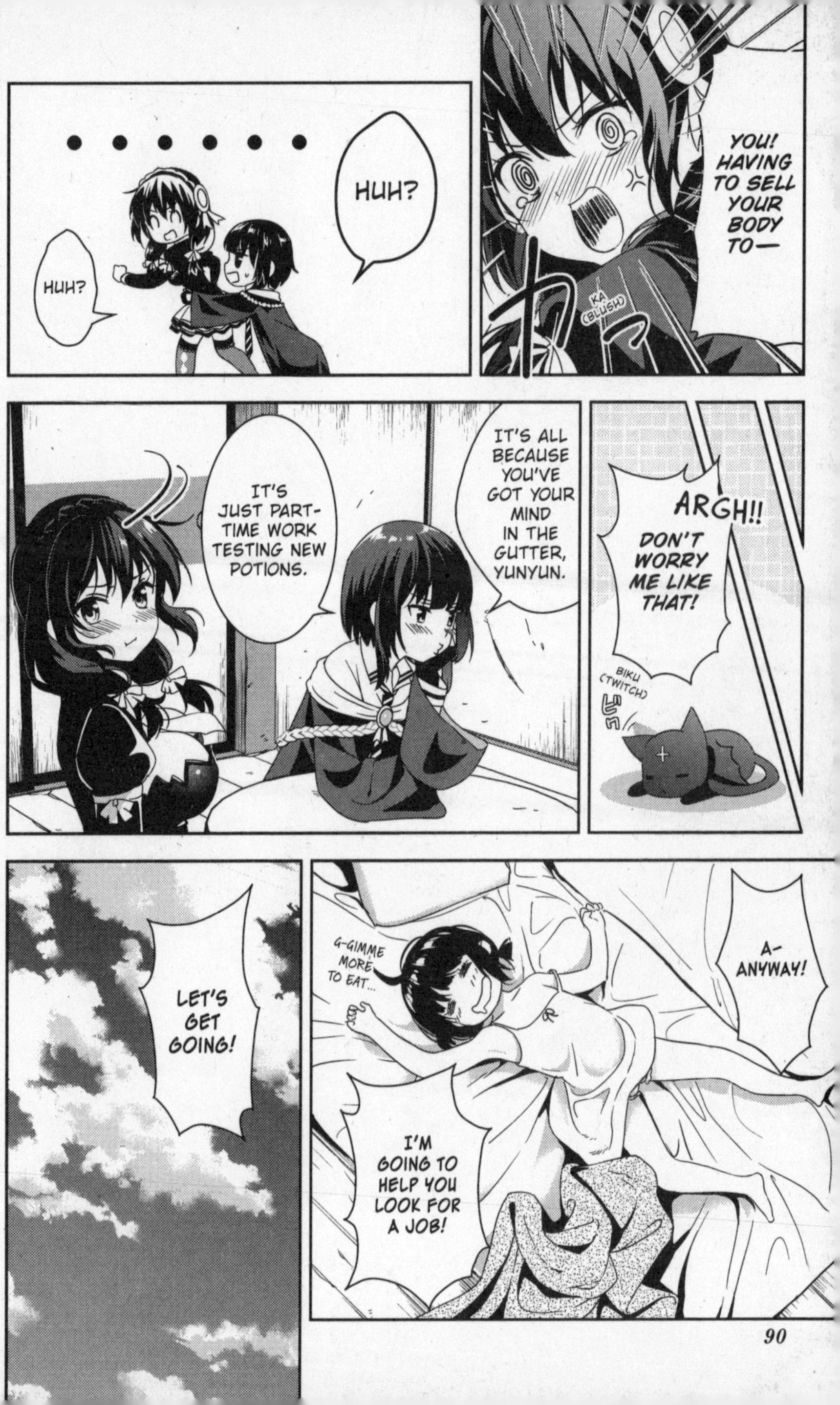
YOU! HAVING TO SELL YOUR BODY TO—
KA (BLUSH)
HUH?
• • • • • •
HUH?
ARGH!!
DON'T WORRY ME LIKE THAT!
BIKU (TWITCH)
IT'S ALL BECAUSE YOU'VE GOT YOUR MIND IN THE GUTTER, YUNYUN.
IT'S JUST PART-TIME WORK TESTING NEW POTIONS.
A-ANYWAY!
G-GIMME MORE TO EAT...
I'M GOING TO HELP YOU LOOK FOR A JOB!
LET'S GET GOING!

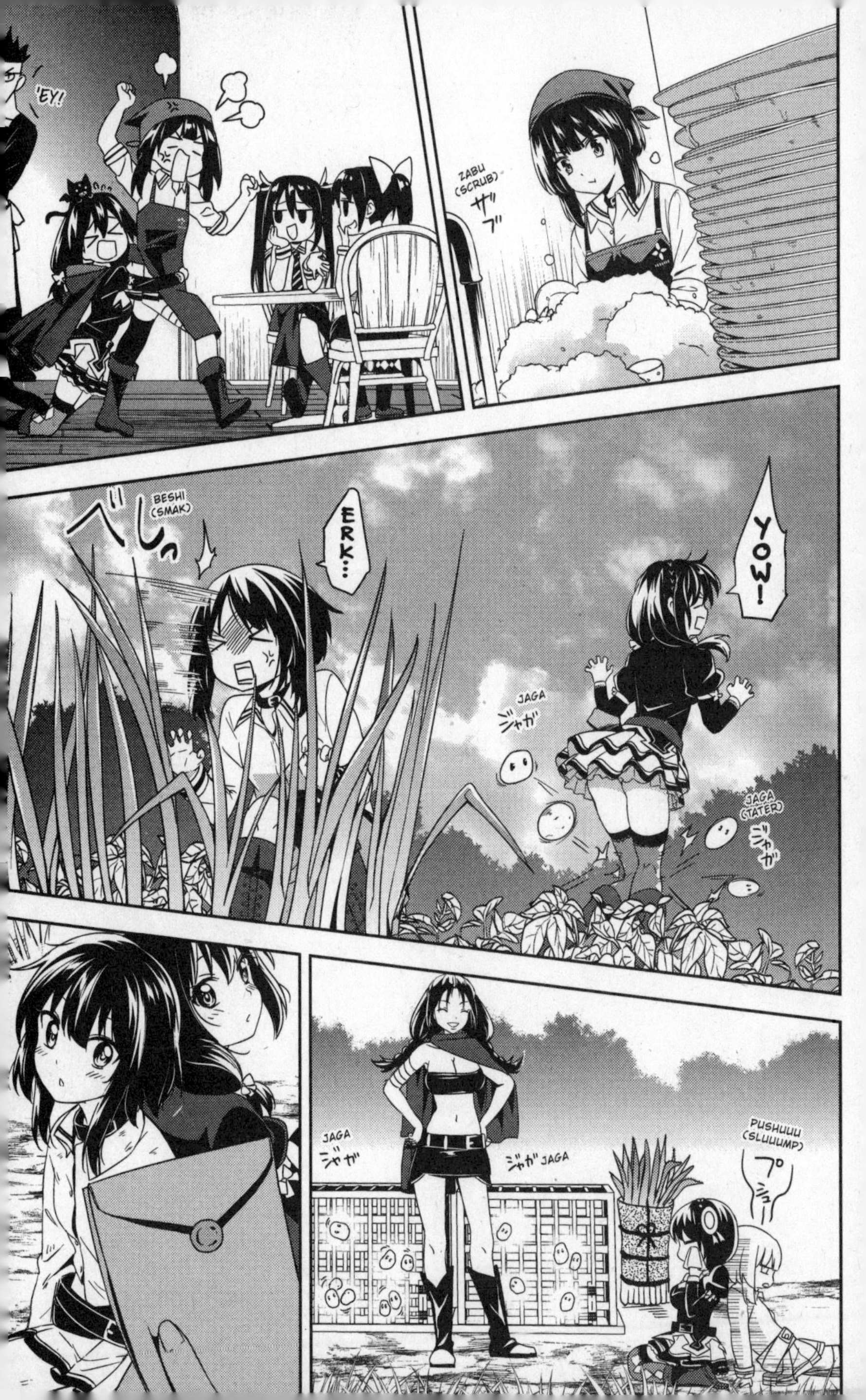
ZABU (SCRUB)
ザブ
'EY!
YOW!
JAGA
ジャガ
JAGA (TATER)
ジャガ
ERK...
BESHI (SMAK)
べしっ
PUSHUUU (SLUUUMP)
プシュー
ジャガ JAGA
JAGA
ジャガ

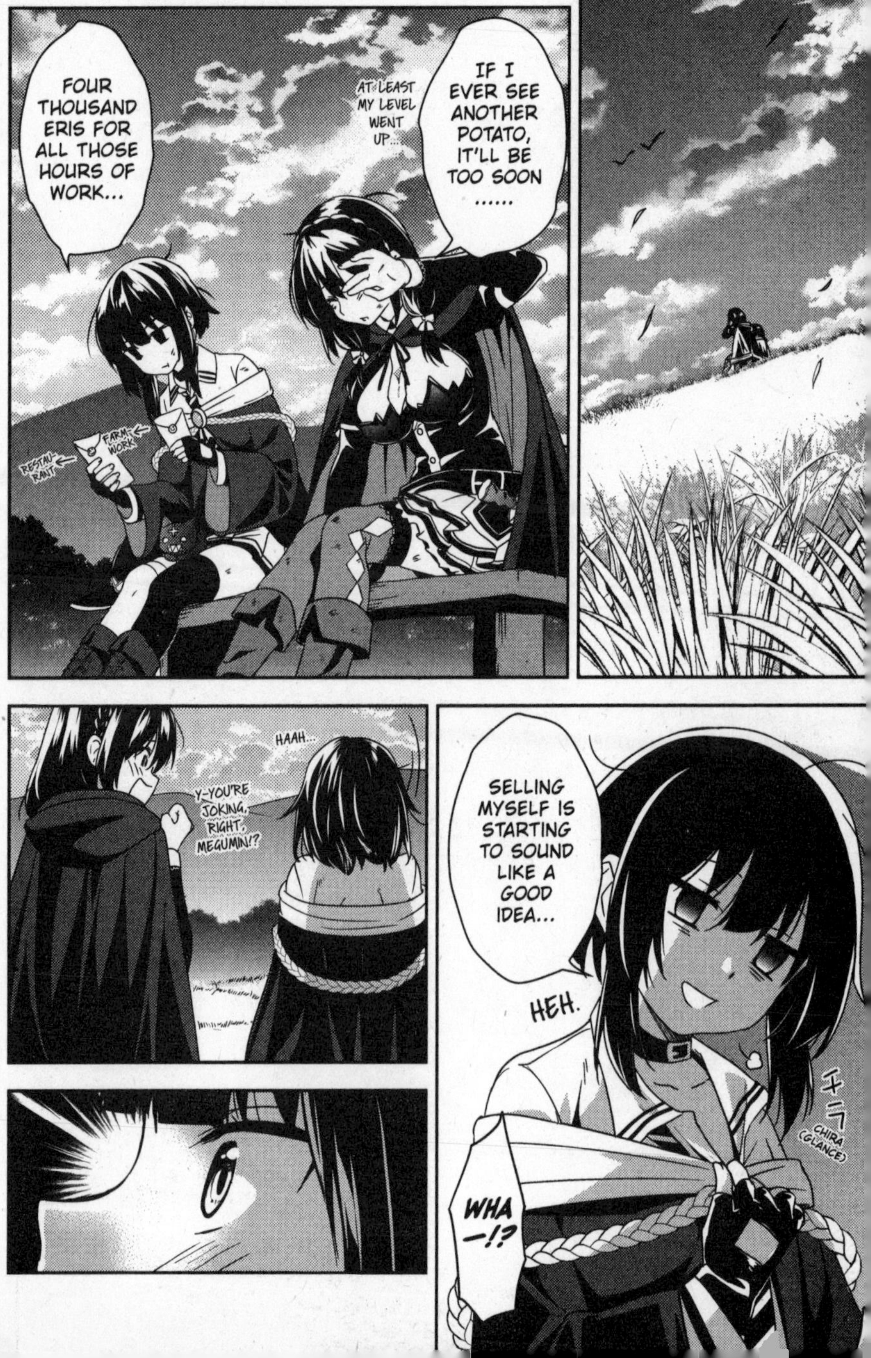
IF I EVER SEE ANOTHER POTATO, IT'LL BE TOO SOON ......
AT LEAST MY LEVEL WENT UP...
FOUR THOUSAND ERIS FOR ALL THOSE HOURS OF WORK...
FARM WORK
RESTAU-RANT
SELLING MYSELF IS STARTING TO SOUND LIKE A GOOD IDEA...
HEH.
CHIRA (GLANCE)
HAAH...
Y-YOU'RE JOKING, RIGHT, MEGUMIN!?
WHA—!?

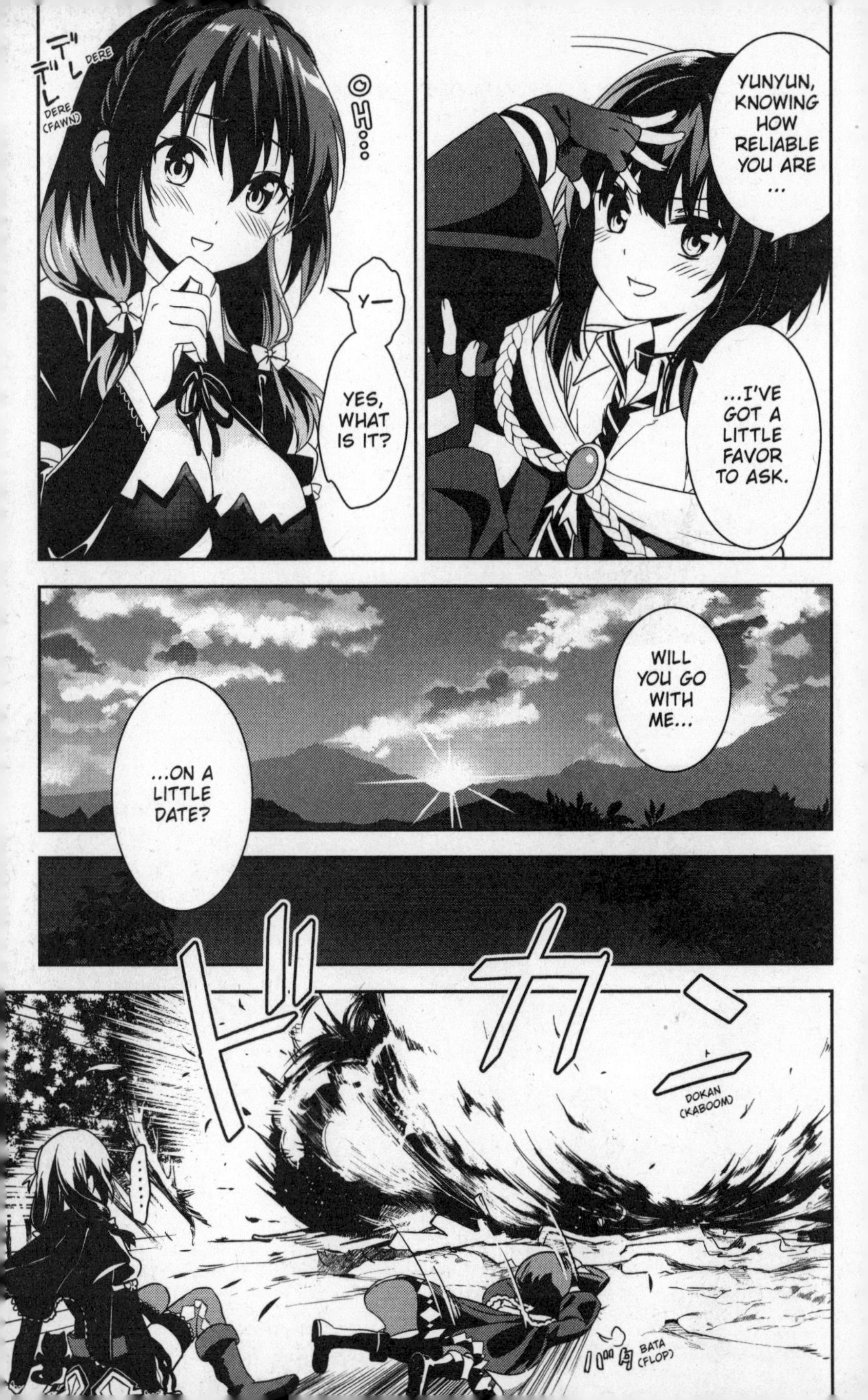
YUNYUN, KNOWING HOW RELIABLE YOU ARE ...
...I'VE GOT A LITTLE FAVOR TO ASK.
OH...
デレデレ
DERE DERE (FAWN)
Y—
YES, WHAT IS IT?
WILL YOU GO WITH ME...
...ON A LITTLE DATE?
ドカーン
DOKAN (KABOOM)
...
バタ
BATA (FLOP)

AHHHHHHHH!
STUPID, STUPID, STUPID ME!
ZUZAZAZA (SHMMMM)
ズザザザ
I WAS AN IDIOT TO THINK IT WOULD BE OKAY TO USE EXPLOSION AS LONG AS WE WERE OUTSIDE THE VILLAGE!
HOW WAS I SUPPOSED TO KNOW A FIRE DRAKE WAS TAKING A NAP RIGHT THERE?
OH, FOR—!
NO MORE EXPLO-SIONS FOR A WHILE!
WHA—!?

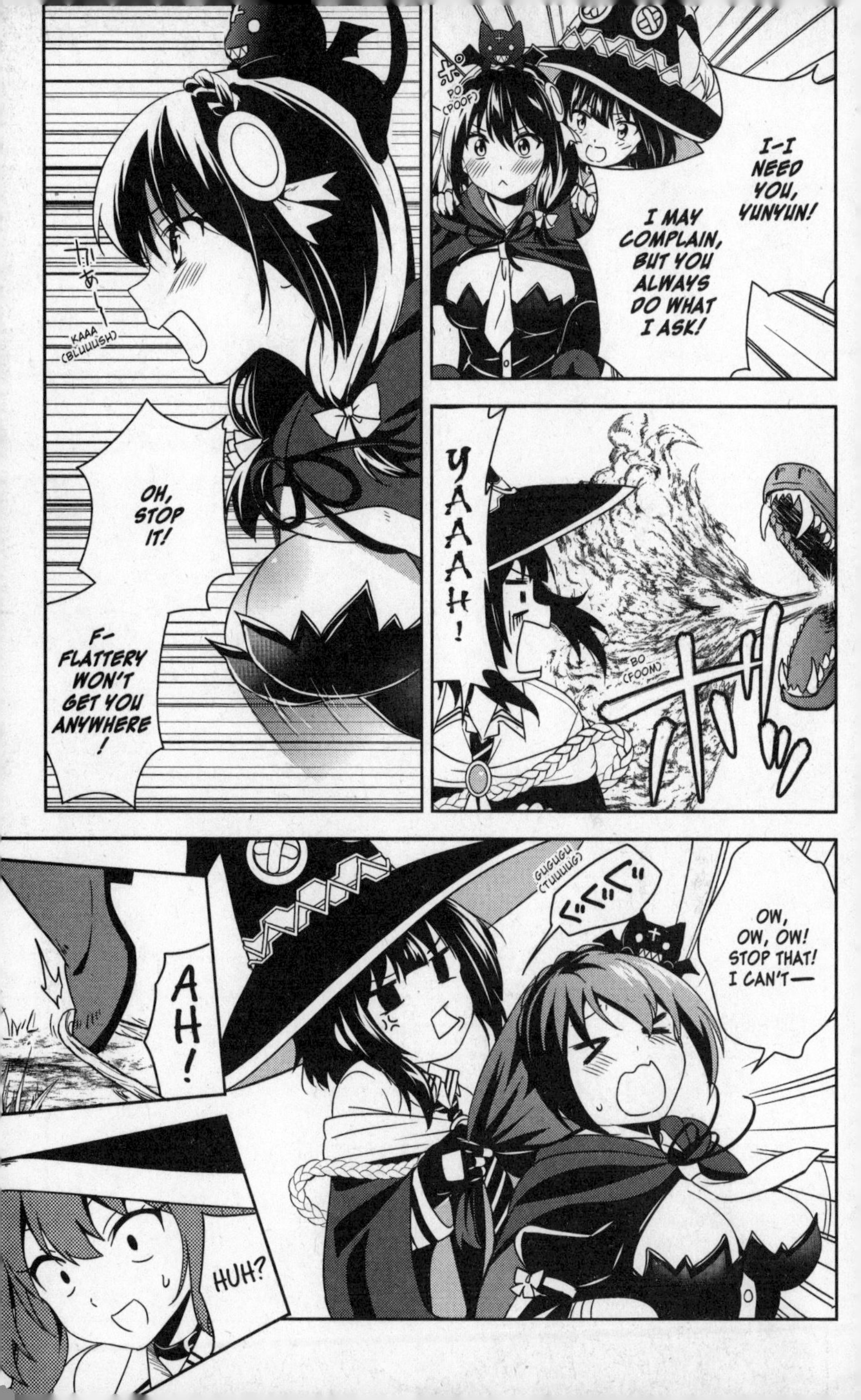
PO (POOF)
I-I NEED YOU, YUNYUN!
I MAY COMPLAIN, BUT YOU ALWAYS DO WHAT I ASK!
YAAAAH!
BO (FOOM)
KAAA (BLUUUSH)
OH, STOP IT!
F-FLATTERY WON'T GET YOU ANYWHERE!
GUGUGU (TUUUUG)
OW, OW, OW! STOP THAT! I CAN'T—
AH!
HUH?

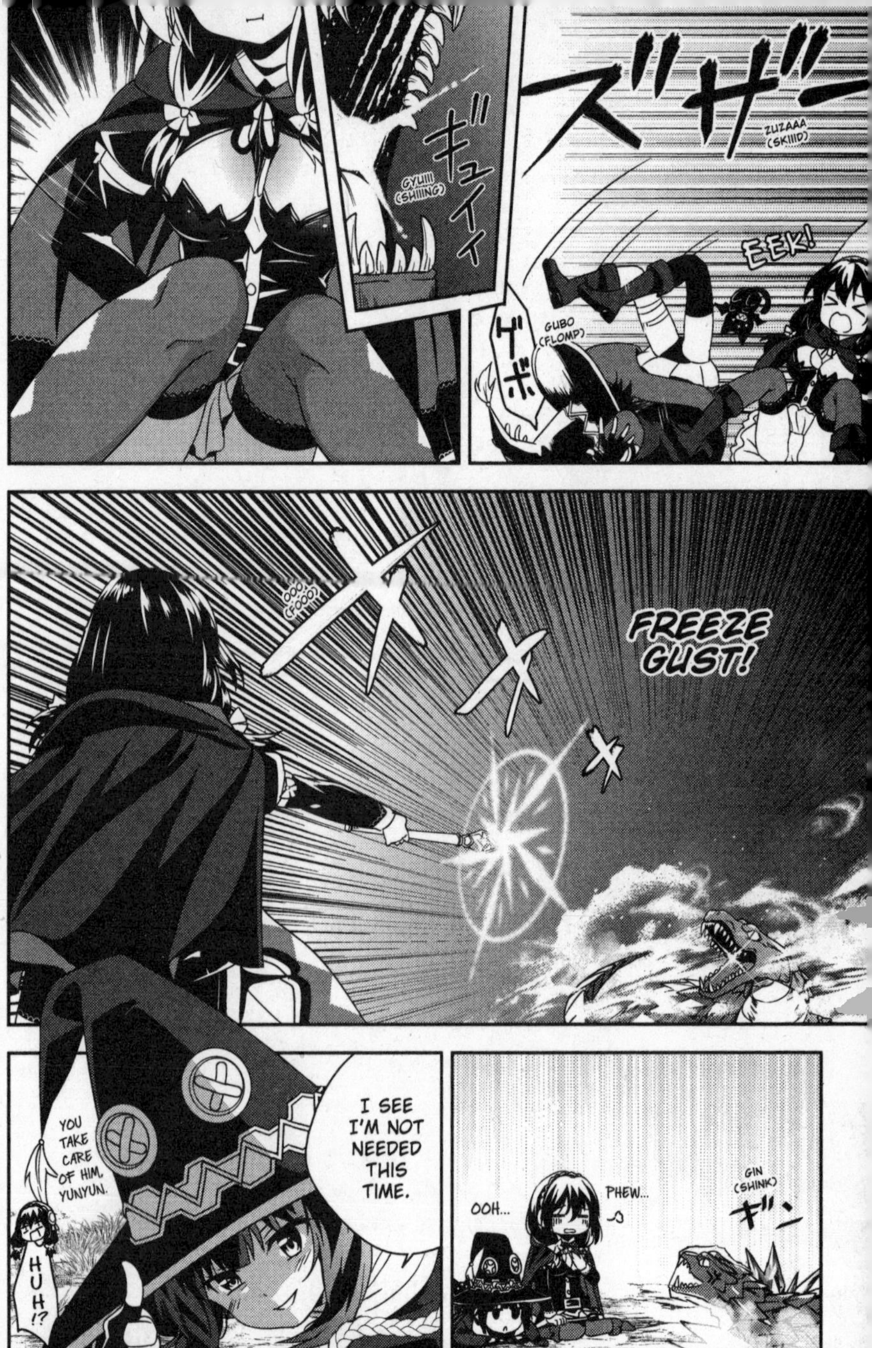
ズザザー
ZUZAAA (SKIIID)
EEK!
ゴボ
GUBO (FLOMP)
ギュイイ
GYUIII (SHIIING)
OOO (FOOO)
FREEZE GUST!
ギン
GIN (SHINK)
PHEW...
OOH...
I SEE I'M NOT NEEDED THIS TIME.
YOU TAKE CARE OF HIM, YUNYUN.
HUH!?

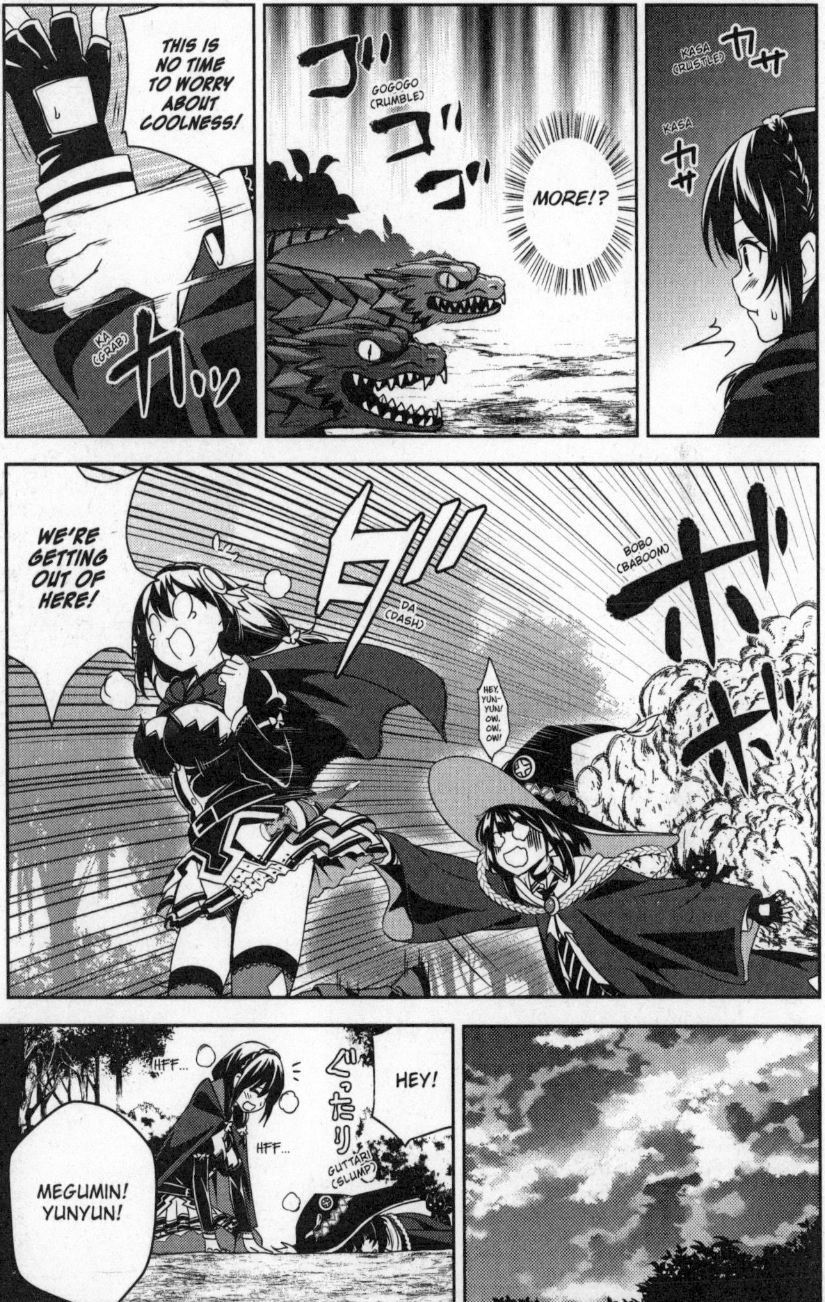
KASA (RUSTLE)
カサ
KASA
カサ
GOGOGO (RUMBLE)
ゴゴゴ
MORE!?
THIS IS NO TIME TO WORRY ABOUT COOLNESS!
KA (GRAB)
ガッ
BOBO (BABOOM)
ボボ
DA (DASH)
ダッ
HEY, YUN-YUN! OW, OW, OW!
WE'RE GETTING OUT OF HERE!
HEY!
ぐったり
GUTTARI (SLUMP)
HFF...
HFF...
MEGUMIN! YUNYUN!

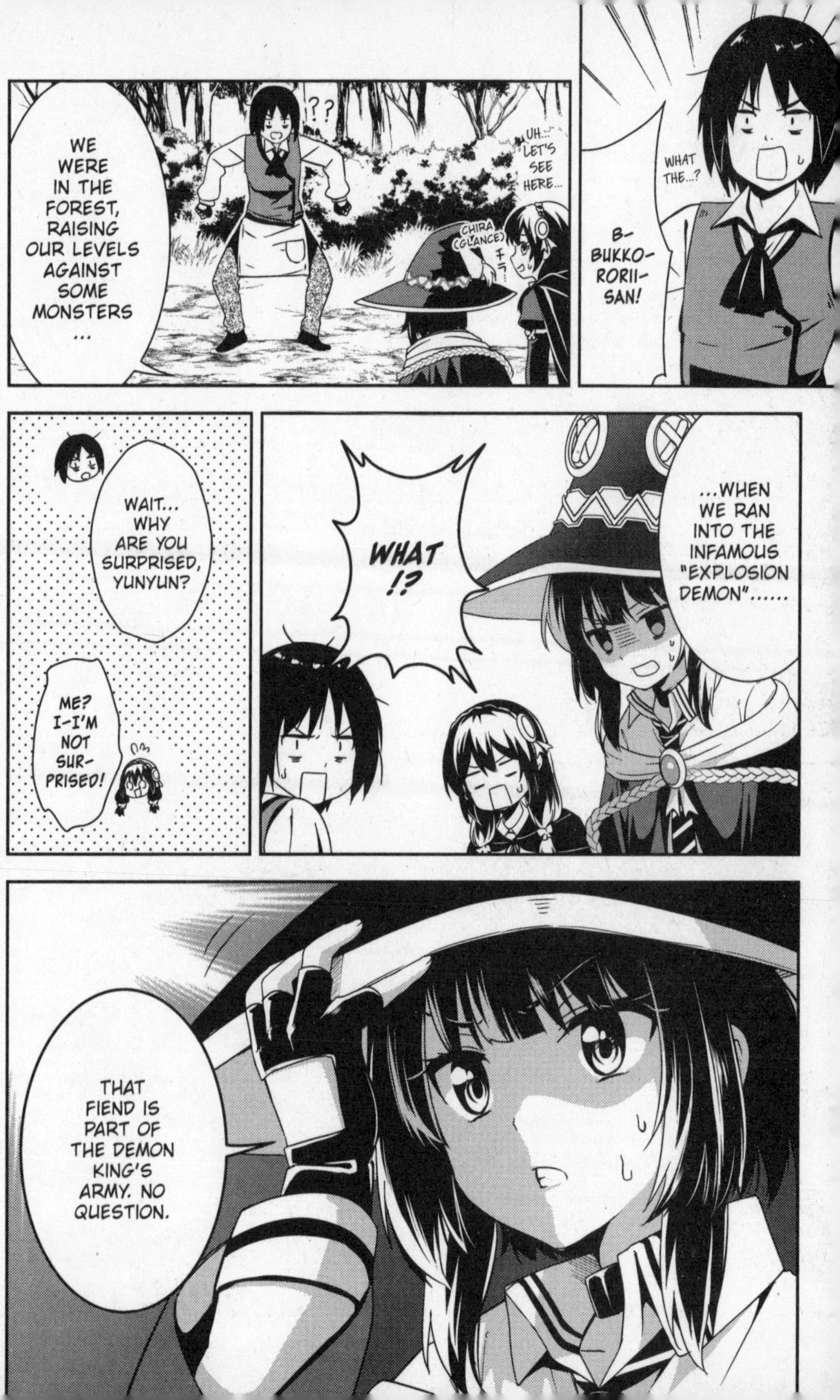
WHAT THE...?
B-BUKKO-RORII-SAN!
UH... LET'S SEE HERE...
??
CHIRA (GLANCE) チラ...
WE WERE IN THE FOREST, RAISING OUR LEVELS AGAINST SOME MONSTERS...
...WHEN WE RAN INTO THE INFAMOUS "EXPLOSION DEMON"......
WHAT!?
WAIT... WHY ARE YOU SURPRISED, YUNYUN?
ME? I-I'M NOT SURPRISED!
THAT FIEND IS PART OF THE DEMON KING'S ARMY. NO QUESTION.

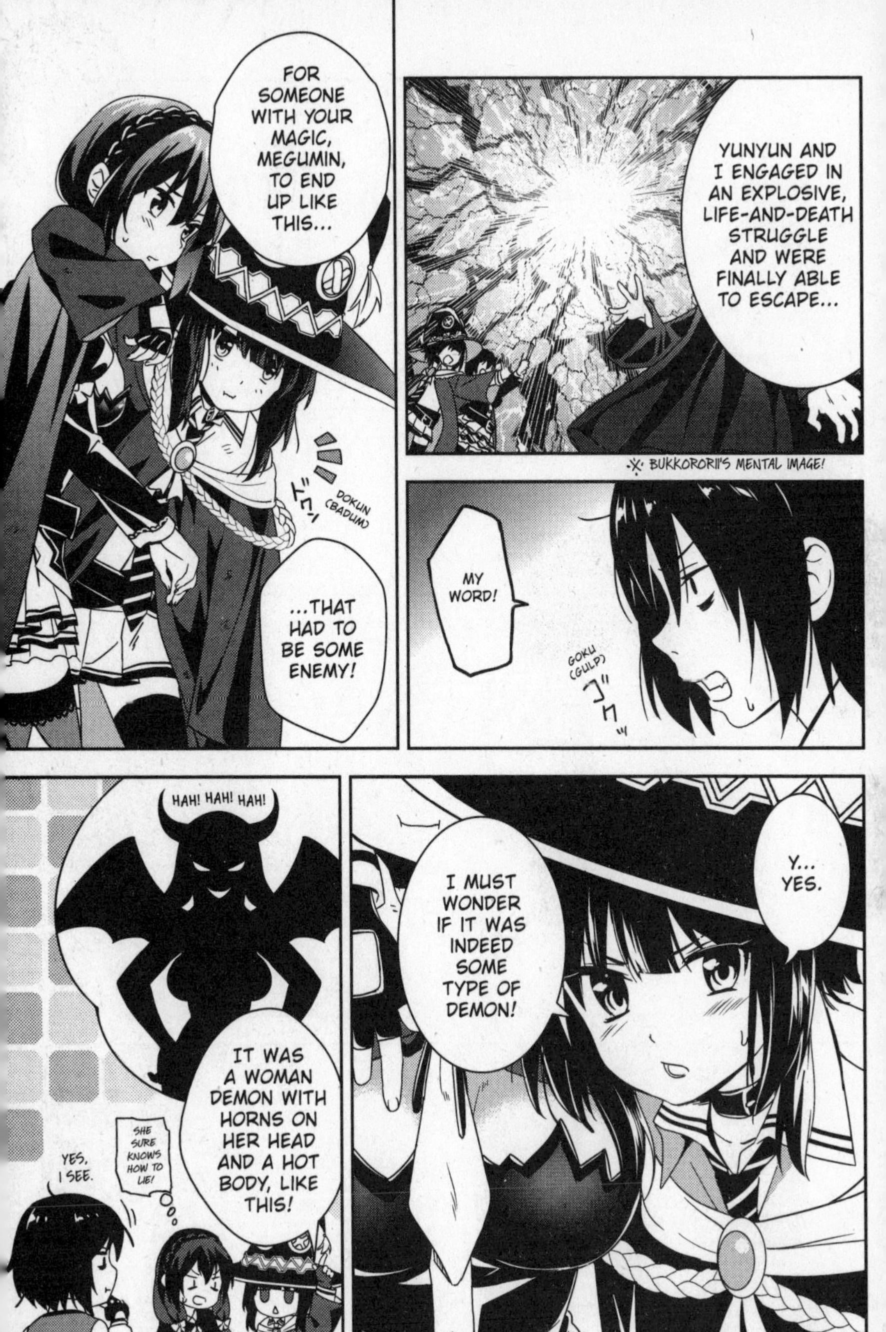
YUNYUN AND I ENGAGED IN AN EXPLOSIVE, LIFE-AND-DEATH STRUGGLE AND WERE FINALLY ABLE TO ESCAPE...
※ BUKKORORII'S MENTAL IMAGE!
MY WORD!
GOKU (GULP)
FOR SOMEONE WITH YOUR MAGIC, MEGUMIN, TO END UP LIKE THIS...
DOKUN (BADUM)
...THAT HAD TO BE SOME ENEMY!
Y... YES.
I MUST WONDER IF IT WAS INDEED SOME TYPE OF DEMON!
HAH! HAH! HAH!
IT WAS A WOMAN DEMON WITH HORNS ON HER HEAD AND A HOT BODY, LIKE THIS!
SHE SURE KNOWS HOW TO LIE!
YES, I SEE.

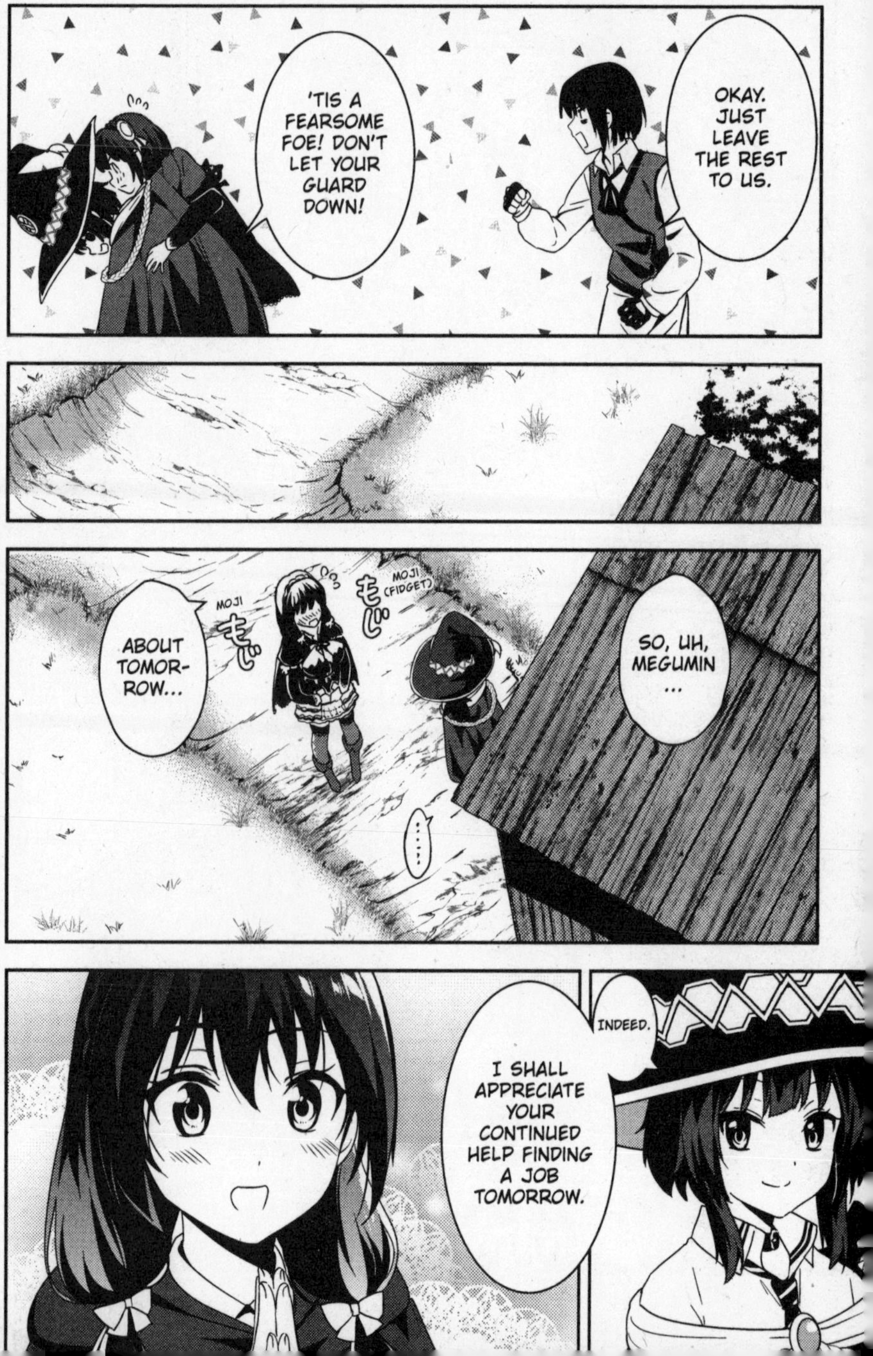
OKAY. JUST LEAVE THE REST TO US.
'TIS A FEARSOME FOE! DON'T LET YOUR GUARD DOWN!
SO, UH, MEGUMIN...
MOJI (FIDGET)
MOJI
ABOUT TOMOR-ROW...
......
INDEED.
I SHALL APPRECIATE YOUR CONTINUED HELP FINDING A JOB TOMORROW.

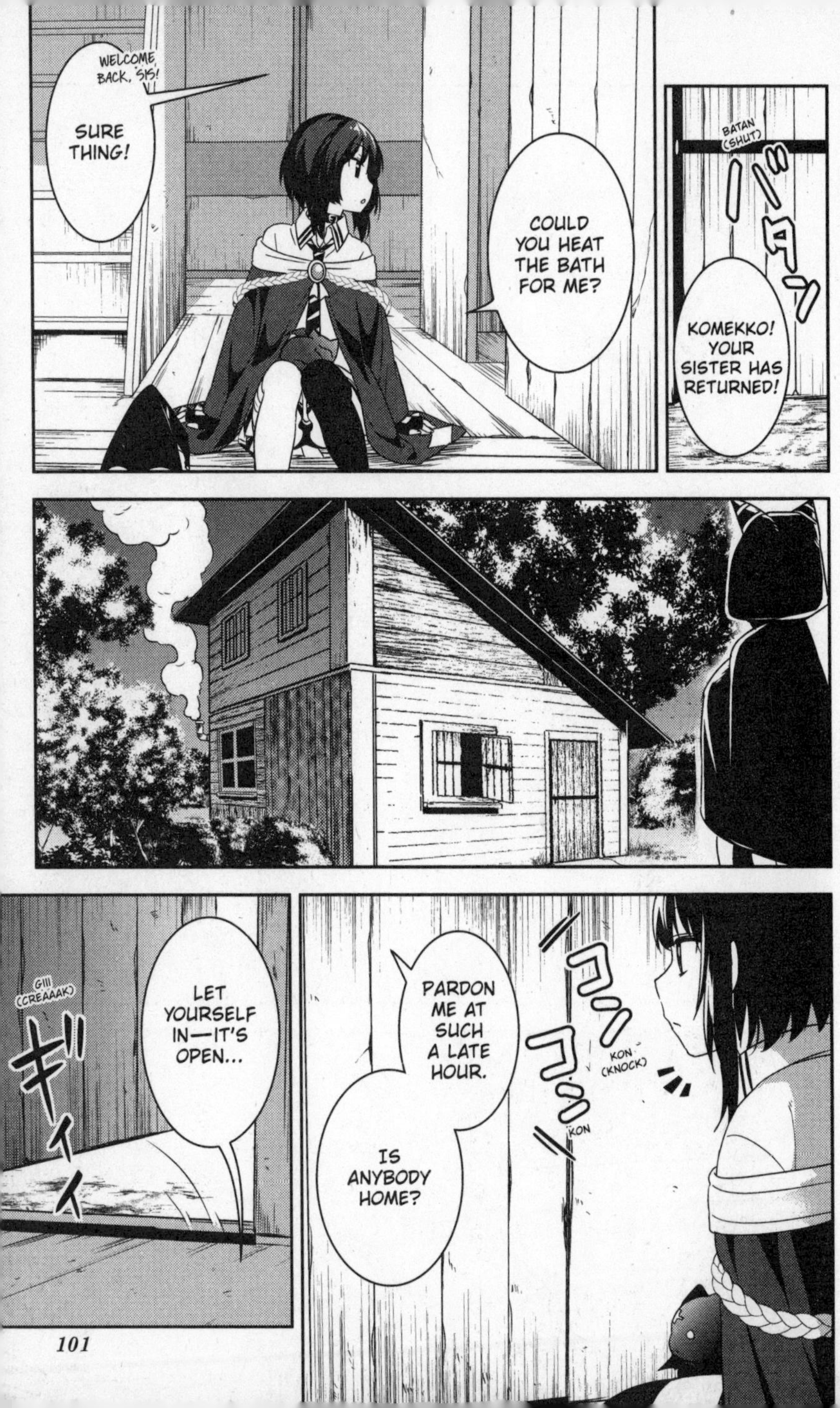

BATAN (SHUT)
KOMEKKO! YOUR SISTER HAS RETURNED!
WELCOME BACK, SIS!
COULD YOU HEAT THE BATH FOR ME?
SURE THING!
KON (KNOCK)
KON
PARDON ME AT SUCH A LATE HOUR.
IS ANYBODY HOME?
GIII (CREAAAK)
LET YOURSELF IN—IT'S OPEN...

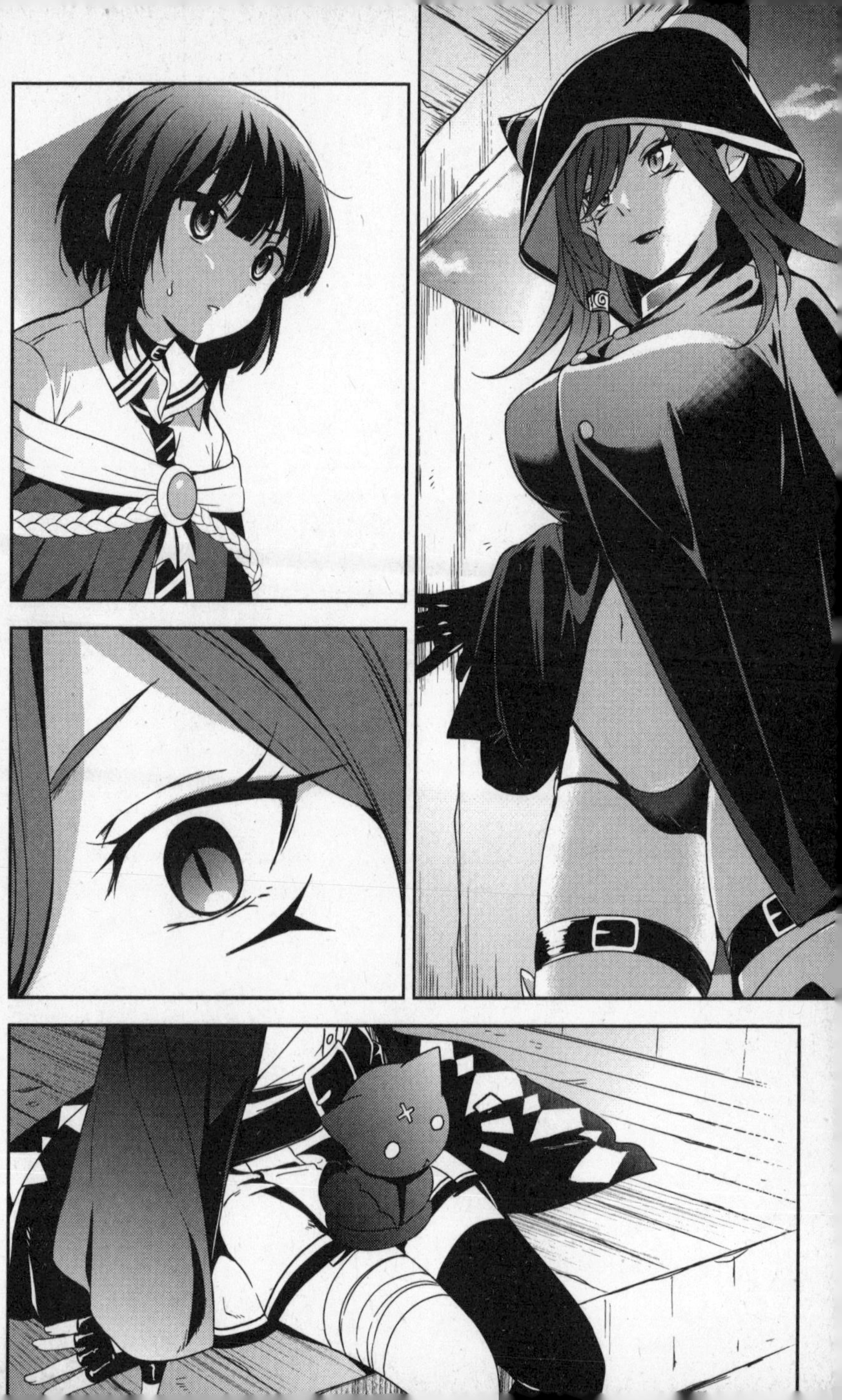

KONOSUBA: AN EXPLOSION ON THIS WONDERFUL WORLD!

KONOSUBA: AN EXPLOSION ON THIS WONDERFUL WORLD!

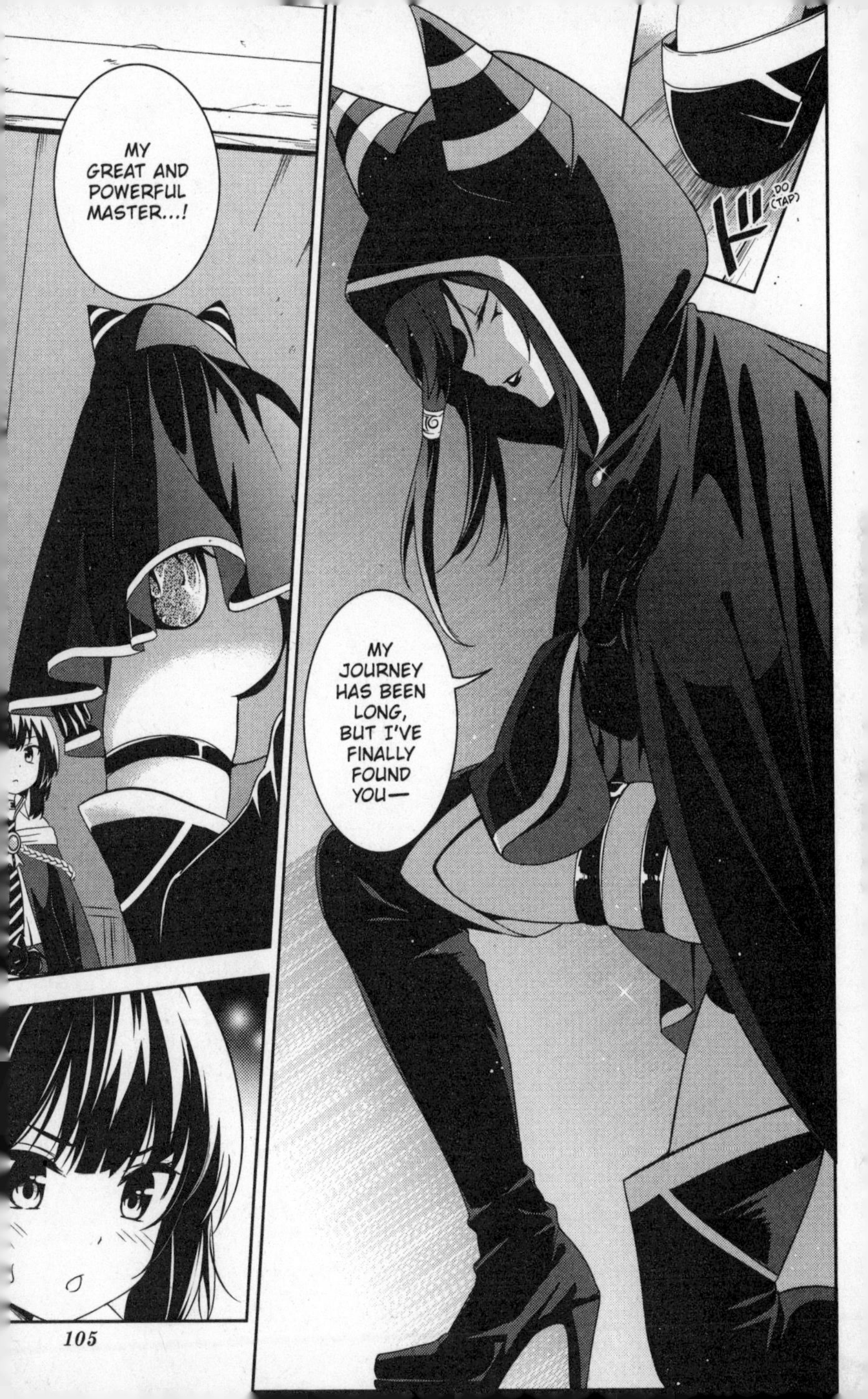
ド
DO (TAP)
MY JOURNEY HAS BEEN LONG, BUT I'VE FINALLY FOUND YOU—
MY GREAT AND POWERFUL MASTER...!

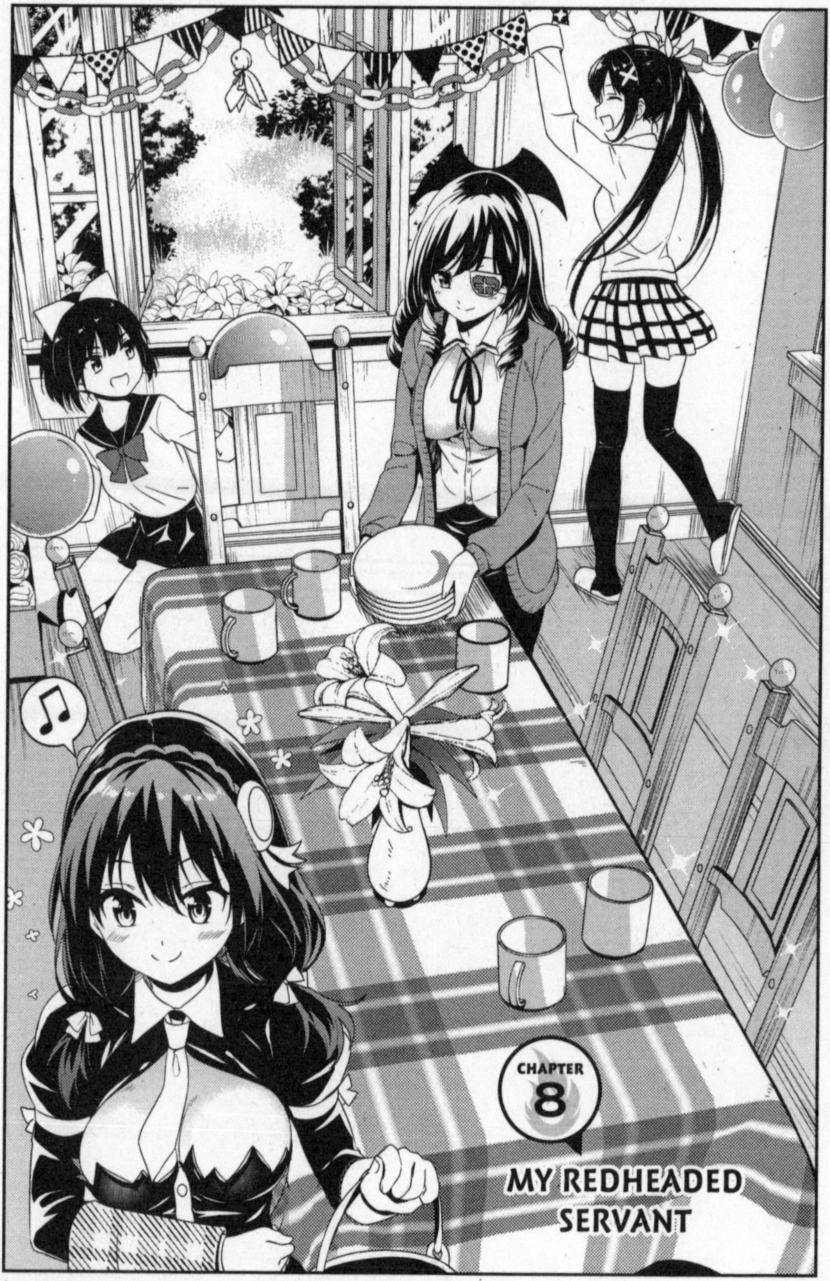
♫
CHAPTER
8
MY REDHEADED SERVANT

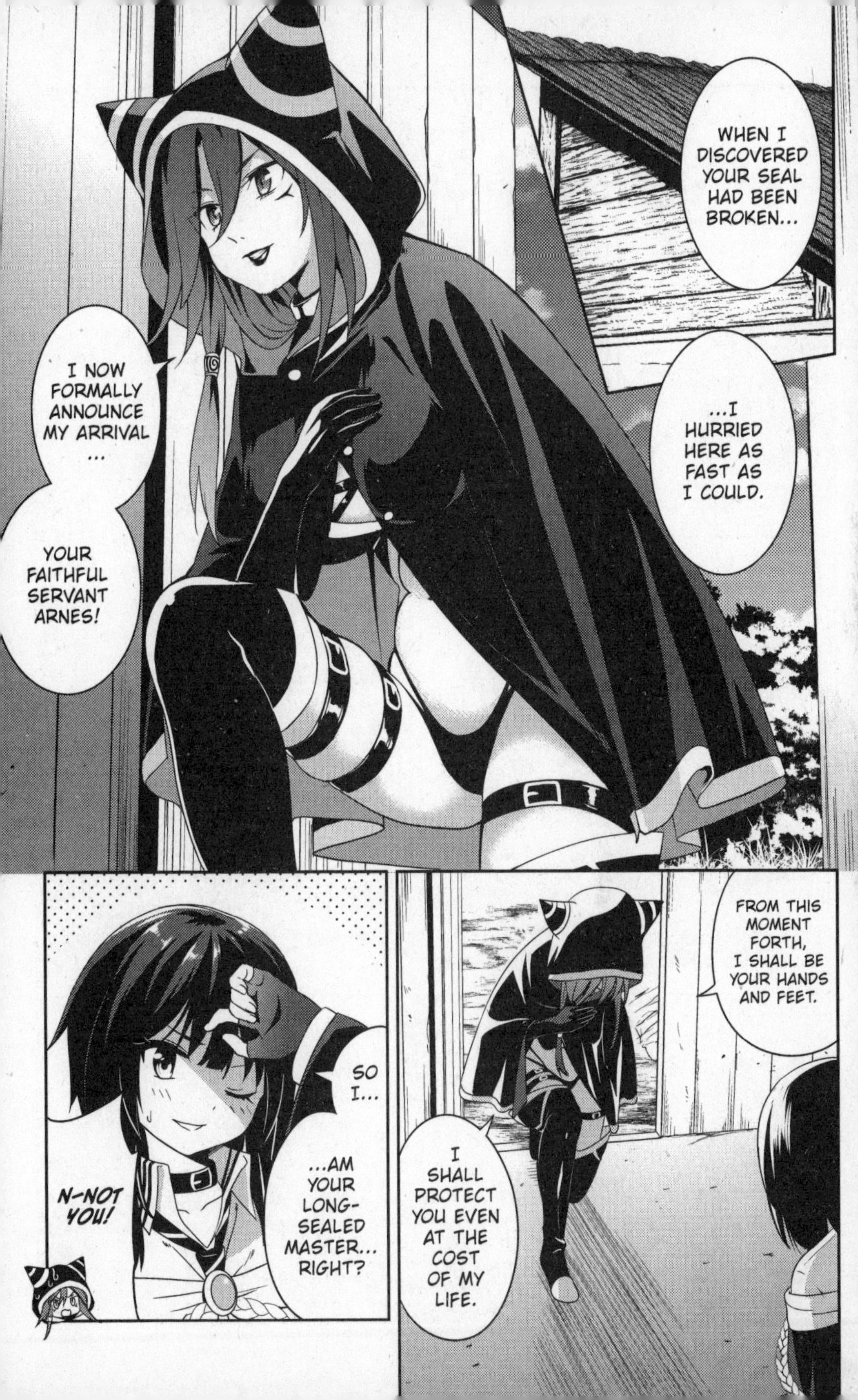
WHEN I DISCOVERED YOUR SEAL HAD BEEN BROKEN...
...I HURRIED HERE AS FAST AS I COULD.
I NOW FORMALLY ANNOUNCE MY ARRIVAL ...
YOUR FAITHFUL SERVANT ARNES!
FROM THIS MOMENT FORTH, I SHALL BE YOUR HANDS AND FEET.
I SHALL PROTECT YOU EVEN AT THE COST OF MY LIFE.
SO I...
...AM YOUR LONG-SEALED MASTER... RIGHT?
N-NOT YOU!

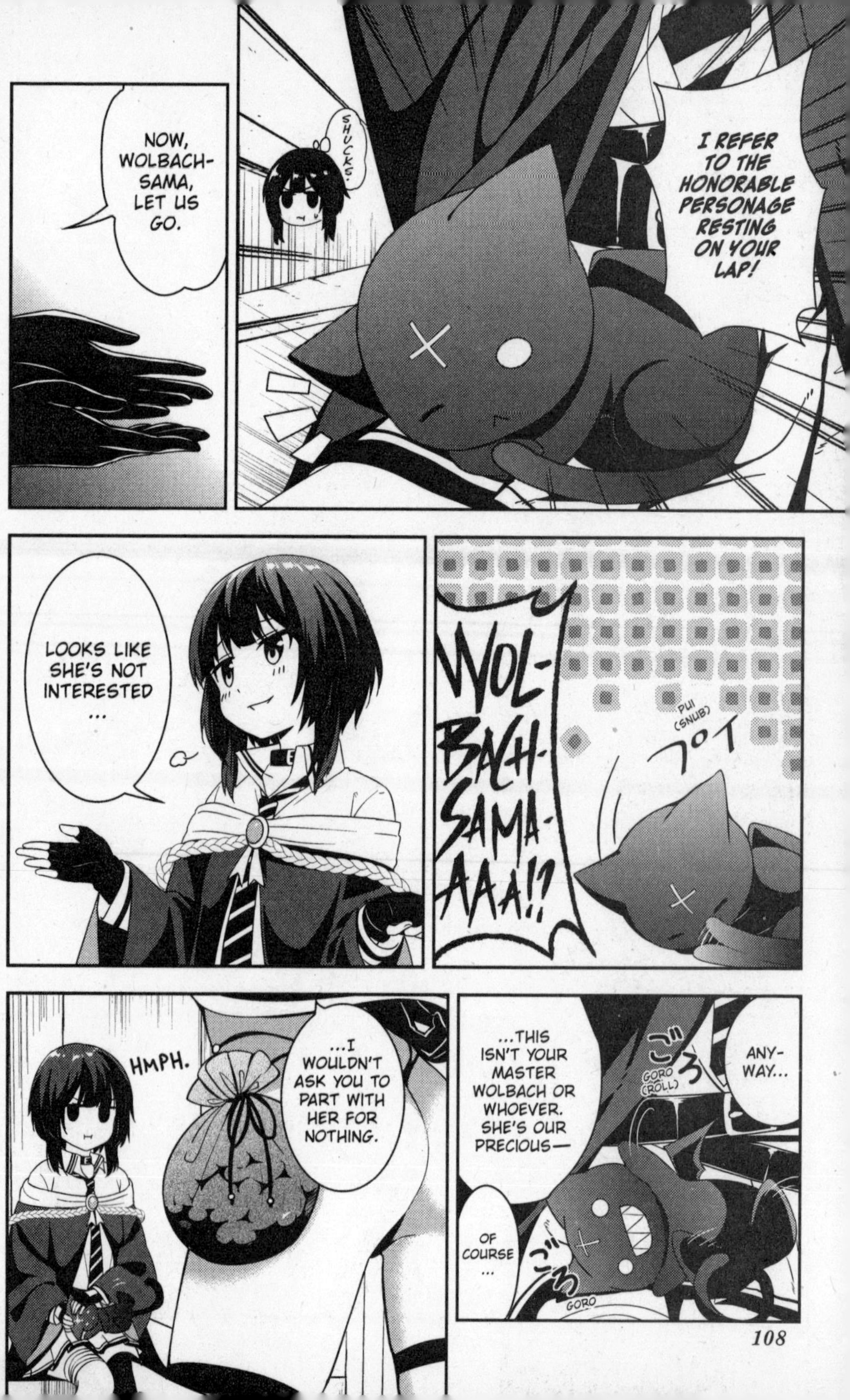
I REFER TO THE HONORABLE PERSONAGE RESTING ON YOUR LAP!
SHUCKS.
NOW, WOLBACH-SAMA, LET US GO.
WOL-BACH-SAMA-AAA!?
PUI (SNUB)
フイ
LOOKS LIKE SHE'S NOT INTERESTED ...
ANY-WAY...
ごろ
GORO (ROLL)
...THIS ISN'T YOUR MASTER WOLBACH OR WHOEVER. SHE'S OUR PRECIOUS—
OF COURSE ...
ごろ
GORO
...I WOULDN'T ASK YOU TO PART WITH HER FOR NOTHING.
HMPH.

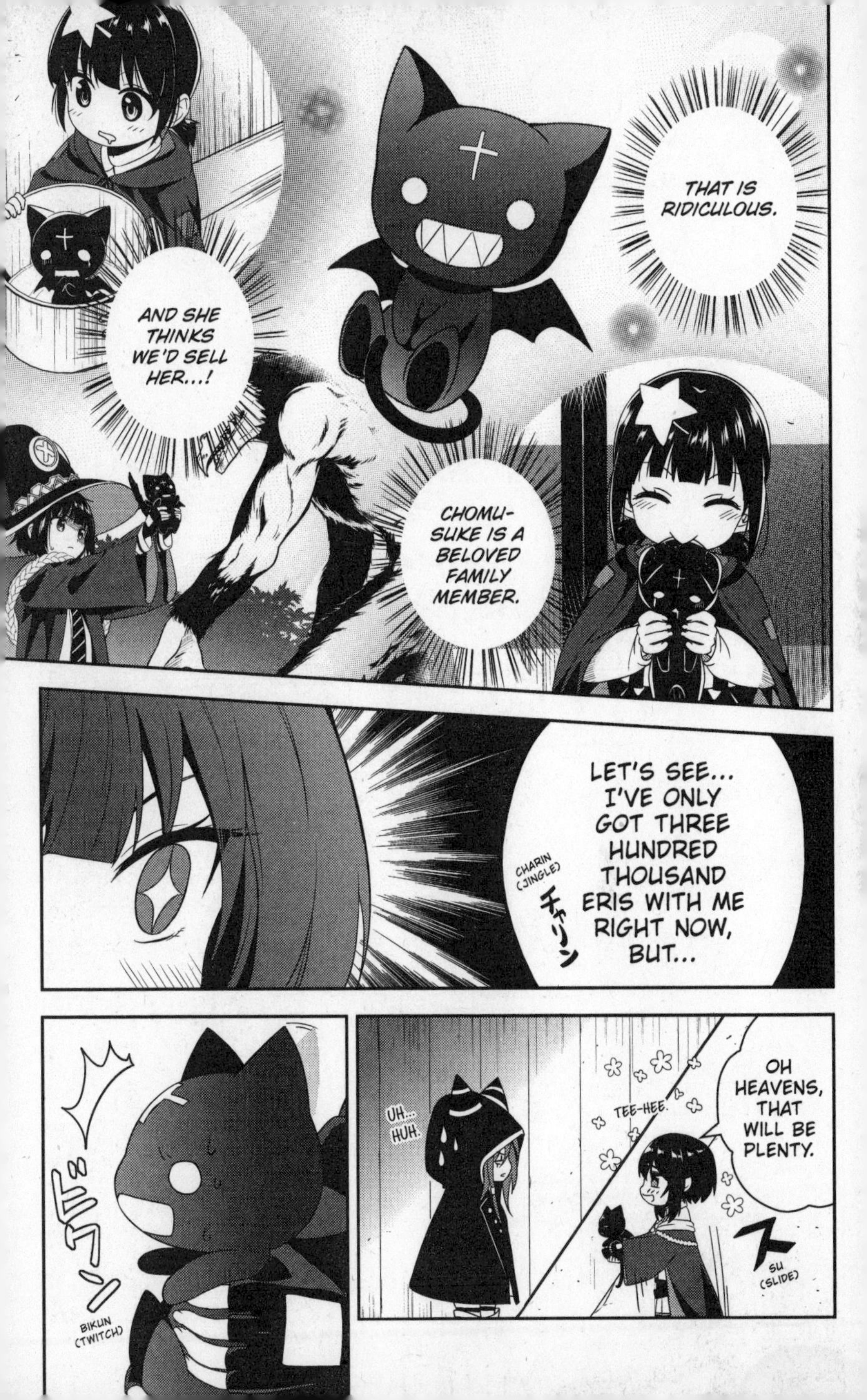
THAT IS RIDICULOUS.
AND SHE THINKS WE'D SELL HER...!
CHOMUSUKE IS A BELOVED FAMILY MEMBER.
LET'S SEE... I'VE ONLY GOT THREE HUNDRED THOUSAND ERIS WITH ME RIGHT NOW, BUT...
CHARIN (JINGLE)
チャリン
OH HEAVENS, THAT WILL BE PLENTY.
TEE-HEE.
UH... HUH.
SU (SLIDE)
BIKUN (TWITCH)

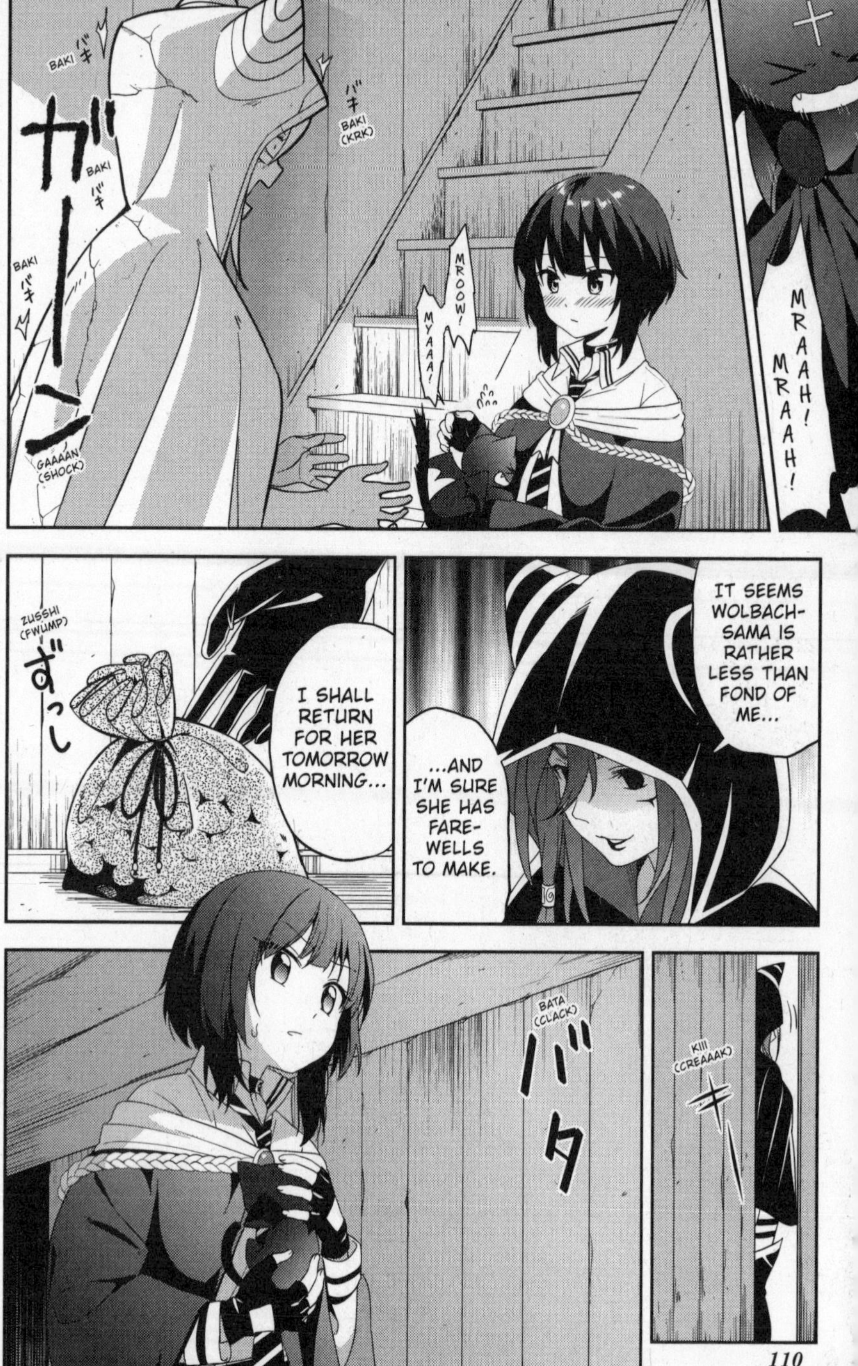
MRAAH! MRAAH!
MROOW!
MYAAA!
バキ BAKI (KRK)
BAKI バキ
BAKI バキ
BAKI バキ
ガーン GAAAAN (SHOCK)
IT SEEMS WOLBACH-SAMA IS RATHER LESS THAN FOND OF ME...
...AND I'M SURE SHE HAS FARE-WELLS TO MAKE.
I SHALL RETURN FOR HER TOMORROW MORNING...
ずっし ZUSSHI (FWUMP)
キィ KIII (CREAAAK)
バタ BATA (CLACK)

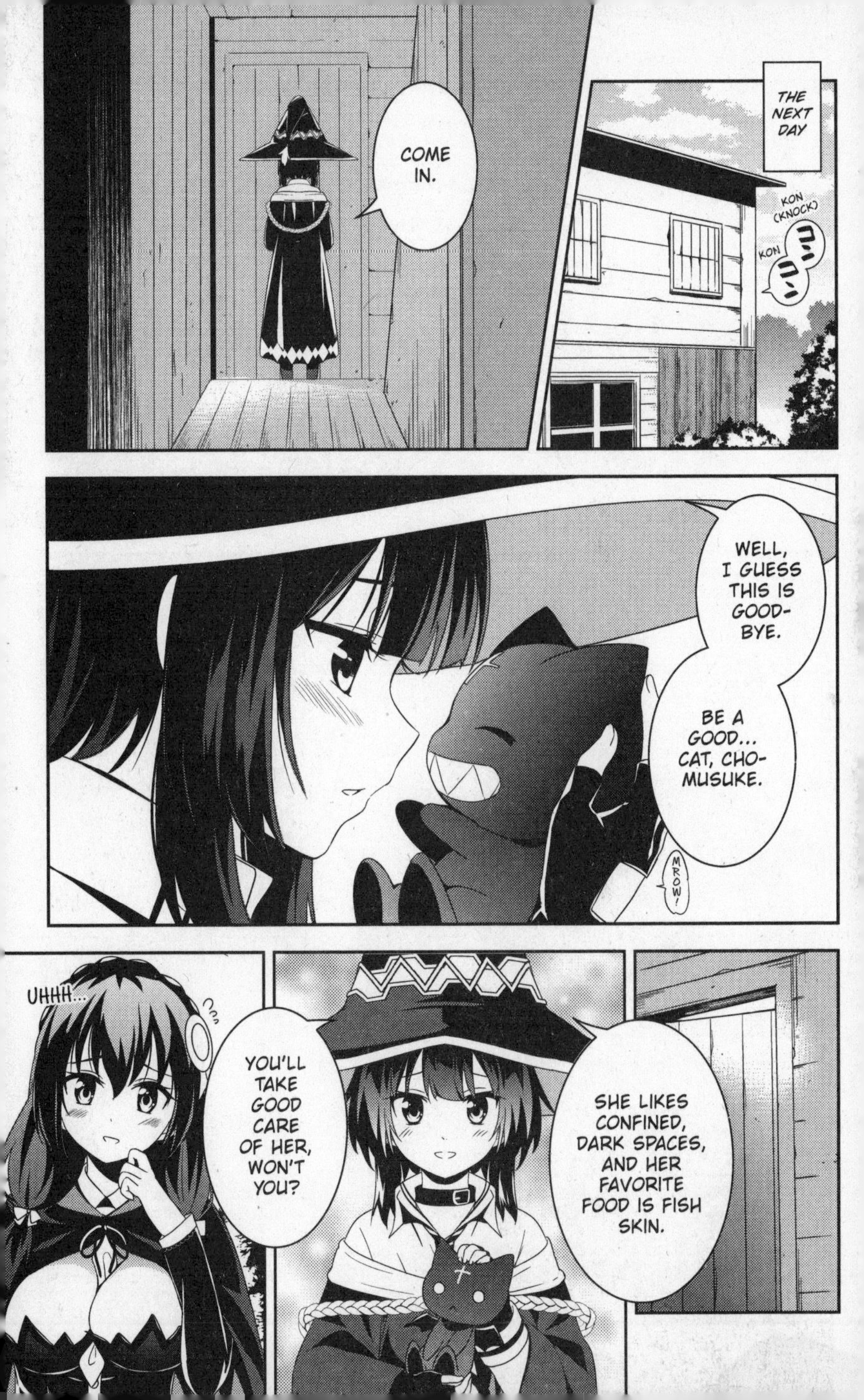
THE NEXT DAY
KON (KNOCK)
KON
COME IN.
WELL, I GUESS THIS IS GOOD-BYE.
BE A GOOD... CAT, CHO-MUSUKE.
MROW!
SHE LIKES CONFINED, DARK SPACES, AND HER FAVORITE FOOD IS FISH SKIN.
YOU'LL TAKE GOOD CARE OF HER, WON'T YOU?
UHHH...

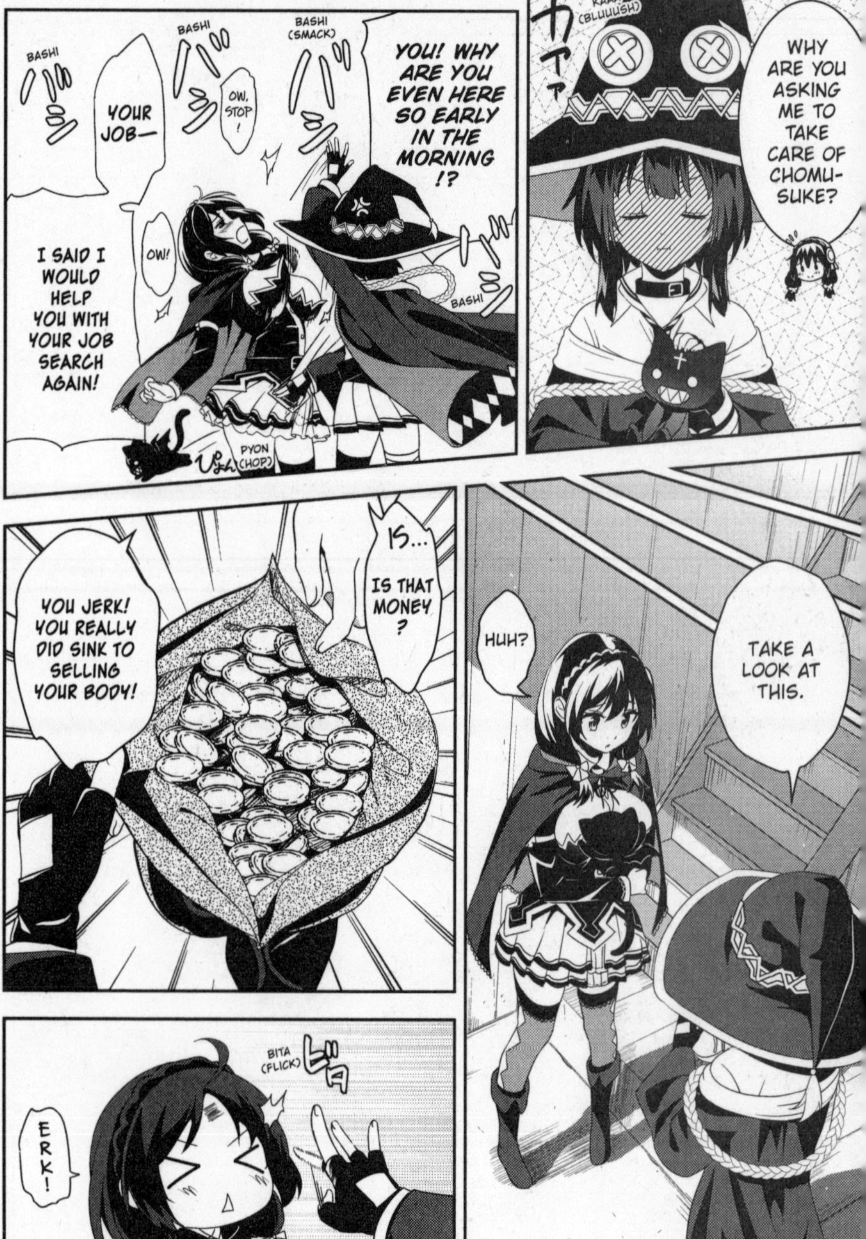
KAAA (BLUUUSH)
WHY ARE YOU ASKING ME TO TAKE CARE OF CHOMU-SUKE?
BASHI (SMACK)
YOU! WHY ARE YOU EVEN HERE SO EARLY IN THE MORNING!?
OW, STOP!
BASHI
YOUR JOB—
BASHI
OW!
BASHI
I SAID I WOULD HELP YOU WITH YOUR JOB SEARCH AGAIN!
PYON (HOP)
TAKE A LOOK AT THIS.
HUH?
IS...
IS THAT MONEY?
YOU JERK! YOU REALLY DID SINK TO SELLING YOUR BODY!
BITA (FLICK)
ERK!

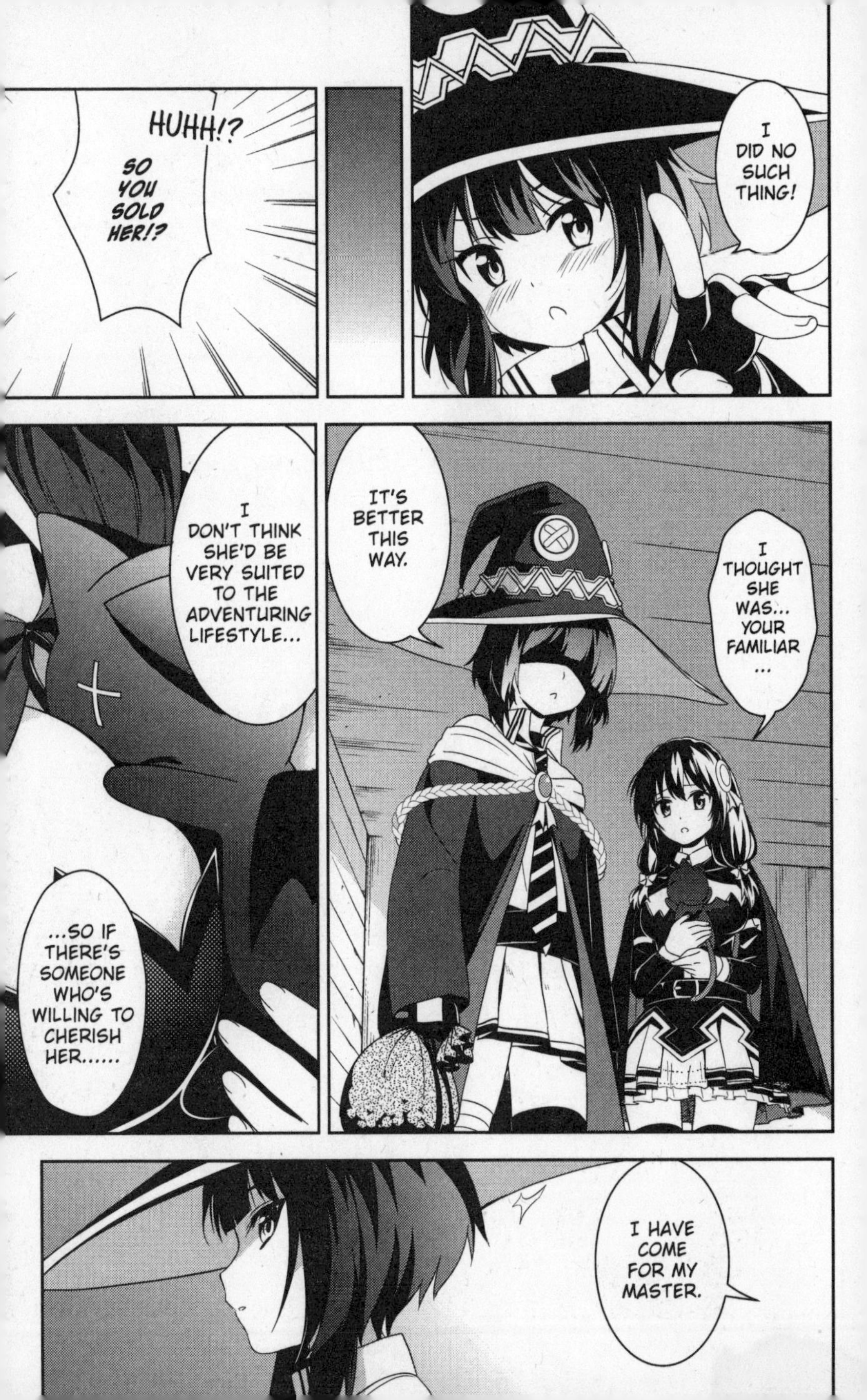
I DID NO SUCH THING!
HUHH!?
SO YOU SOLD HER!?
I THOUGHT SHE WAS... YOUR FAMILIAR ...
IT'S BETTER THIS WAY.
I DON'T THINK SHE'D BE VERY SUITED TO THE ADVENTURING LIFESTYLE...
...SO IF THERE'S SOMEONE WHO'S WILLING TO CHERISH HER......
I HAVE COME FOR MY MASTER.

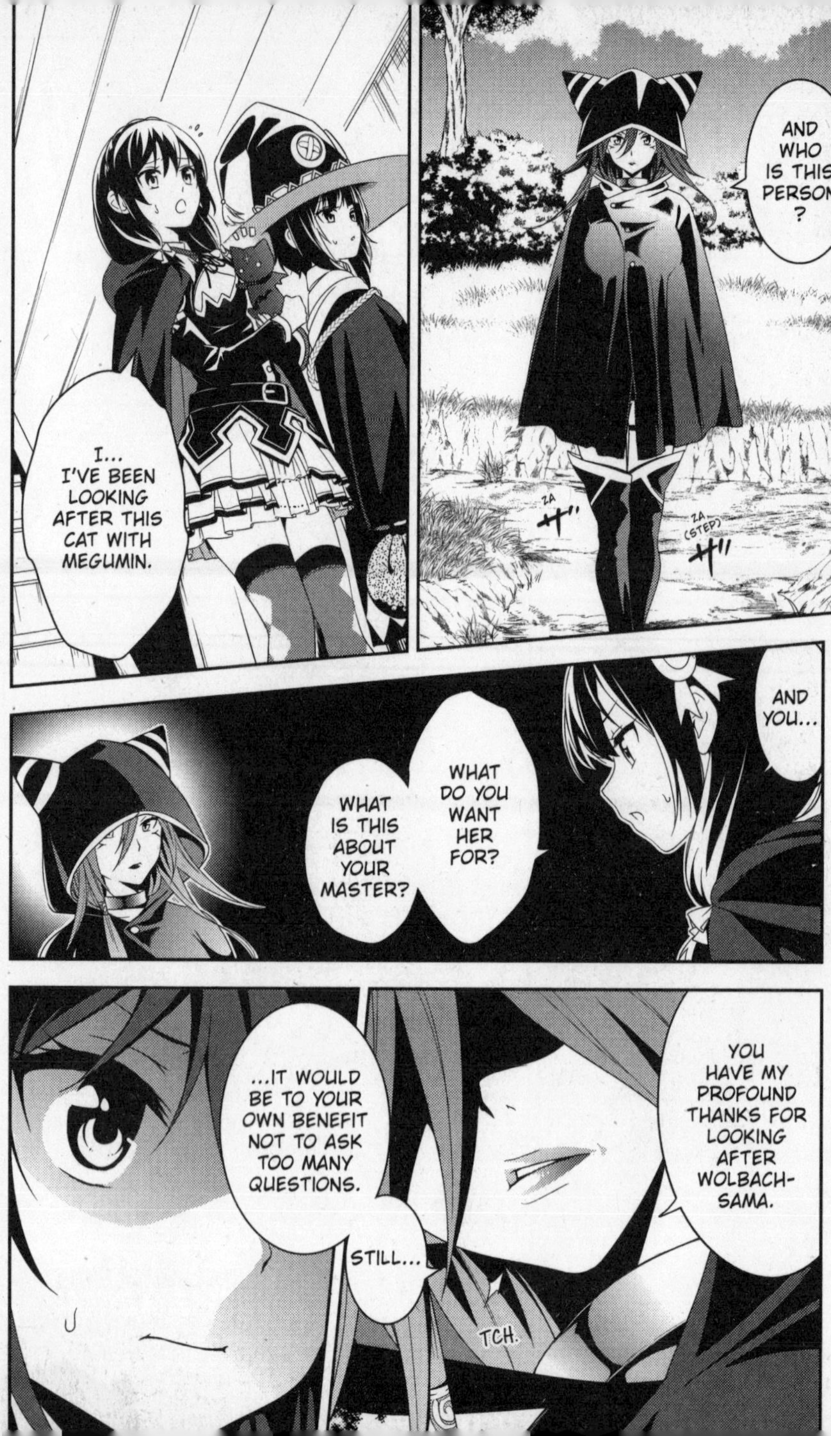
AND WHO IS THIS PERSON?
ZA
ZA (STEP)
I... I'VE BEEN LOOKING AFTER THIS CAT WITH MEGUMIN.
AND YOU...
WHAT DO YOU WANT HER FOR?
WHAT IS THIS ABOUT YOUR MASTER?
YOU HAVE MY PROFOUND THANKS FOR LOOKING AFTER WOLBACH-SAMA.
STILL...
...IT WOULD BE TO YOUR OWN BENEFIT NOT TO ASK TOO MANY QUESTIONS.
TCH.

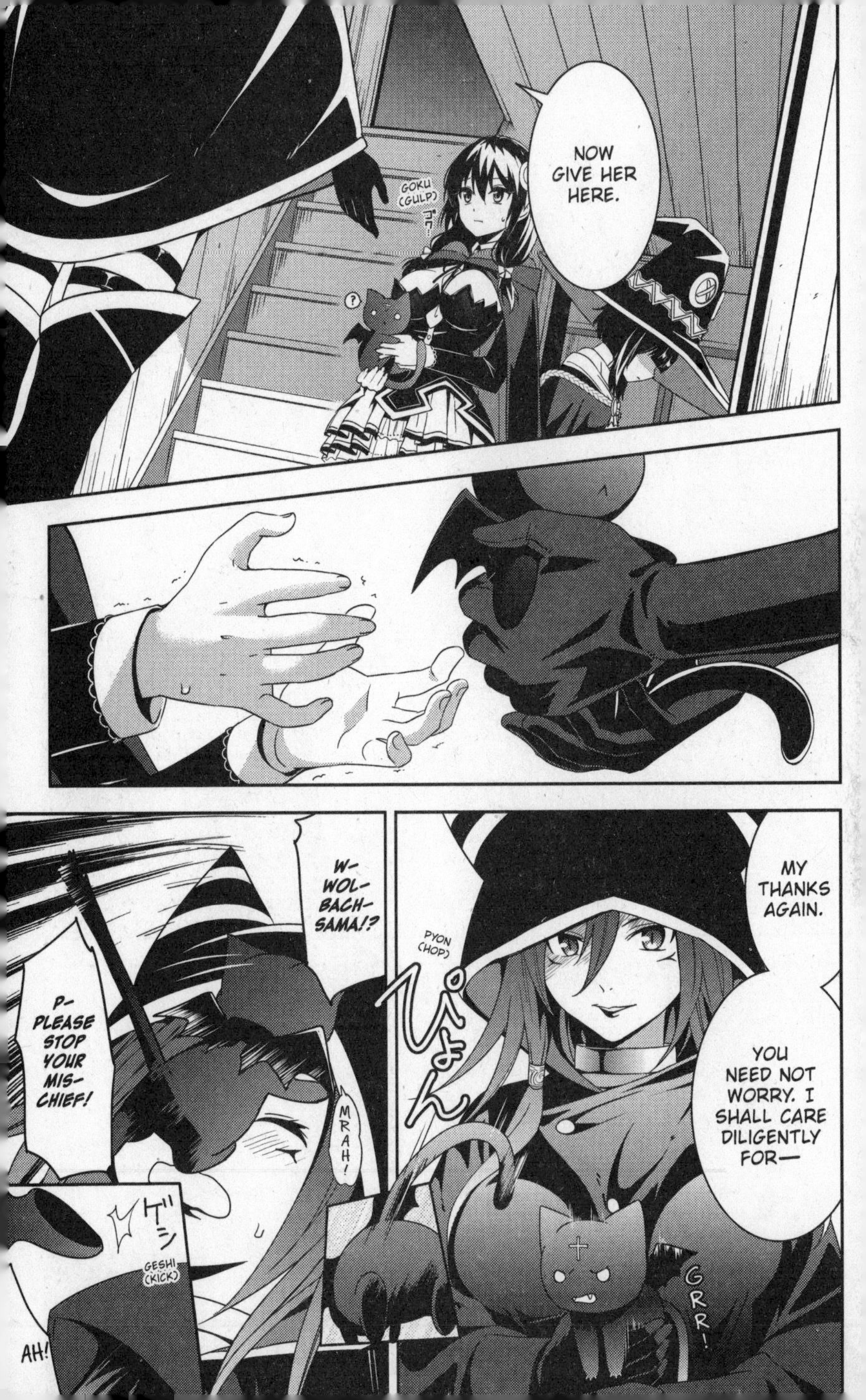
NOW GIVE HER HERE.
GOKU (GULP)
ゴク…
?
MY THANKS AGAIN.
PYON (HOP)
ぴょん
YOU NEED NOT WORRY. I SHALL CARE DILIGENTLY FOR—
GRR!
W-WOL-BACH-SAMA!?
P-PLEASE STOP YOUR MIS-CHIEF!
MRAH!
ゲシ
GESHI (KICK)
AH!

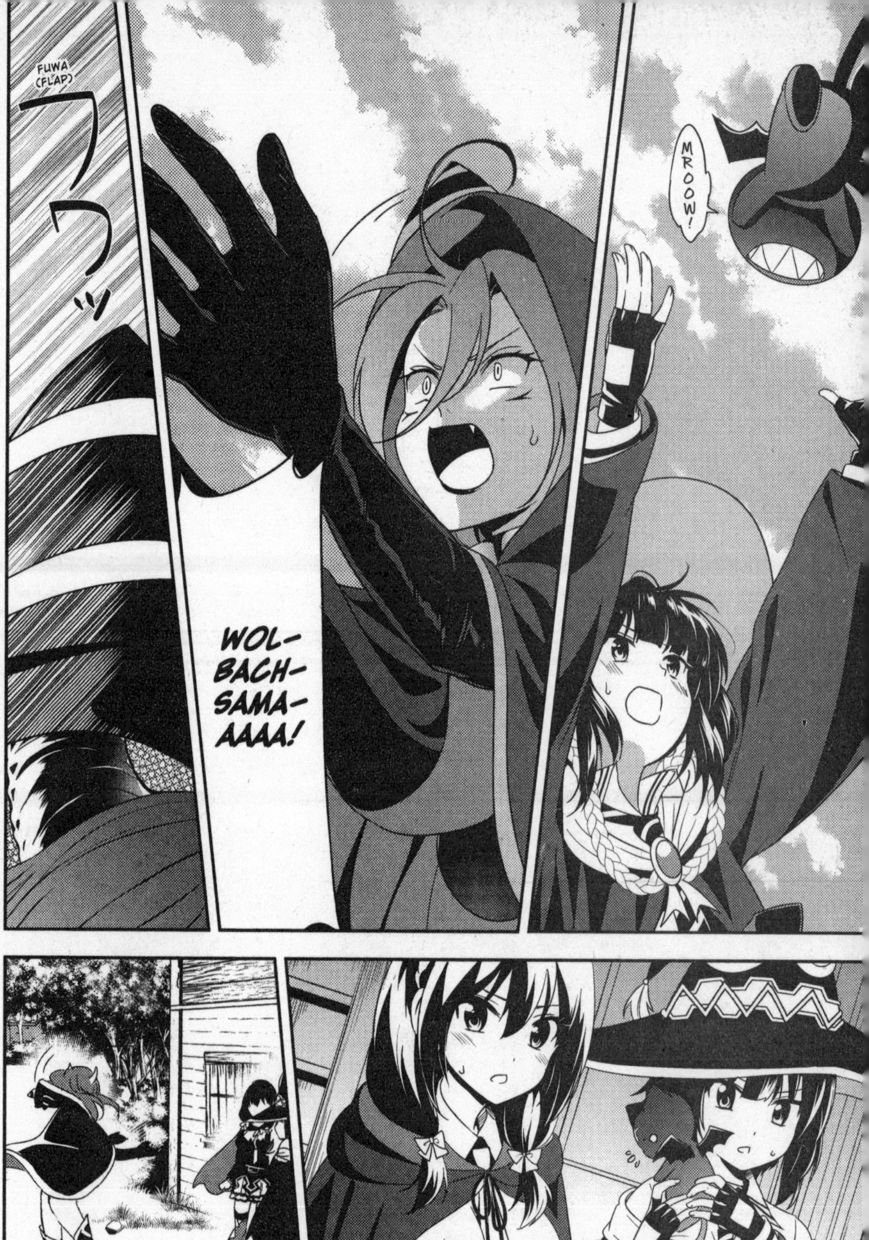
MROOW!
WOL-BACH-SAMA-AAAA!
FUWA (FLAP)

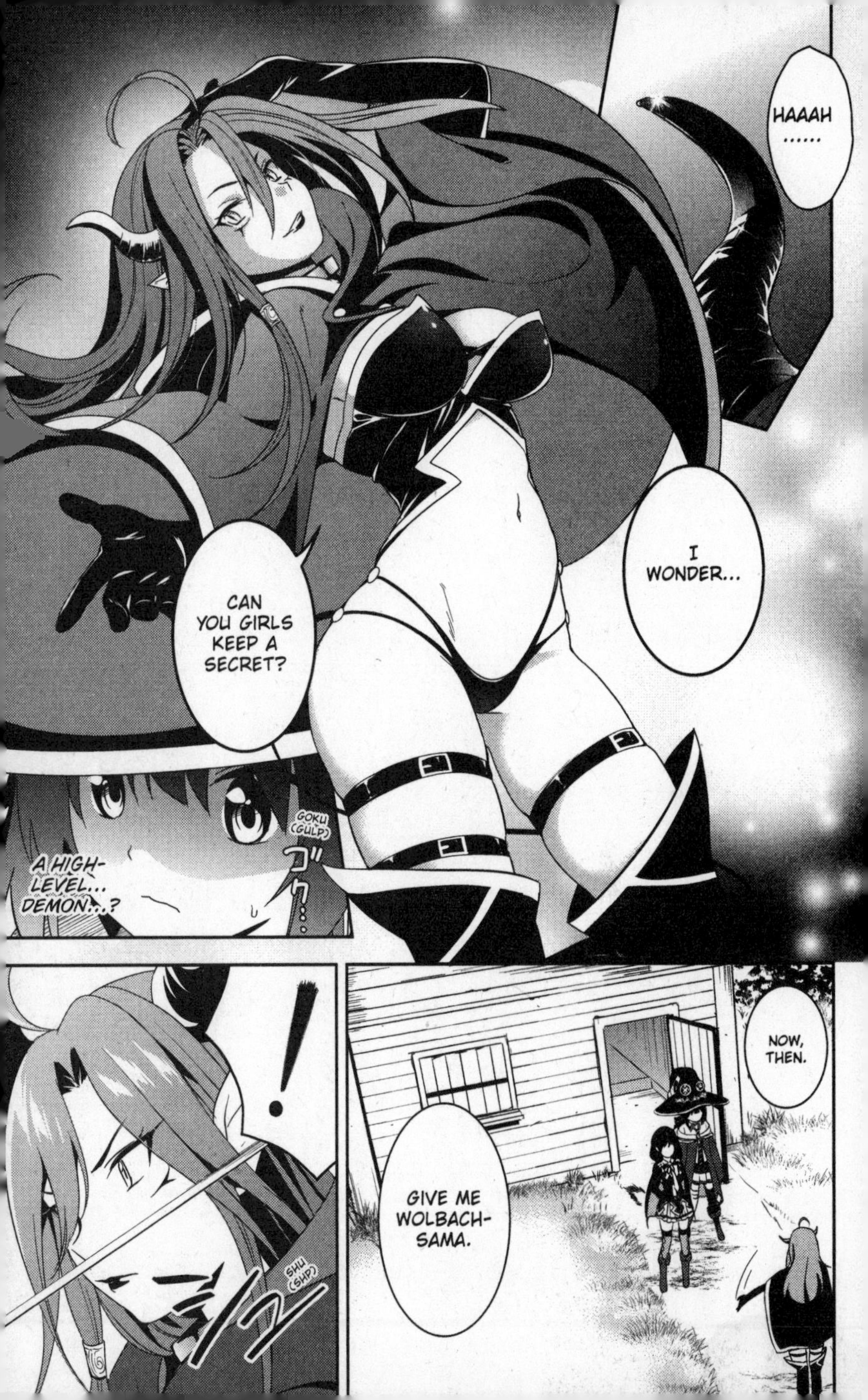
HAAAH ......
I WONDER...
CAN YOU GIRLS KEEP A SECRET?
GOKU (GULP)
A HIGH-LEVEL... DEMON...?
NOW, THEN.
GIVE ME WOLBACH-SAMA.
!
SHU (SHP)

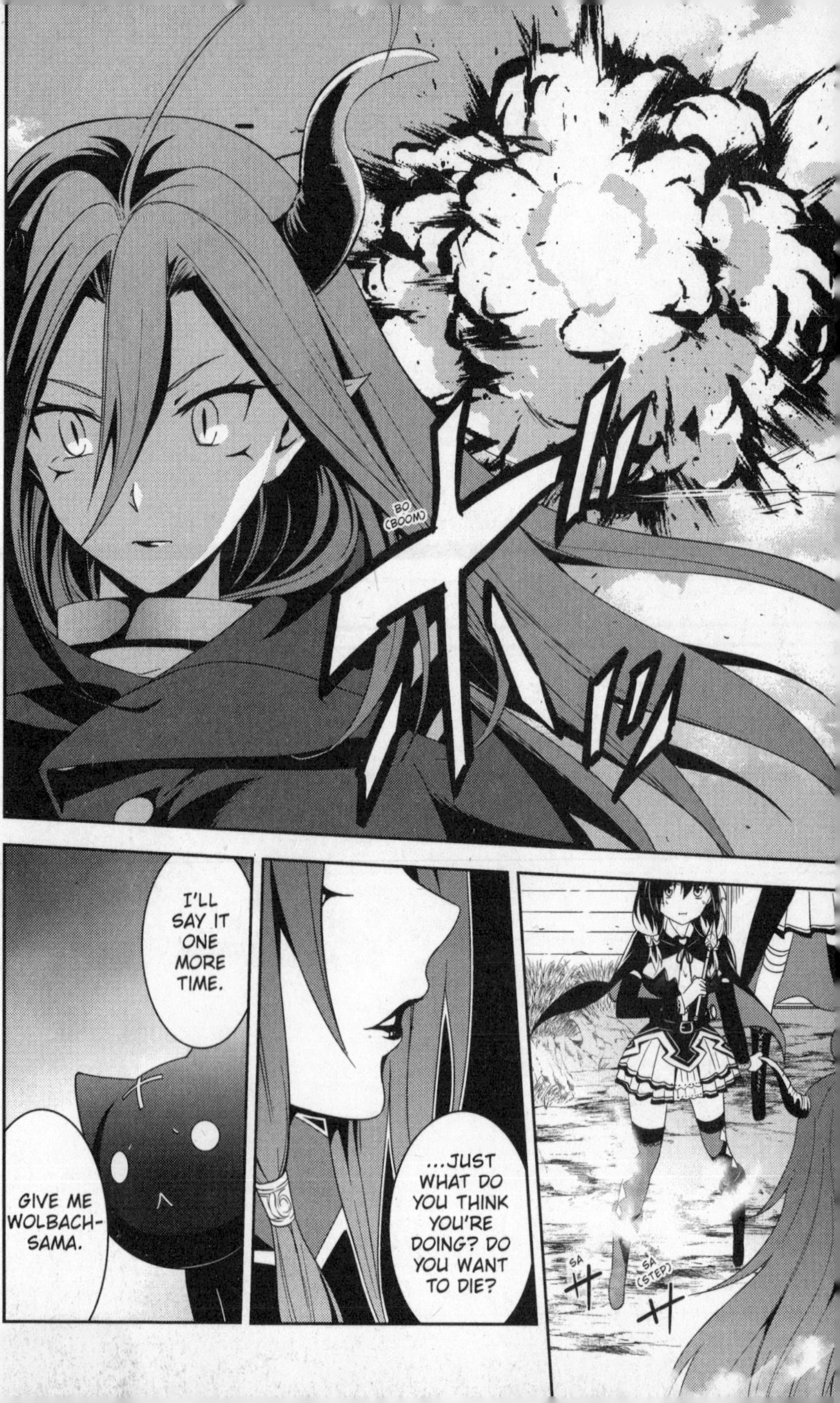
BO (BOOM)
SA (STEP)
SA
...JUST WHAT DO YOU THINK YOU'RE DOING? DO YOU WANT TO DIE?
I'LL SAY IT ONE MORE TIME.
GIVE ME WOLBACH-SAMA.

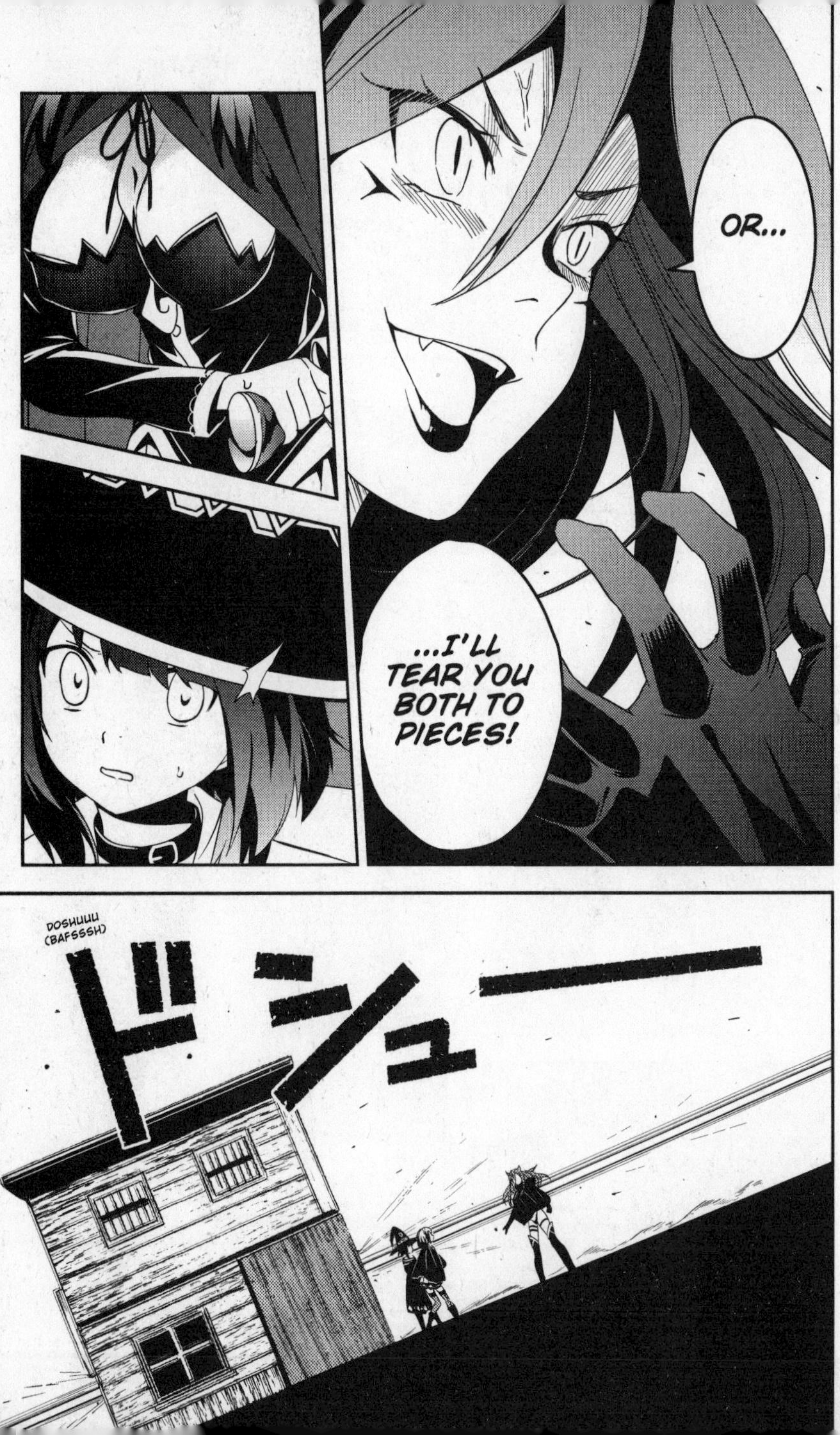
OR...
...I'LL TEAR YOU BOTH TO PIECES!
DOSHUUU (BAFSSSH)
ドシュー

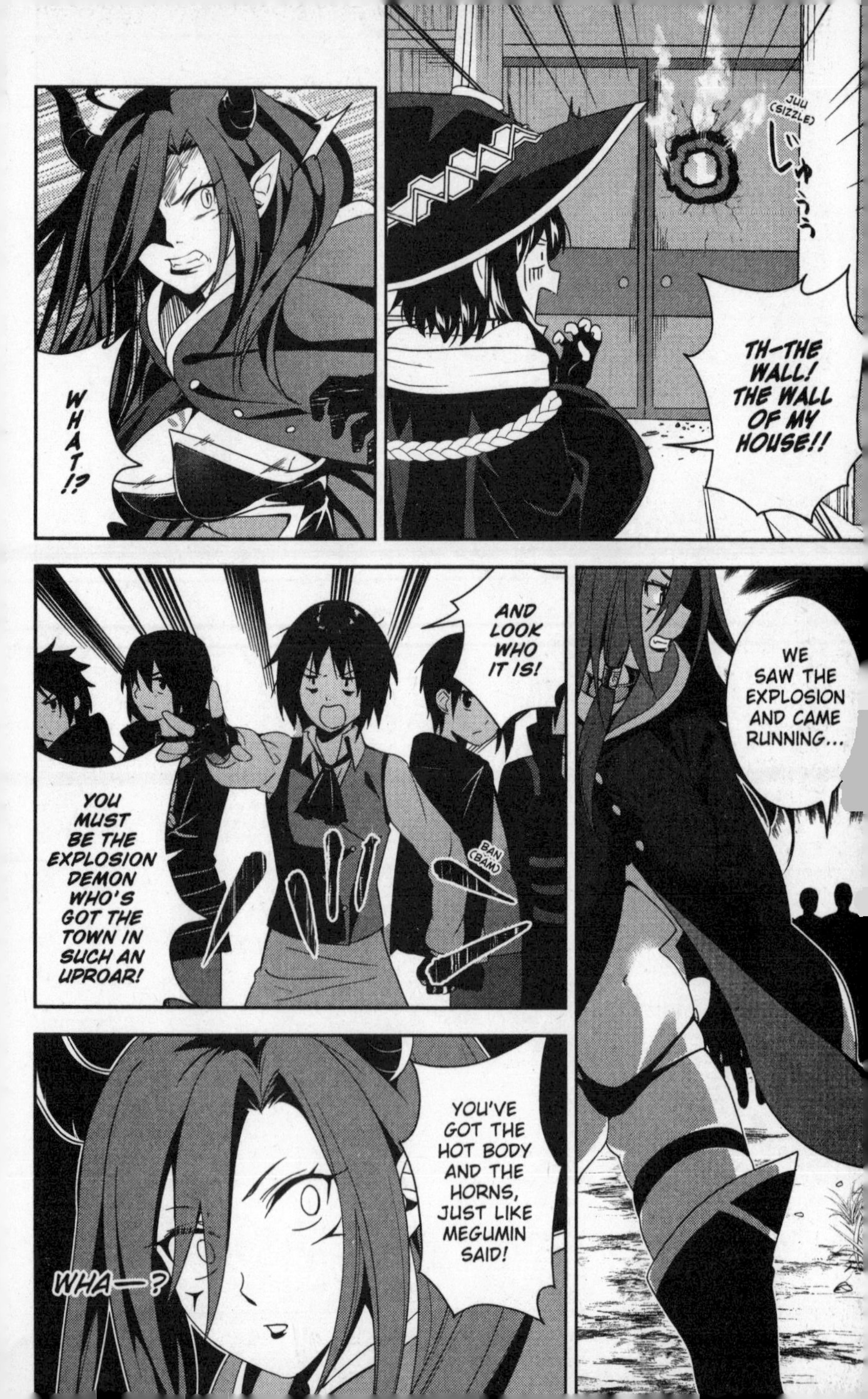
JUU (SIZZLE)
TH—THE WALL! THE WALL OF MY HOUSE!!
WHAT!?
WE SAW THE EXPLOSION AND CAME RUNNING...
AND LOOK WHO IT IS!
BAN (BAM)
YOU MUST BE THE EXPLOSION DEMON WHO'S GOT THE TOWN IN SUCH AN UPROAR!
YOU'VE GOT THE HOT BODY AND THE HORNS, JUST LIKE MEGUMIN SAID!
WHA—?

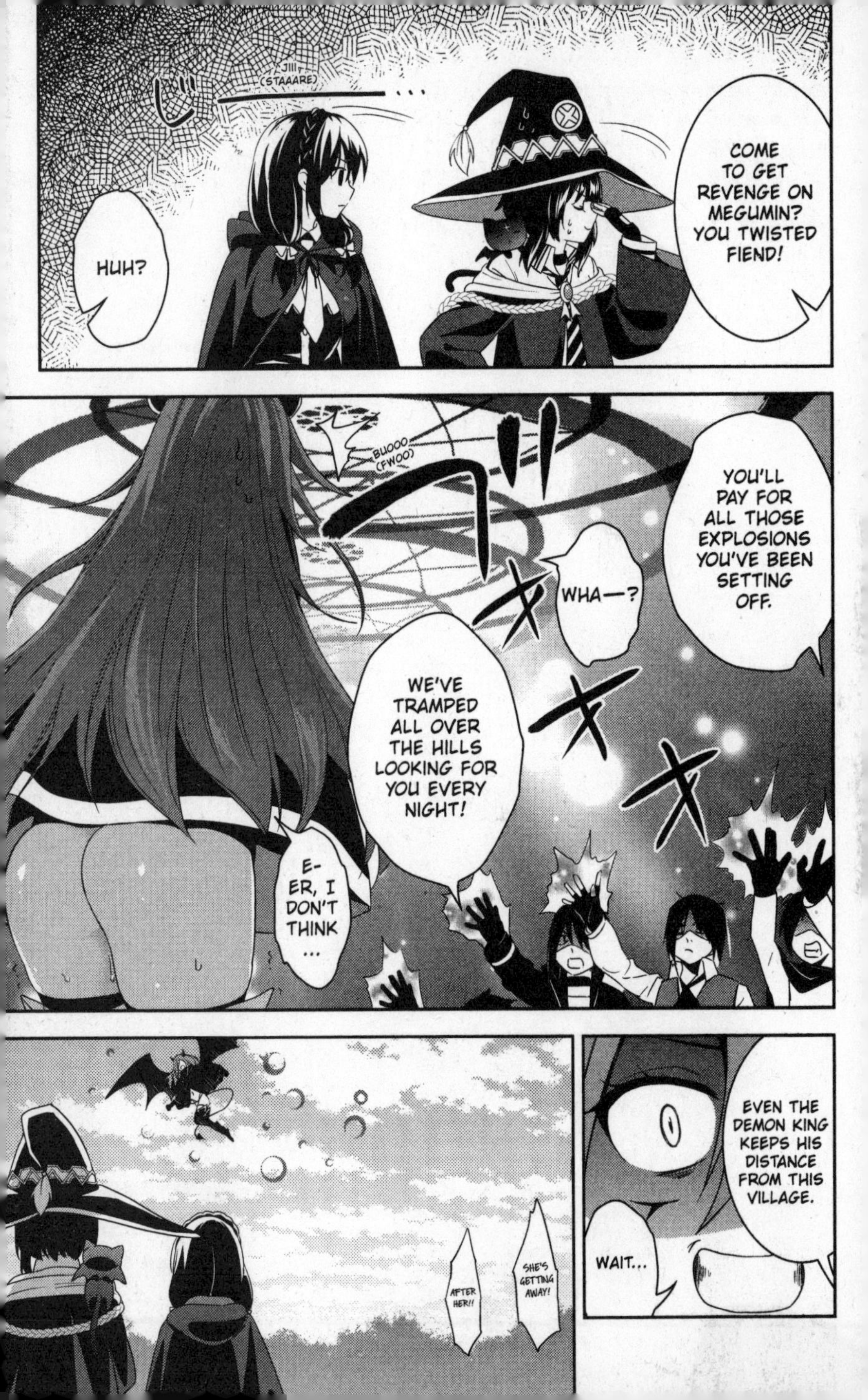
COME TO GET REVENGE ON MEGUMIN? YOU TWISTED FIEND!
じ
JIII (STAAARE)
HUH?
YOU'LL PAY FOR ALL THOSE EXPLOSIONS YOU'VE BEEN SETTING OFF.
WHA—?
BUOOO (FWOO)
WE'VE TRAMPED ALL OVER THE HILLS LOOKING FOR YOU EVERY NIGHT!
E-ER, I DON'T THINK...
EVEN THE DEMON KING KEEPS HIS DISTANCE FROM THIS VILLAGE.
WAIT...
SHE'S GETTING AWAY!
AFTER HER!!

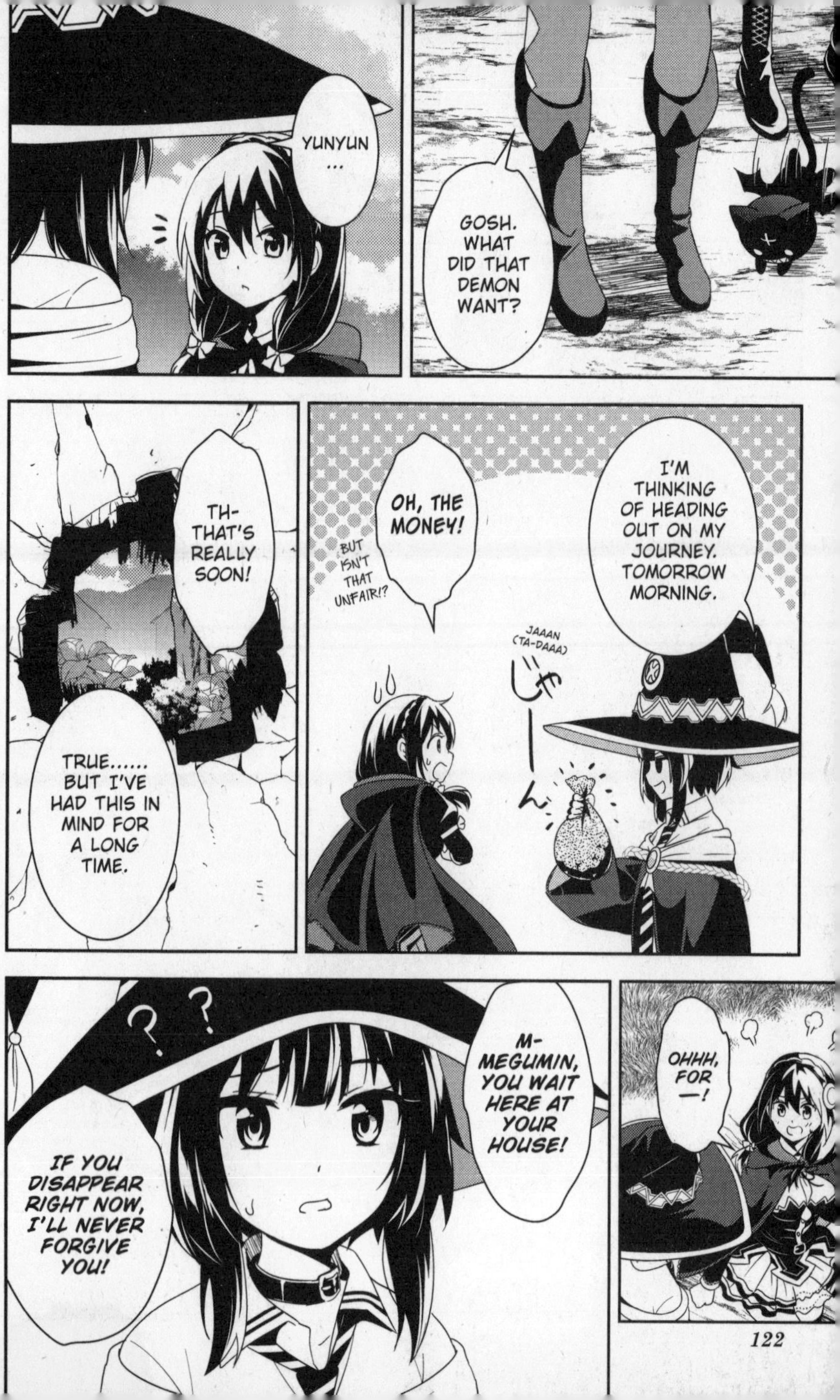
GOSH. WHAT DID THAT DEMON WANT?
YUNYUN ...
I'M THINKING OF HEADING OUT ON MY JOURNEY. TOMORROW MORNING.
JAAAN (TA-DAAA)
じゃーん
OH, THE MONEY!
BUT ISN'T THAT UNFAIR!?
TH-THAT'S REALLY SOON!
TRUE...... BUT I'VE HAD THIS IN MIND FOR A LONG TIME.
OHHH, FOR—!
M-MEGUMIN, YOU WAIT HERE AT YOUR HOUSE!
IF YOU DISAPPEAR RIGHT NOW, I'LL NEVER FORGIVE YOU!

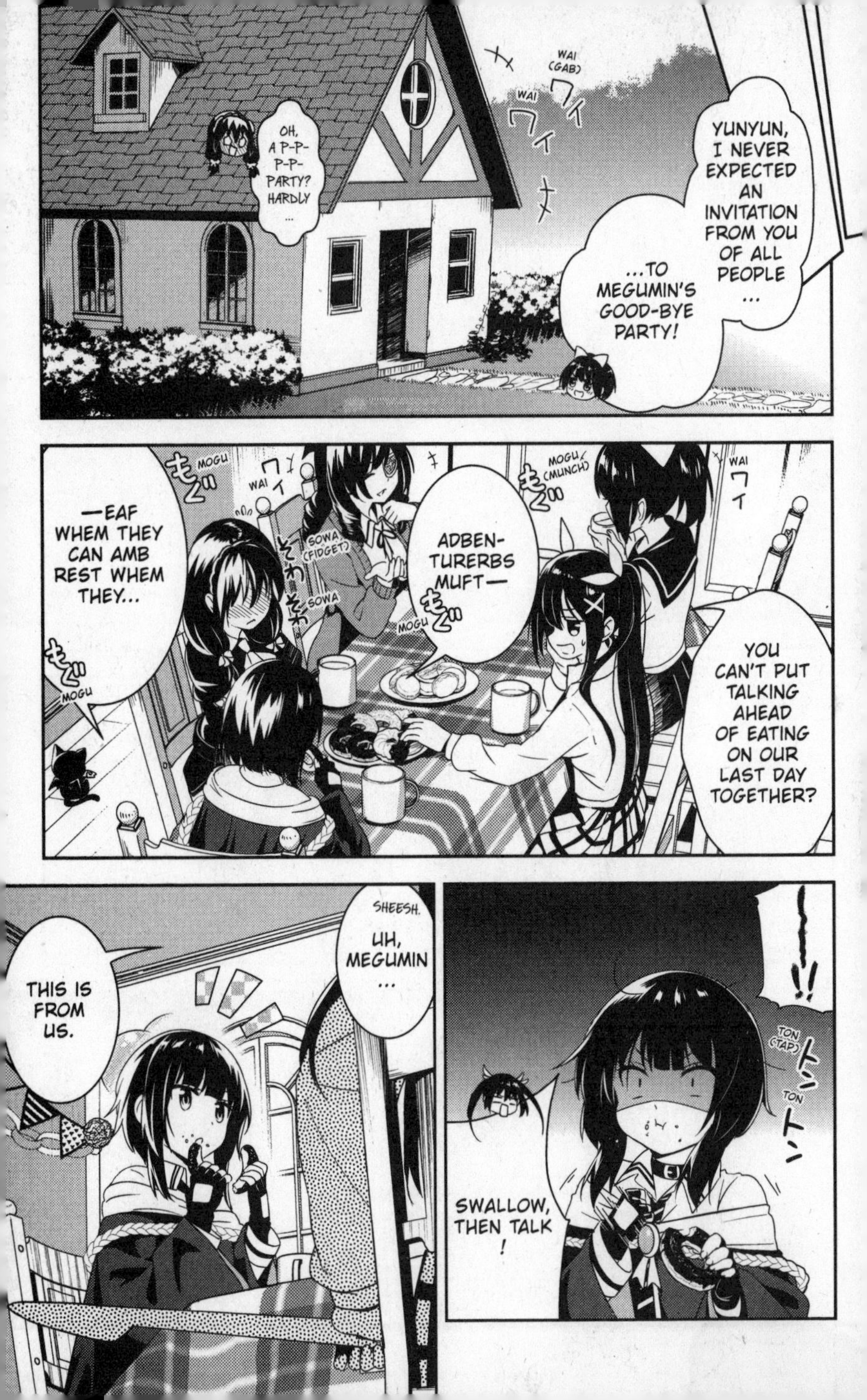
YUNYUN, I NEVER EXPECTED AN INVITATION FROM YOU OF ALL PEOPLE...
...TO MEGUMIN'S GOOD-BYE PARTY!
WAI (GAB)
WAI
OH, A P-P-P-P-PARTY? HARDLY...
WAI
MOGU/ (MUNCH)
YOU CAN'T PUT TALKING AHEAD OF EATING ON OUR LAST DAY TOGETHER?
ADBEN-TURERBS MUFT—
MOGU
SOWA (FIDGET)
SOWA
WAI
MOGU
—EAF WHEM THEY CAN AMB REST WHEM THEY...
MOGU
!!
TON (TAP)
TON
SWALLOW, THEN TALK!
SHEESH.
UH, MEGUMIN...
THIS IS FROM US.

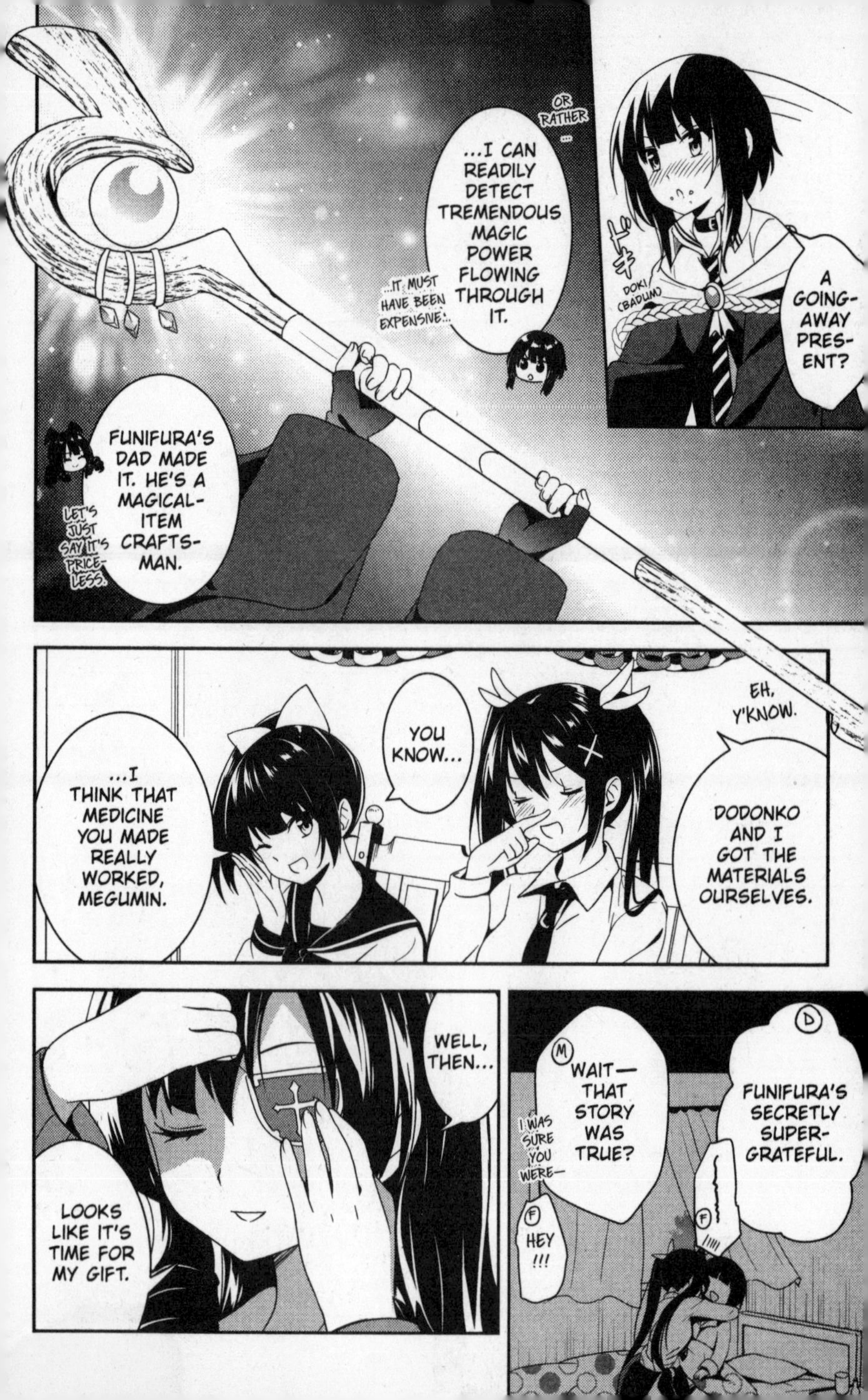
A GOING-AWAY PRESENT?
DOKI (BADUM)
OR RATHER...
...I CAN READILY DETECT TREMENDOUS MAGIC POWER FLOWING THROUGH IT.
...IT MUST HAVE BEEN EXPENSIVE...
FUNIFURA'S DAD MADE IT. HE'S A MAGICAL-ITEM CRAFTSMAN.
LET'S JUST SAY IT'S PRICELESS.
EH, Y'KNOW.
DODONKO AND I GOT THE MATERIALS OURSELVES.
YOU KNOW...
...I THINK THAT MEDICINE YOU MADE REALLY WORKED, MEGUMIN.
D
FUNIFURA'S SECRETLY SUPER-GRATEFUL.
M
WAIT—THAT STORY WAS TRUE?
I WAS SURE YOU WERE—
F
HEY!!!
F
WELL, THEN...
LOOKS LIKE IT'S TIME FOR MY GIFT.

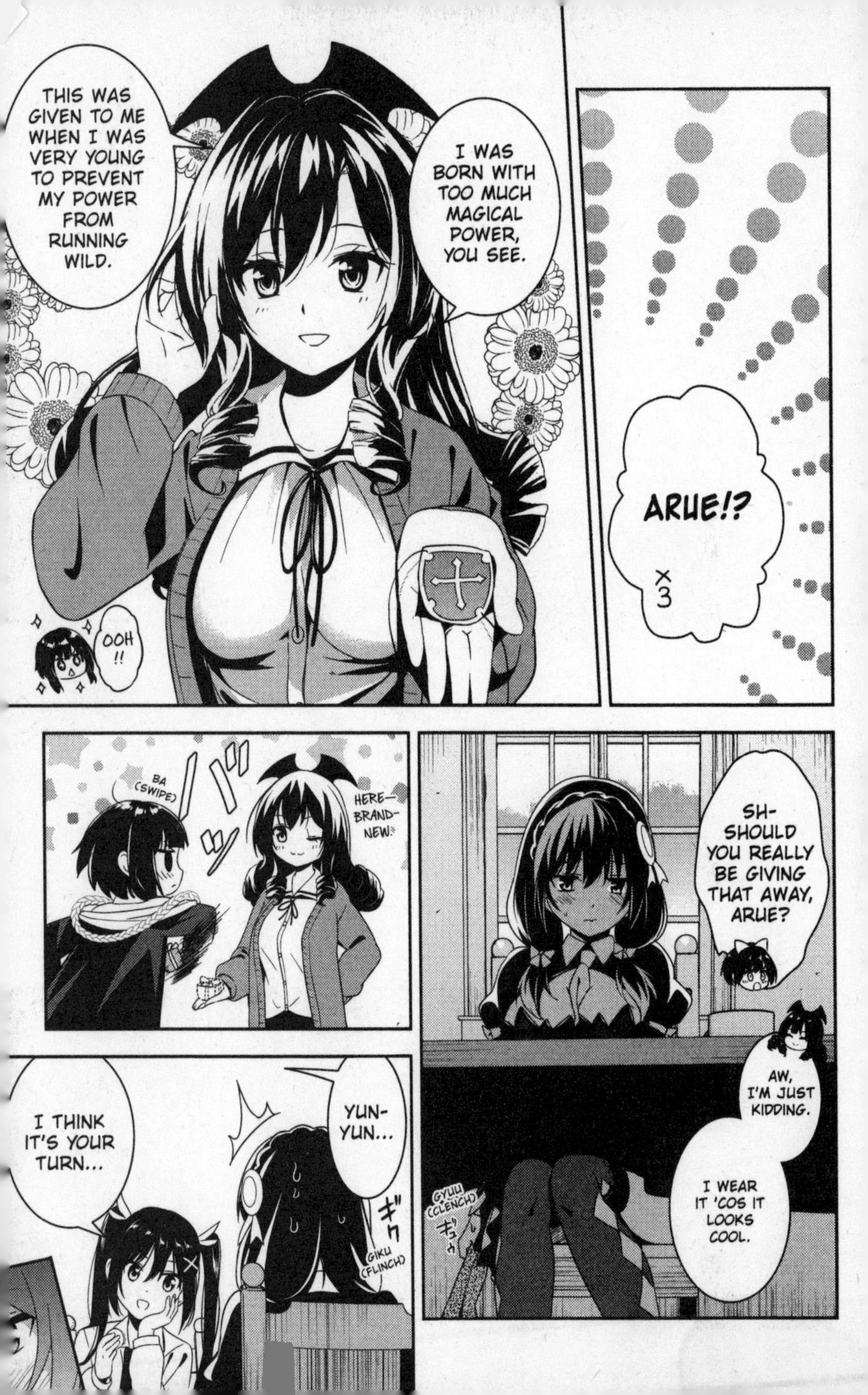
ARUE!?
×3
I WAS BORN WITH TOO MUCH MAGICAL POWER, YOU SEE.
THIS WAS GIVEN TO ME WHEN I WAS VERY YOUNG TO PREVENT MY POWER FROM RUNNING WILD.
OOH !!
SH-SHOULD YOU REALLY BE GIVING THAT AWAY, ARUE?
AW, I'M JUST KIDDING.
I WEAR IT 'COS IT LOOKS COOL.
GYUU (CLENCH)
HERE—BRAND-NEW.
BA (SWIPE)
YUN-YUN...
GIKU (FLINCH)
I THINK IT'S YOUR TURN...

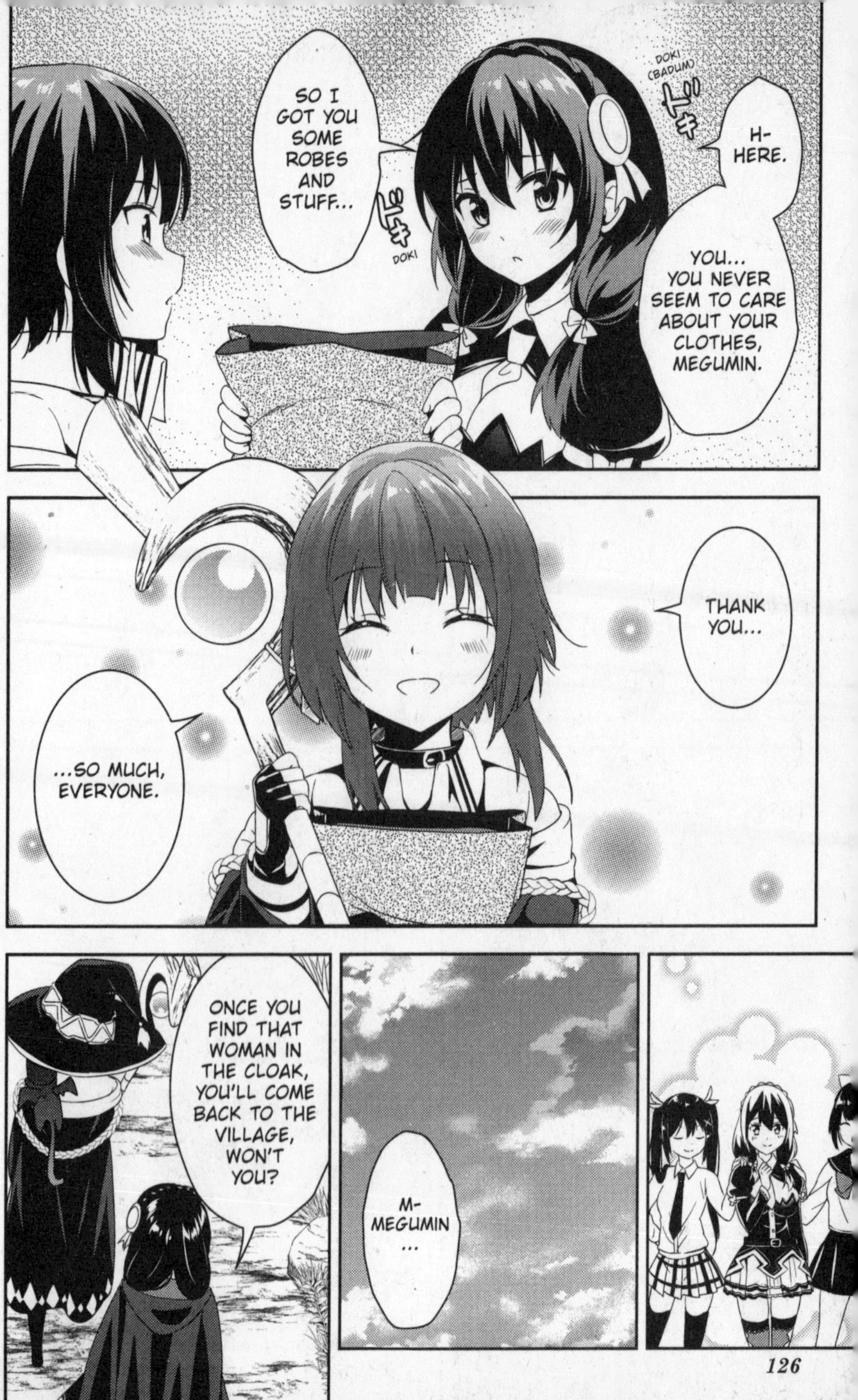
DOKI (BADUM)
H-HERE.
YOU... YOU NEVER SEEM TO CARE ABOUT YOUR CLOTHES, MEGUMIN.
SO I GOT YOU SOME ROBES AND STUFF...
DOKI
THANK YOU...
...SO MUCH, EVERYONE.
M-MEGUMIN...
ONCE YOU FIND THAT WOMAN IN THE CLOAK, YOU'LL COME BACK TO THE VILLAGE, WON'T YOU?

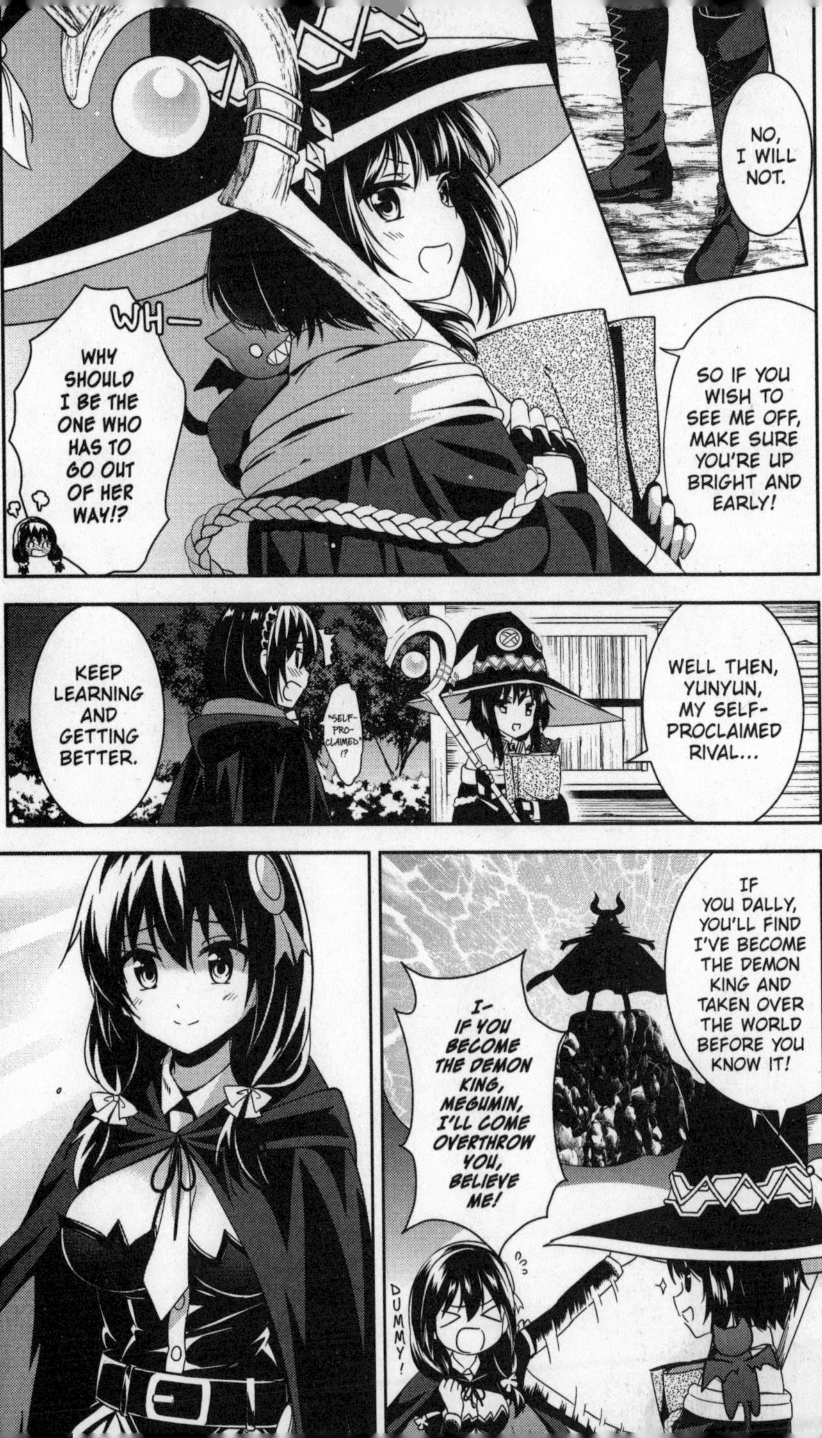
NO, I WILL NOT.
SO IF YOU WISH TO SEE ME OFF, MAKE SURE YOU'RE UP BRIGHT AND EARLY!
WH—
WHY SHOULD I BE THE ONE WHO HAS TO GO OUT OF HER WAY!?
WELL THEN, YUNYUN, MY SELF-PROCLAIMED RIVAL...
"SELF-PROCLAIMED"!?
KEEP LEARNING AND GETTING BETTER.
IF YOU DALLY, YOU'LL FIND I'VE BECOME THE DEMON KING AND TAKEN OVER THE WORLD BEFORE YOU KNOW IT!
I- IF YOU BECOME THE DEMON KING, MEGUMIN, I'LL COME OVERTHROW YOU, BELIEVE ME!
DUMMY!

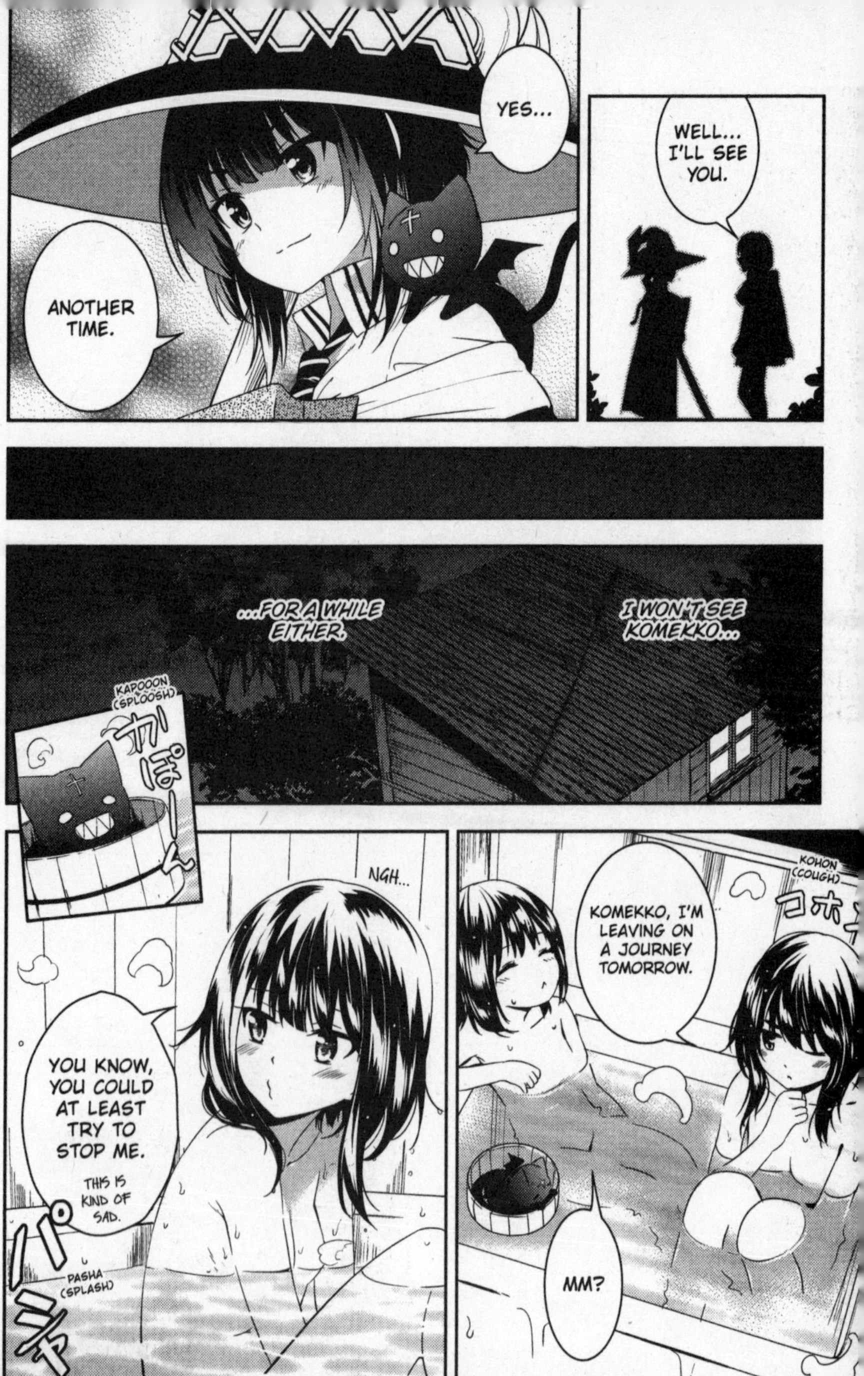
WELL... I'LL SEE YOU.
YES...
ANOTHER TIME.
I WON'T SEE KOMEKKO...
...FOR A WHILE EITHER.
KAPOOON (SPLOOSH)
かぽーん
KOHON (COUGH)
コホ
KOMEKKO, I'M LEAVING ON A JOURNEY TOMORROW.
MM?
NGH...
YOU KNOW, YOU COULD AT LEAST TRY TO STOP ME.
THIS IS KIND OF SAD.
PASHA (SPLASH)
パシャ

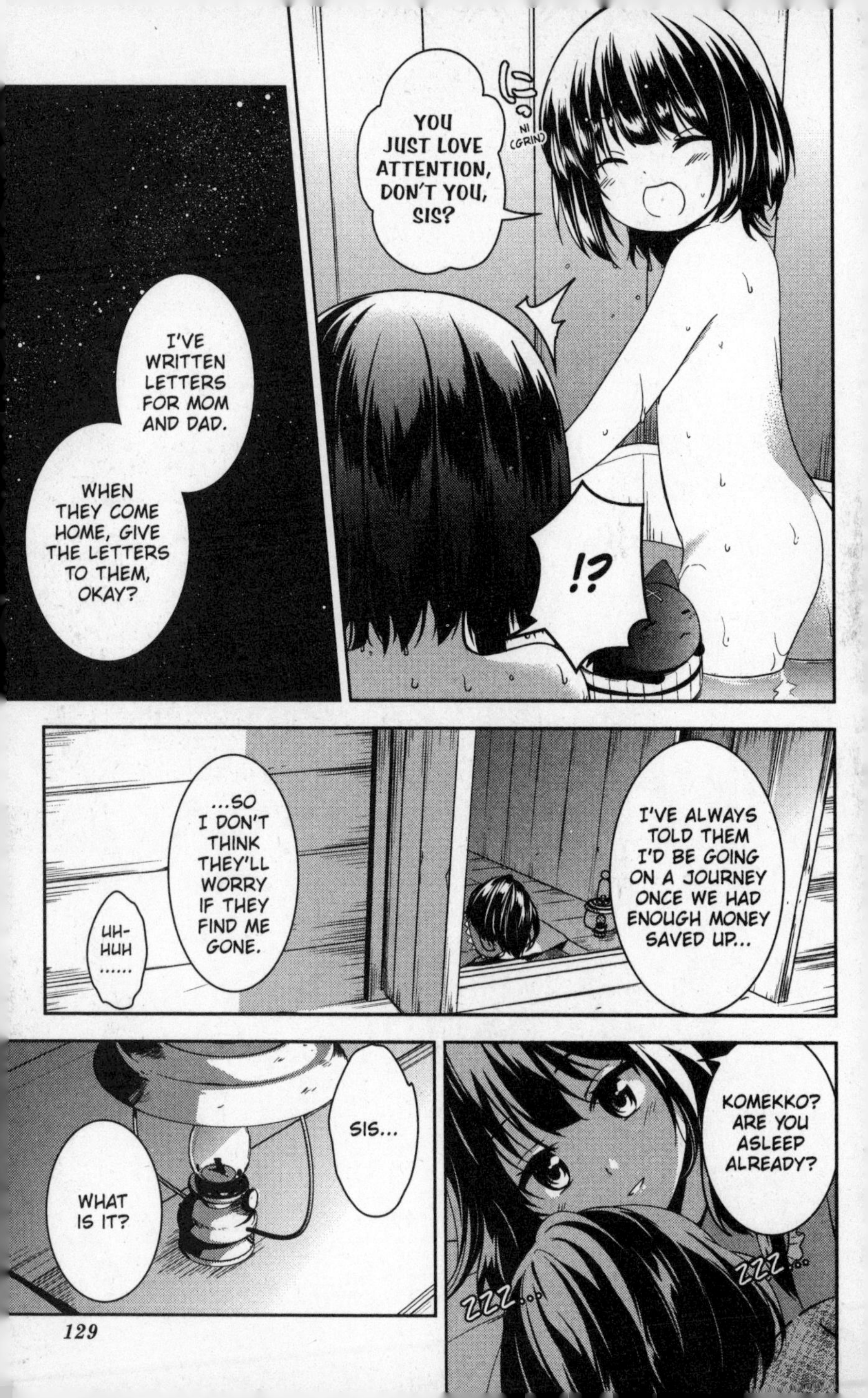

YOU JUST LOVE ATTENTION, DON'T YOU, SIS?
NI (GRIN)
!?
I'VE WRITTEN LETTERS FOR MOM AND DAD.
WHEN THEY COME HOME, GIVE THE LETTERS TO THEM, OKAY?
I'VE ALWAYS TOLD THEM I'D BE GOING ON A JOURNEY ONCE WE HAD ENOUGH MONEY SAVED UP...
...SO I DON'T THINK THEY'LL WORRY IF THEY FIND ME GONE.
UH-HUH......
KOMEKKO? ARE YOU ASLEEP ALREADY?
ZZZ...
ZZZ...
SIS...
WHAT IS IT?

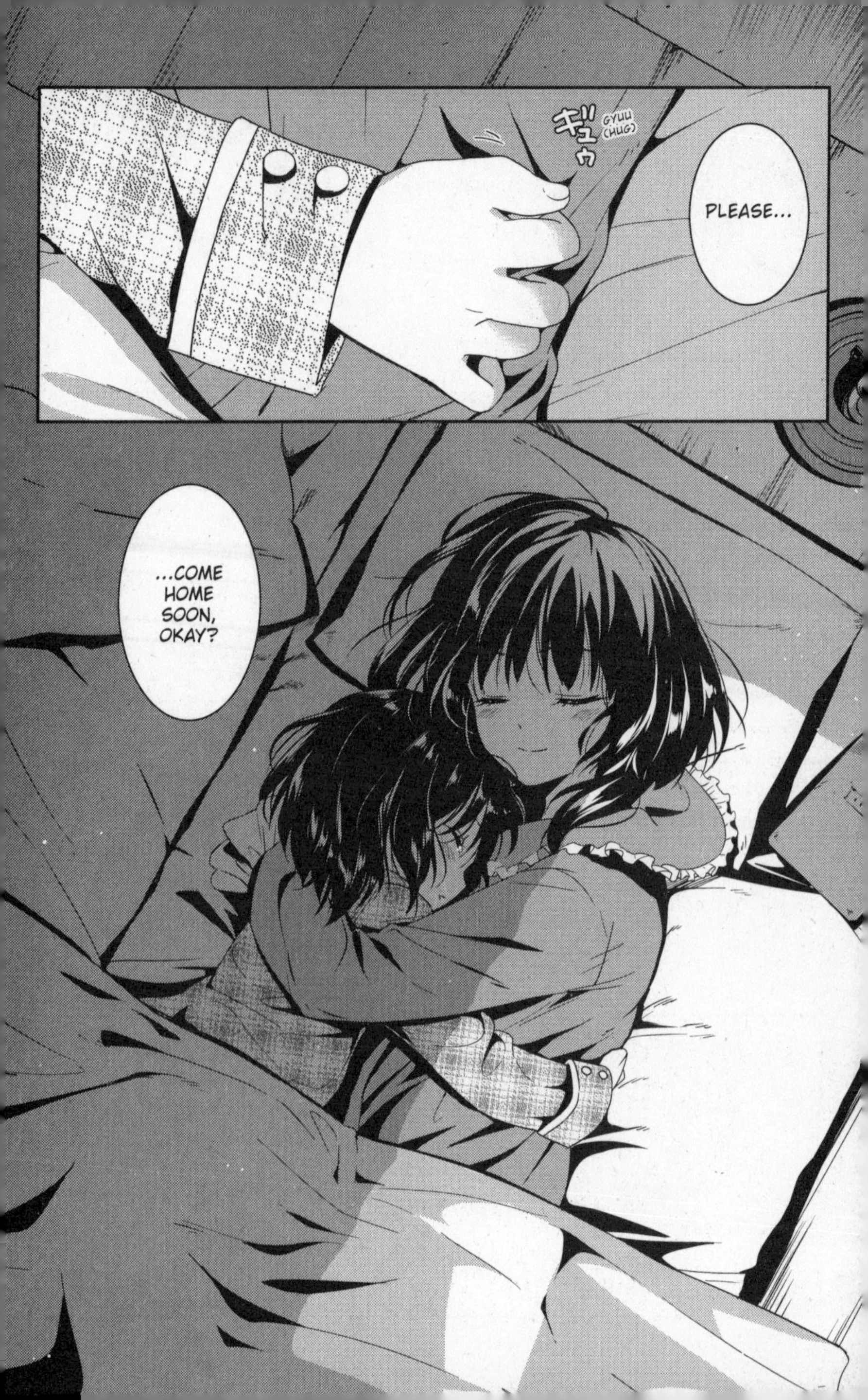
ギュッ
GYUU (HUG)
PLEASE...
...COME HOME SOON, OKAY?

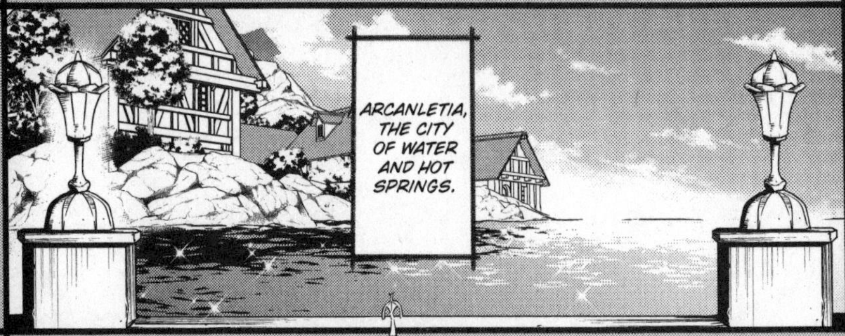
ARCANLETIA, THE CITY OF WATER AND HOT SPRINGS.

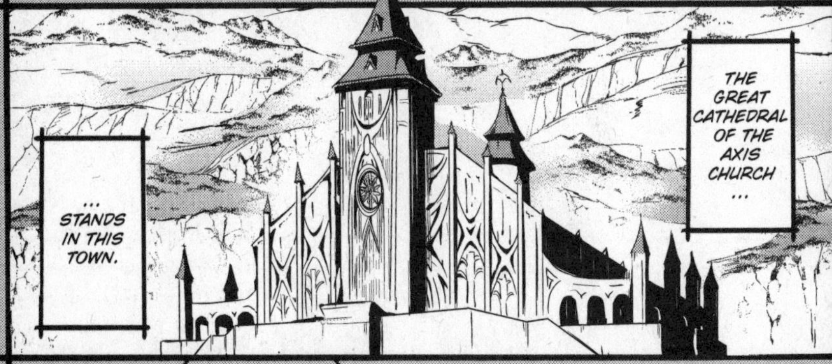
THE GREAT CATHEDRAL OF THE AXIS CHURCH...
...STANDS IN THIS TOWN.

INTERLUDE THEATRE 1

CECILY'S STORY

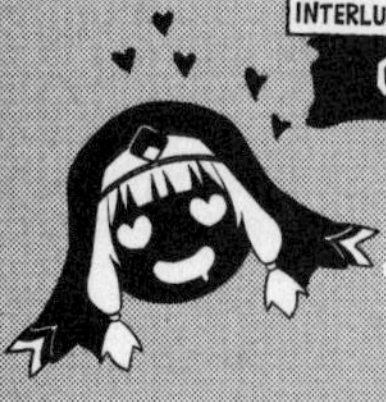

Aqua-sama, I Won't Let Him Escape!

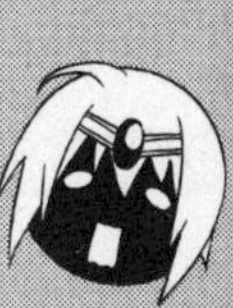

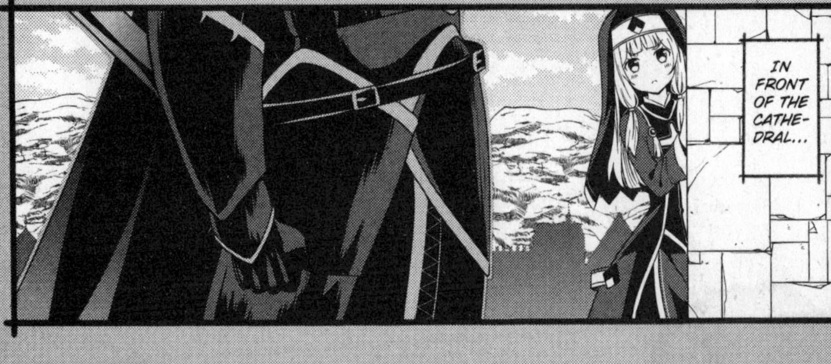
IN FRONT OF THE CATHE-DRAL...

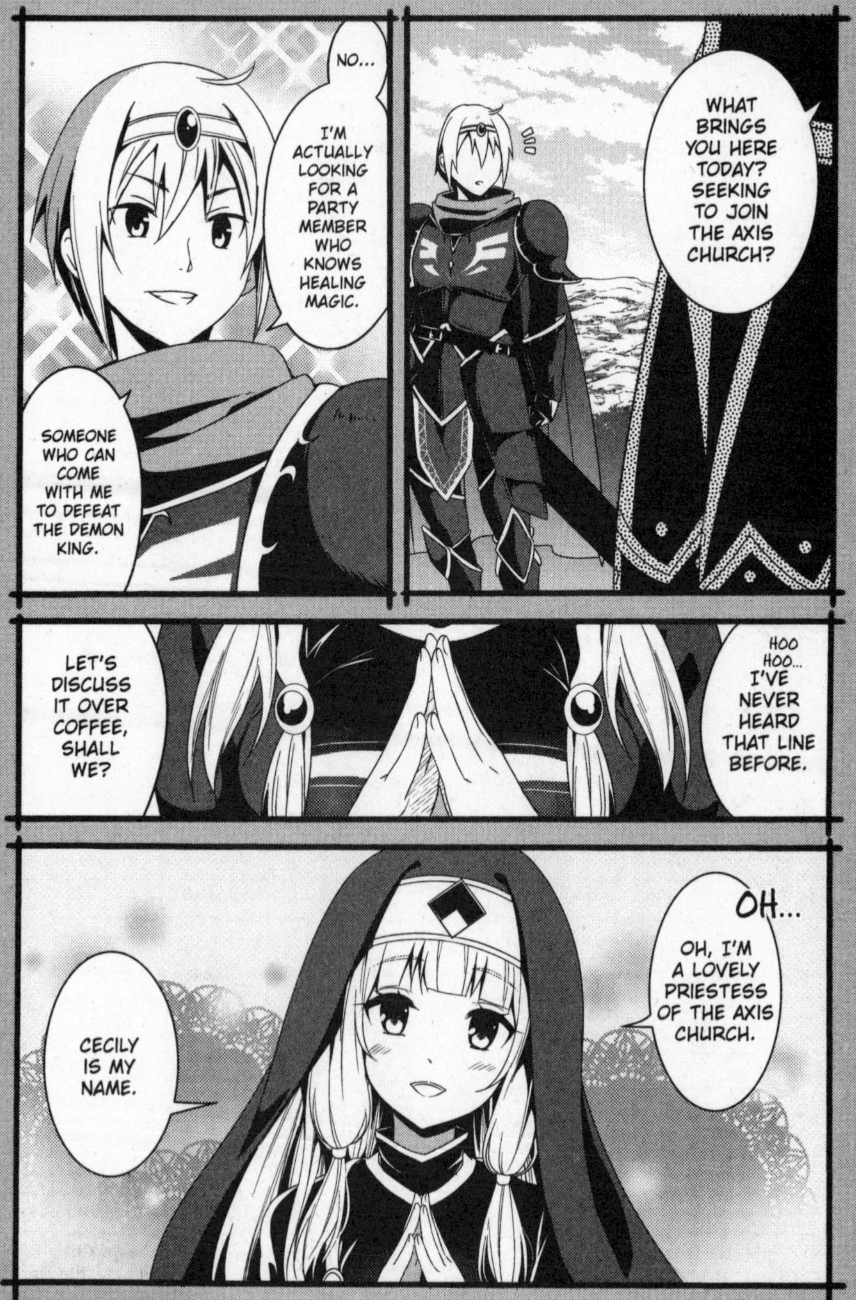
WHAT BRINGS YOU HERE TODAY? SEEKING TO JOIN THE AXIS CHURCH?
NO...
I'M ACTUALLY LOOKING FOR A PARTY MEMBER WHO KNOWS HEALING MAGIC.
SOMEONE WHO CAN COME WITH ME TO DEFEAT THE DEMON KING.
HOO HOO... I'VE NEVER HEARD THAT LINE BEFORE.
LET'S DISCUSS IT OVER COFFEE, SHALL WE?
OH...
OH, I'M A LOVELY PRIESTESS OF THE AXIS CHURCH.
CECILY IS MY NAME.

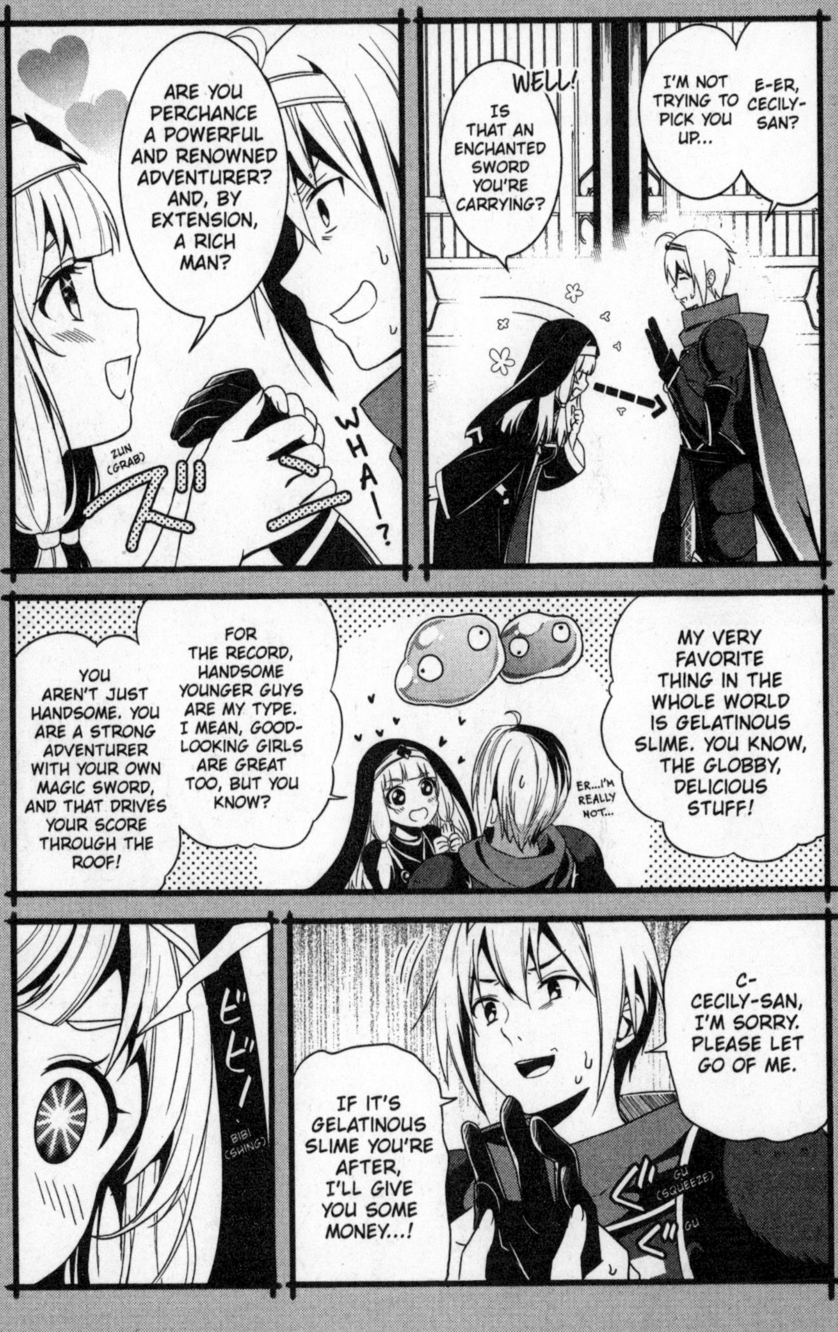
E-ER, CECILY-SAN?
I'M NOT TRYING TO PICK YOU UP...
WELL!
IS THAT AN ENCHANTED SWORD YOU'RE CARRYING?
ARE YOU PERCHANCE A POWERFUL AND RENOWNED ADVENTURER? AND, BY EXTENSION, A RICH MAN?
WHA!?
ZUN (GRAB)
MY VERY FAVORITE THING IN THE WHOLE WORLD IS GELATINOUS SLIME. YOU KNOW, THE GLOBBY, DELICIOUS STUFF!
ER...I'M REALLY NOT...
FOR THE RECORD, HANDSOME YOUNGER GUYS ARE MY TYPE. I MEAN, GOOD-LOOKING GIRLS ARE GREAT TOO, BUT YOU KNOW?
YOU AREN'T JUST HANDSOME. YOU ARE A STRONG ADVENTURER WITH YOUR OWN MAGIC SWORD, AND THAT DRIVES YOUR SCORE THROUGH THE ROOF!
C-CECILY-SAN, I'M SORRY. PLEASE LET GO OF ME.
GU (SQUEEZE)
GU
IF IT'S GELATINOUS SLIME YOU'RE AFTER, I'LL GIVE YOU SOME MONEY...!
BIBI (SHING)

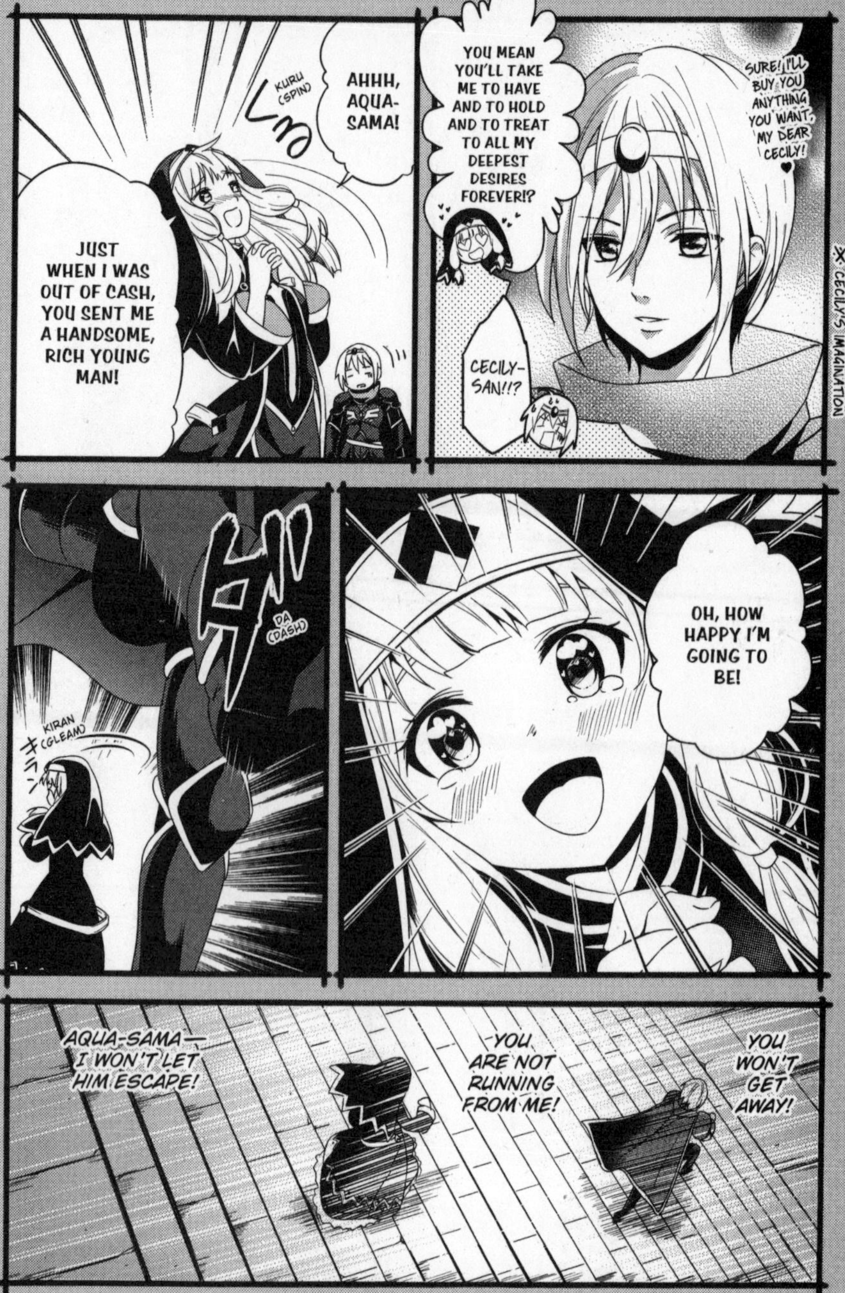
※ CECILY'S IMAGINATION
YOU MEAN YOU'LL TAKE ME TO HAVE AND TO HOLD AND TO TREAT TO ALL MY DEEPEST DESIRES FOREVER!?
SURE! I'LL BUY YOU ANYTHING YOU WANT, MY DEAR CECILY! ♥
CECILY-SAN!!?
AHHH, AQUA-SAMA!
KURU (SPIN)
JUST WHEN I WAS OUT OF CASH, YOU SENT ME A HANDSOME, RICH YOUNG MAN!
OH, HOW HAPPY I'M GOING TO BE!
DA (DASH)
KIRAN (GLEAM)
YOU WON'T GET AWAY!
YOU ARE NOT RUNNING FROM ME!
AQUA-SAMA— I WON'T LET HIM ESCAPE!

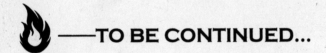——TO BE CONTINUED...

KONOSUBA: AN EXPLOSION ON THIS WONDERFUL WORLD!

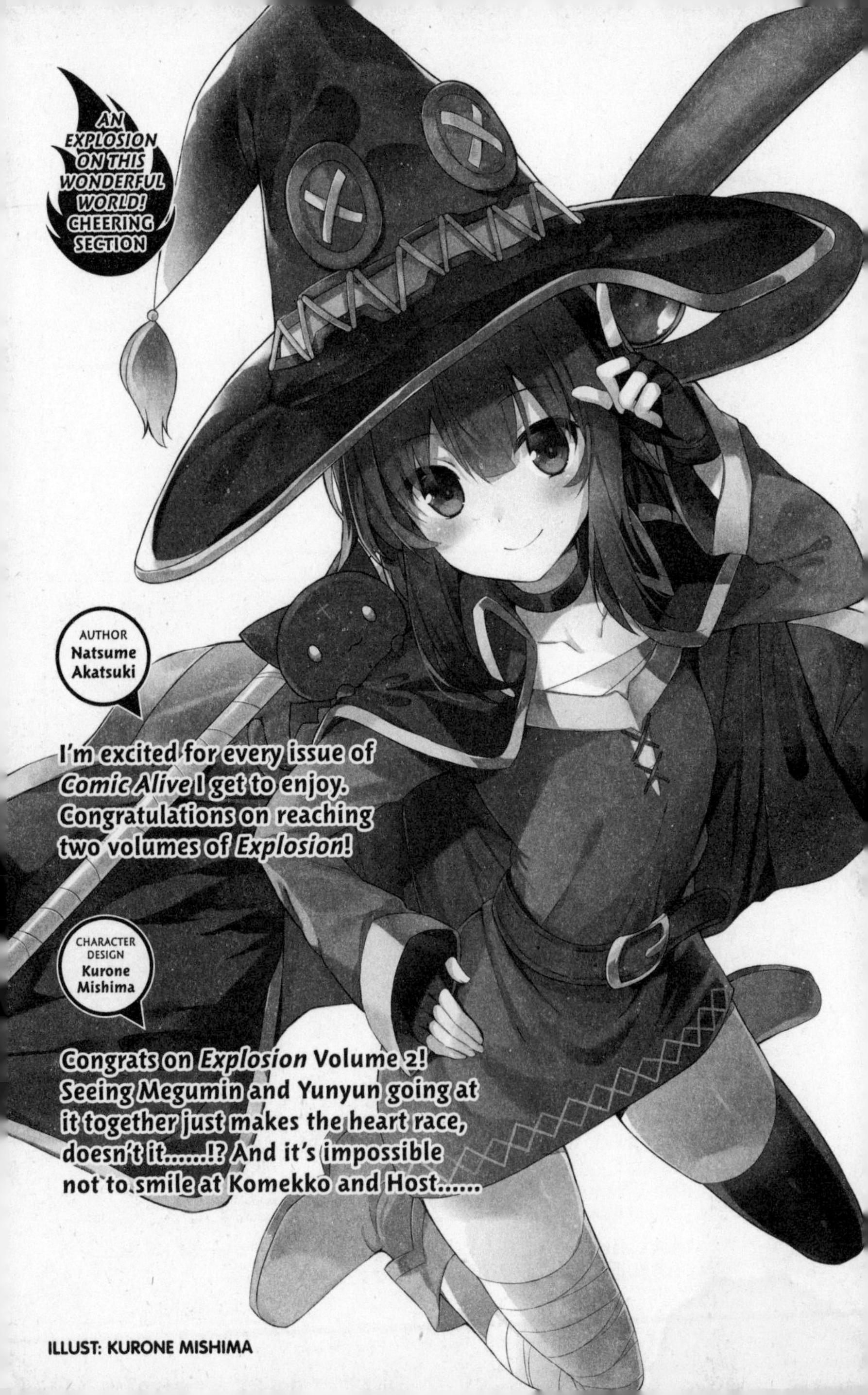
AN EXPLOSION ON THIS WONDERFUL WORLD! CHEERING SECTION
AUTHOR Natsume Akatsuki
I'm excited for every issue of *Comic Alive* I get to enjoy. Congratulations on reaching two volumes of *Explosion*!
CHARACTER DESIGN Kurone Mishima
Congrats on *Explosion* Volume 2! Seeing Megumin and Yunyun going at it together just makes the heart race, doesn't it......!? And it's impossible not to smile at Komekko and Host......
ILLUST: KURONE MISHIMA

AFTERWORD

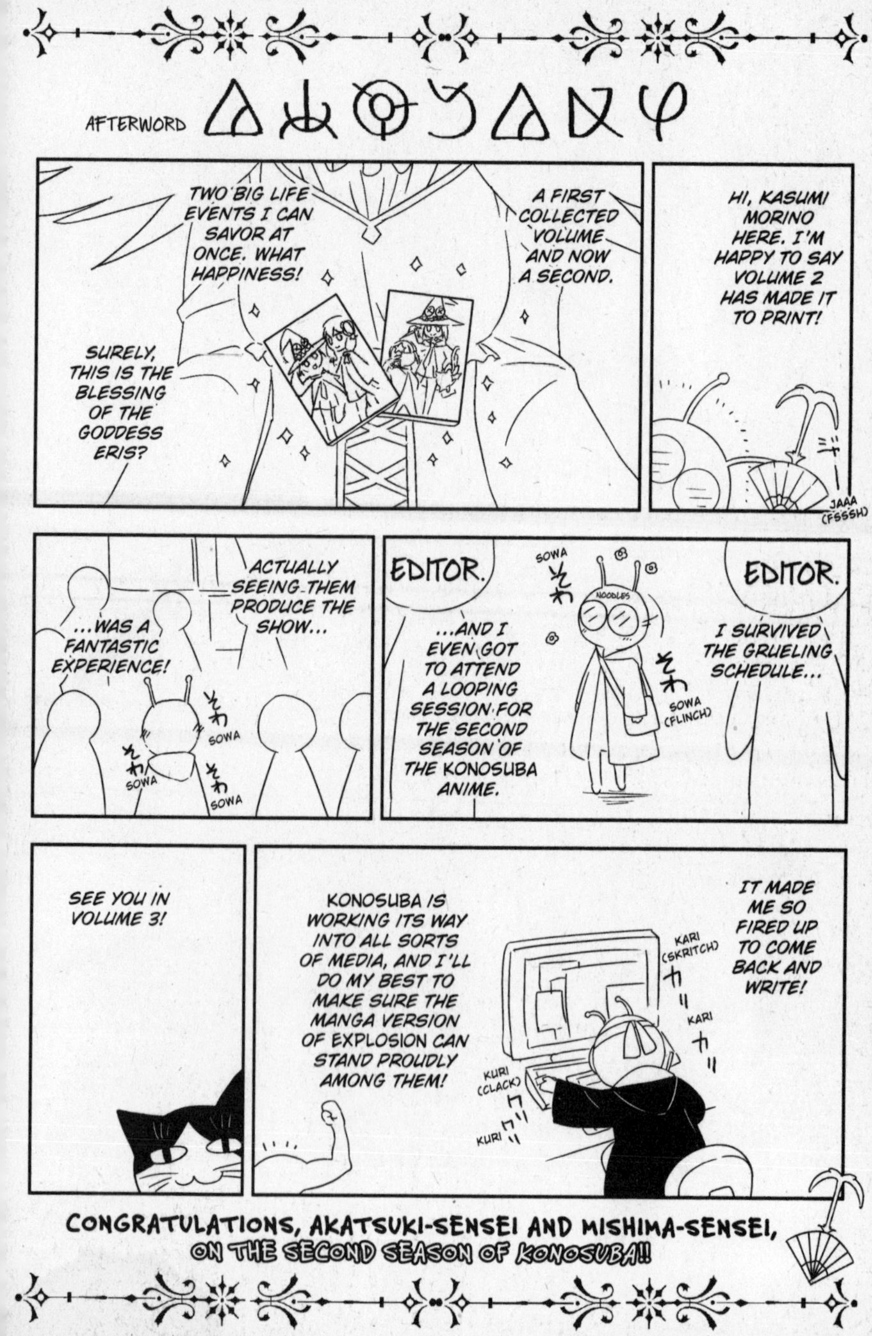

HI, KASUMI MORINO HERE. I'M HAPPY TO SAY VOLUME 2 HAS MADE IT TO PRINT!
JAAA (FSSSH)
A FIRST COLLECTED VOLUME AND NOW A SECOND.
TWO BIG LIFE EVENTS I CAN SAVOR AT ONCE. WHAT HAPPINESS!
SURELY, THIS IS THE BLESSING OF THE GODDESS ERIS?
EDITOR.
I SURVIVED THE GRUELING SCHEDULE...
SOWA
NOODLES
SOWA (FLINCH)
EDITOR.
...AND I EVEN GOT TO ATTEND A LOOPING SESSION FOR THE SECOND SEASON OF THE KONOSUBA ANIME.
ACTUALLY SEEING THEM PRODUCE THE SHOW...
...WAS A FANTASTIC EXPERIENCE!
SOWA
SOWA
SOWA
IT MADE ME SO FIRED UP TO COME BACK AND WRITE!
KARI (SKRITCH)
KARI
KONOSUBA IS WORKING ITS WAY INTO ALL SORTS OF MEDIA, AND I'LL DO MY BEST TO MAKE SURE THE MANGA VERSION OF EXPLOSION CAN STAND PROUDLY AMONG THEM!
KURI (CLACK)
KURI
SEE YOU IN VOLUME 3!

CONGRATULATIONS, AKATSUKI-SENSEI AND MISHIMA-SENSEI, ON THE SECOND SEASON OF *KONOSUBA*!!

KONOSUBA: AN EXPLOSION ON THIS WONDERFUL WORLD!

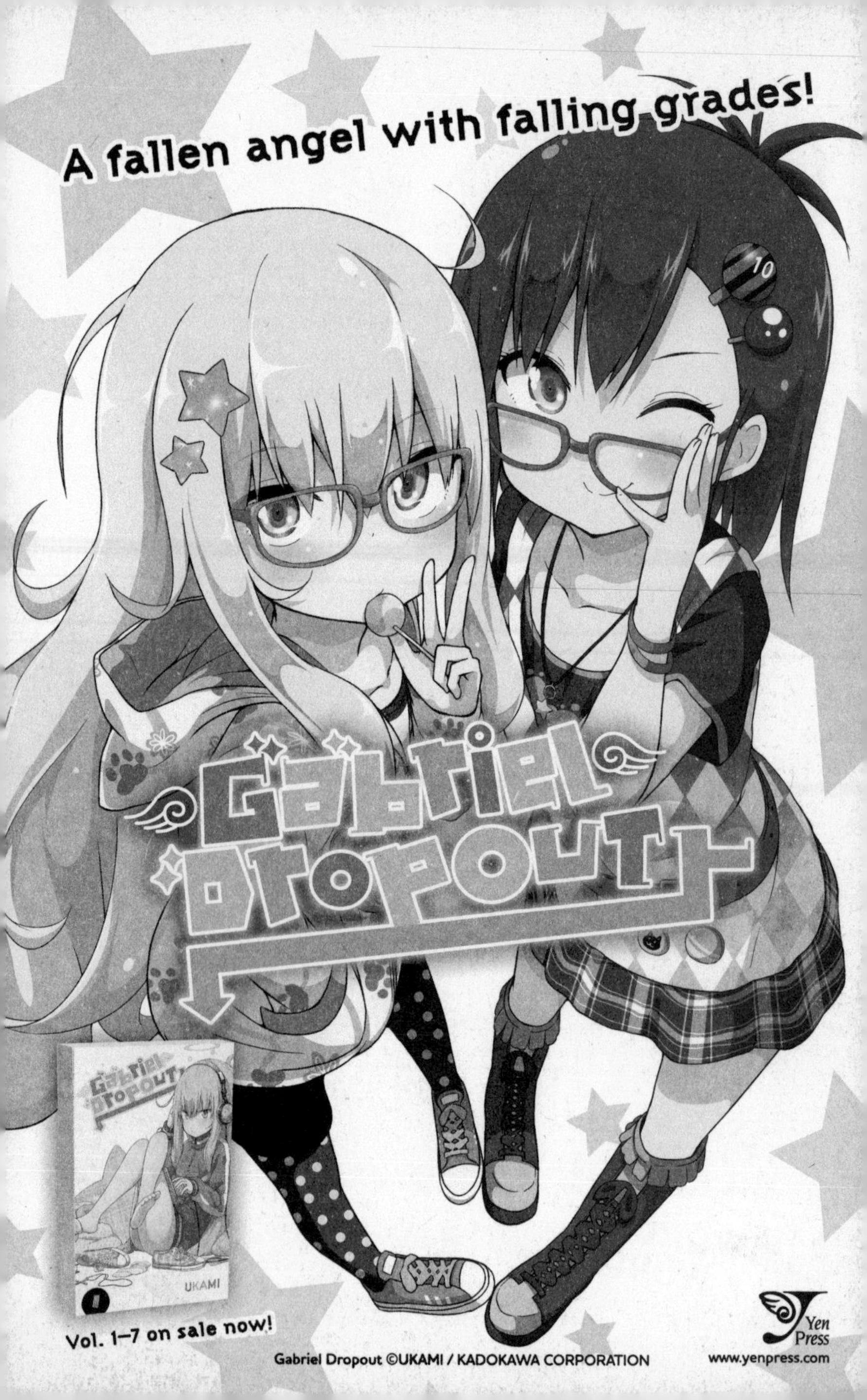
A fallen angel with falling grades!
Gabriel Dropout
Gabriel Dropout
UKAMI
Vol. 1–7 on sale now!
Gabriel Dropout ©UKAMI / KADOKAWA CORPORATION
Yen Press
www.yenpress.com

ENJOY EVERYTHING.

YOU SHOULD COME PLAY WITH YOTSUBA TOO!

Join Yotsuba as she delights in the things many of us take for granted in this Eisner-nominated series.

VOLUMES 1-14 AVAILABLE NOW!

Visit our website at www.yenpress.com.

Yen Press

Hello! This is YOTSUBA!

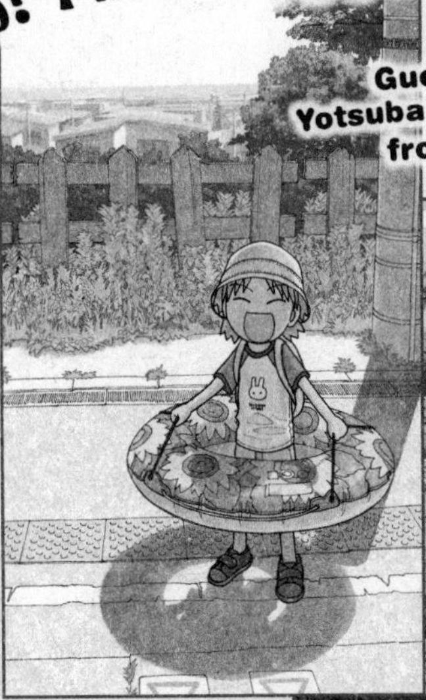

Guess what? Guess what? Yotsuba and Daddy just moved here from waaaay over there!

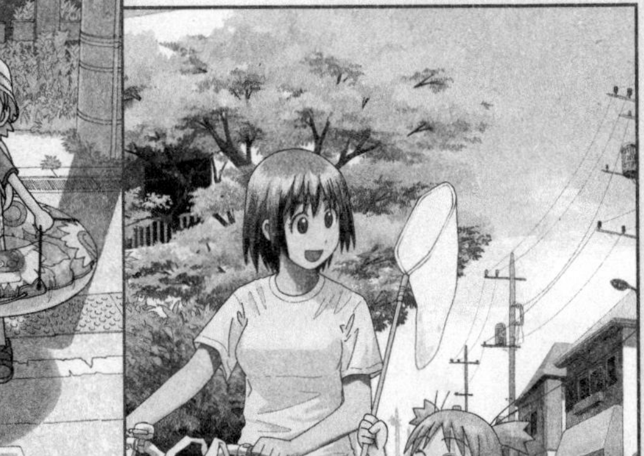

And Yotsuba met these nice people next door and made new friends to play with!

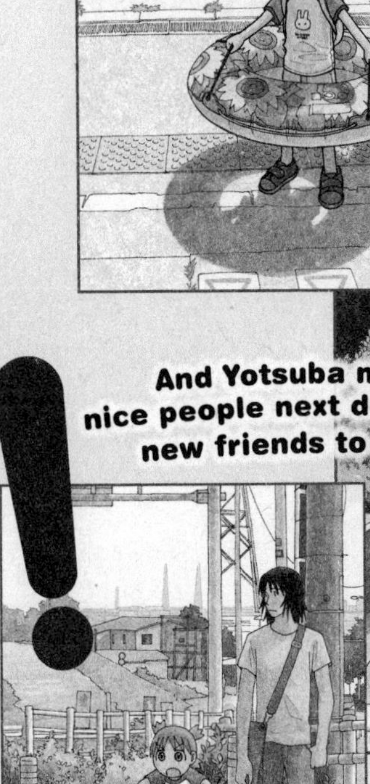

The pretty one took Yotsuba on a bike ride!
(Whoooa! There was a big hill!)

And Ena's a good drawer!
(Almost as good as Yotsuba!)

And their mom always gives Yotsuba ice cream!
(Yummy!)

And...
And...
OHHHH!

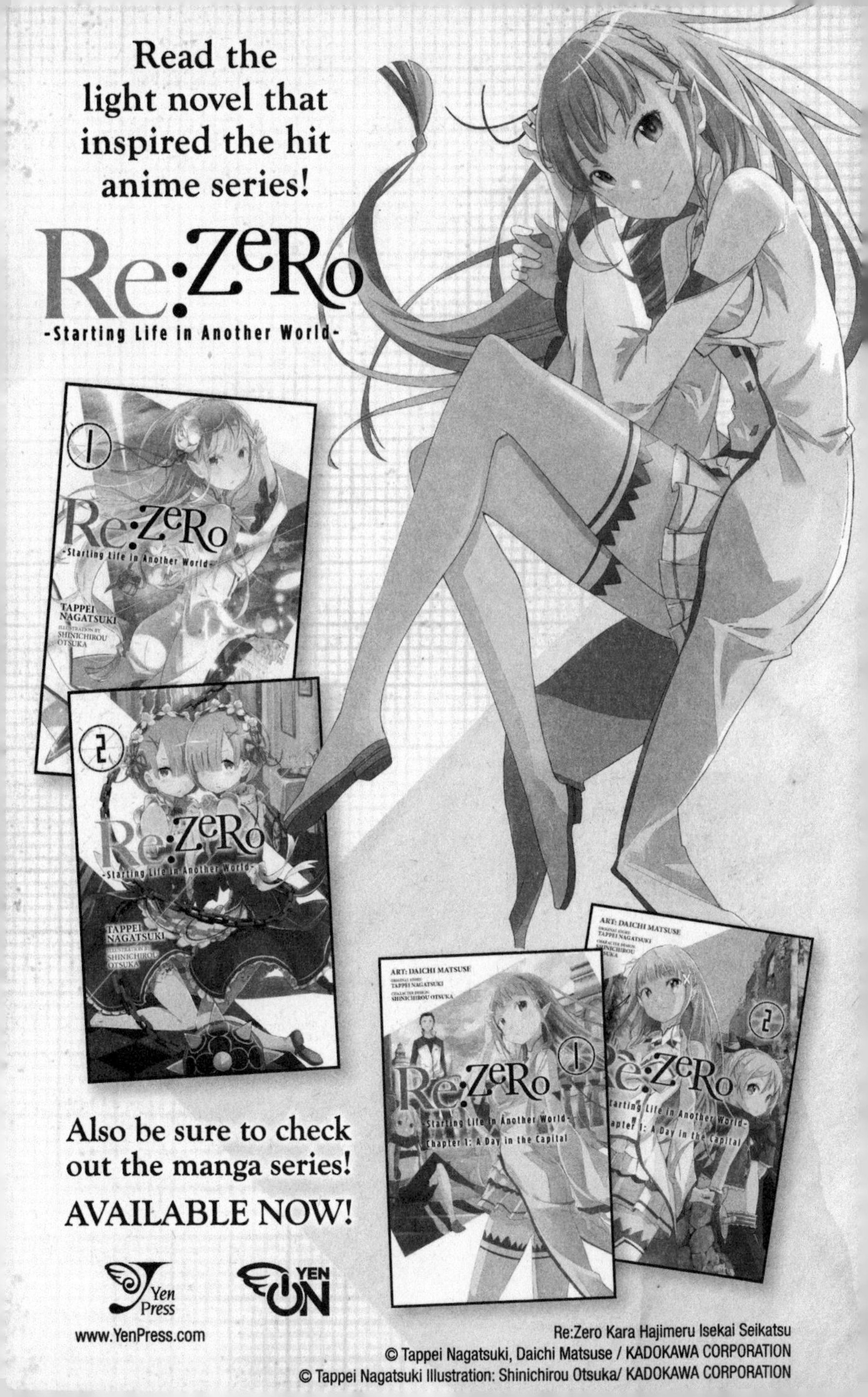
Read the light novel that inspired the hit anime series!
Re:ZeRo
-Starting Life in Another World-
1
Re:ZeRo
-Starting Life in Another World-
TAPPEI NAGATSUKI
ILLUSTRATION BY SHINICHIROU OTSUKA
2
Re:ZeRo
-Starting Life in Another World-
TAPPEI NAGATSUKI
ILLUSTRATION BY SHINICHIROU OTSUKA
ART: DAICHI MATSUSE
ORIGINAL STORY: TAPPEI NAGATSUKI
CHARACTER DESIGN: SHINICHIROU OTSUKA
1
Re:ZeRo
-Starting Life in Another World-
Chapter 1: A Day in the Capital
ART: DAICHI MATSUSE
ORIGINAL STORY: TAPPEI NAGATSUKI
2
Re:ZeRo
-Starting Life in Another World-
Chapter 1: A Day in the Capital
Also be sure to check out the manga series!
AVAILABLE NOW!
Yen Press
YEN ON
www.YenPress.com
Re:Zero Kara Hajimeru Isekai Seikatsu
© Tappei Nagatsuki, Daichi Matsuse / KADOKAWA CORPORATION
© Tappei Nagatsuki Illustration: Shinichirou Otsuka/ KADOKAWA CORPORATION

TRANSLATION: Kevin Steinbach ● **LETTERING: Rochelle Gancio**

KONO SUBARASHII SEKAI NI BAKUEN WO! Volume 2
©Kasumi Morino 2017
©Natsume Akatsuki, Kurone Mishima 2017
First published in Japan in 2017 by KADOKAWA CORPORATION, Tokyo.
English translation rights arranged with KADOKAWA CORPORATION, Tokyo
through Tuttle-Mori Agency, Inc., Tokyo.

English translation © 2019 by Yen Press, LLC

Yen Press
150 West 30th Street, 19th Floor
New York, NY 10001

Visit us at yenpress.com
facebook.com/yenpress
twitter.com/yenpress
yenpress.tumblr.com
instagram.com/yenpress

First Yen Press Edition: September 2019

Yen Press is an imprint of Yen Press, LLC.
The Yen Press name and logo are trademarks of Yen Press, LLC.

The publisher is not responsible for websites (or their content) that are not owned
by the publisher.

Library of Congress Control Number: 2019935209

ISBNs: 978-1-9753-0597-0 (paperback)
        978-1-9753-0598-7 (ebook)

10 9 8 7 6 5 4 3 2 1

WOR

Printed in the United States of America